2013 Yearbook of Immigration Statistics

Office of Immigration Statistics

August 2014

U.S. DEPARTMENT OF HOMELAND SECURITY

Jeh Johnson
Secretary

Office of Policy

Alan Bersin
Acting Assistant Secretary

Office of Immigration Statistics

Nancy F. Rytina
Director

Homeland
Security

Suggested Citation

United States. Department of Homeland Security. *Yearbook of Immigration Statistics: 2013.* Washington, D.C.: U.S. Department of Homeland Security, Office of Immigration Statistics, 2014.

Library of Congress
National Serials Program

CONTENTS

CONTENTS – *Continued*

NATURALIZATIONS

NONIMMIGRANT ADMISSIONS

ENFORCEMENT ACTIONS

INTRODUCTION

Statistical data on immigration have been published annually by the U.S. government since the 1890s. Over the years, the federal agencies responsible for reporting on immigration have changed, as have the content, format, and title of the annual publication. Currently, immigration data are published in the *Yearbook of Immigration Statistics* by the Office of Immigration Statistics in the Policy Directorate of the Department of Homeland Security.

The *2013 Yearbook of Immigration Statistics* consists of a compendium of tables organized by subject matter, including:

Lawful Permanent Residents (Tables 1 to 12)

Lawful permanent residents (LPRs) are persons who have been granted lawful permanent residence in the United States. They are also known as "green card" recipients.

Refugees and Asylees (Tables 13 to 19)

Refugees and asylees are persons who sought residence in the United States in order to avoid persecution in their country of origin. Persons granted refugee status applied for admission while outside the United States. Persons granted asylum applied either at a port of entry or at some point after their entry into the United States.

Naturalizations (Tables 20 to 24)

Naturalizations refer to persons aged 18 and over who become citizens of the United States. Most legal permanent residents are eligible to apply for naturalization within five years after obtaining LPR status.

Nonimmigrant Admissions (Tables 25 to 32)

Nonimmigrant admissions refer to arrivals of persons who are authorized to stay in the United States for a limited period of time. Most nonimmigrants enter the United States as tourists or business travelers, but some come to work, study, or engage in cultural exchange programs.

Enforcement Actions (Tables 33 to 41)

Enforcement actions include foreign nationals who are inadmissible, apprehended, removed or returned for violating the Immigration and Nationality Act. These actions occur at the borders of the United States, in the interior of the country, and at designated sites outside the United States.

Technical Data Notes

The data presented in the *2013 Yearbook* were obtained primarily from workload and case tracking systems of the U.S. Department of Homeland Security. Definitions by subject matter and information on data sources are available in the publications section of the website of the Office of Immigration Statistics at: http://www.dhs.gov/immigration-statistics. Note that numbers appearing for a given year may change in subsequent *Yearbooks* due to updating of data series.

Confidentiality

The Office of Immigration Statistics is committed to protecting the identity of individuals reported in the *Yearbook of Immigration Statistics*. All data tables, therefore, have been edited to avoid divulging information about any individual by either direct or indirect means. The practice of cell suppression has been employed by placing a "D" (disclosure standards not met) in any cell that would show a count of 1 or 2, or in any associated cell that might be used to reveal such a count through calculation. The process of suppression does not change the marginal totals, so the integrity of the data is not affected.

Countries and Regions

The Office of Immigration Statistics categorizes countries and their territories and dependencies into specific regional groups. The following lists the countries included in each region.

Africa includes Algeria, Angola, Benin, Botswana, Burkina Faso, Burundi, Cameroon, Cape Verde, Central African Republic, Chad, Comoros, Cote d'Ivoire, Democratic Republic of the Congo, Djibouti, Egypt, Equatorial Guinea, Eritrea, Ethiopia, Gabon, Gambia, Ghana, Guinea, Guinea-Bissau, Kenya, Lesotho, Liberia, Libya, Madagascar, Malawi, Mali, Mauritania, Mauritius, Morocco, Mozambique, Namibia, Niger, Nigeria, Republic of the Congo, Reunion, Rwanda, Saint Helena, Sao Tome and Principe, Senegal, Seychelles, Sierra Leone, Somalia, South Africa, South Sudan, Sudan, Swaziland, Tanzania, Togo, Tunisia, Uganda, Western Sahara, Zambia, and Zimbabwe.

Asia includes Afghanistan, Armenia, Azerbaijan, Bahrain, Bangladesh, Bhutan, Brunei, Burma, Cambodia, China, Cyprus, East Timor, Georgia, Hong Kong, India, Indonesia, Iran, Iraq, Israel, Japan, Jordan, Kazakhstan, Kuwait, Kyrgyzstan, Laos, Lebanon, Macau, Malaysia, Maldives, Mongolia, Nepal, North Korea, Oman, Pakistan, Philippines, Qatar, Saudi Arabia, Singapore, South Korea, Sri Lanka, Syria, Taiwan, Tajikistan, Thailand, Turkey, Turkmenistan, United Arab Emirates, Uzbekistan, Vietnam, and Yemen.

Europe includes Albania, Andorra, Austria, Belarus, Belgium, Bosnia and Herzegovina, Bulgaria, Croatia, Czech Republic, Denmark, Estonia, Finland, France, Germany, Gibraltar, Greece, Holy See, Hungary, Iceland, Ireland, Italy, Kosovo, Latvia, Liechtenstein, Lithuania, Luxembourg, Macedonia, Malta, Moldova, Monaco, Montenegro, Netherlands, Norway, Poland, Portugal, Romania, Russia, San Marino, Serbia, Serbia and Montenegro, Slovak Republic, Slovenia, Spain, Sweden, Switzerland, Ukraine, and the United Kingdom.

North America includes Canada, Greenland, Mexico, Saint Pierre and Miquelon, United States, and the countries within the regions of the Caribbean and Central America. *Caribbean* includes Anguilla, Antigua and Barbuda, Aruba, Bahamas, Barbados, Bermuda, British Virgin Islands, Cayman Islands, Cuba, Dominica, Dominican Republic, Grenada, Guadeloupe, Haiti, Jamaica, Martinique, Montserrat, Netherlands Antilles, Puerto Rico, Saint Kitts and Nevis, Saint Lucia, Saint Vincent and the Grenadines, Trinidad and Tobago, Turks and Caicos Islands, and U.S. Virgin Islands. *Central America* includes Belize, Costa Rica, El Salvador, Guatemala, Honduras, Nicaragua, and Panama.

Oceania includes American Samoa, Australia, Christmas Island, Cocos (Keeling) Islands, Cook Islands, Federated States of Micronesia, Fiji, French Polynesia, Guam, Kiribati, Marshall Islands, Nauru, New Caledonia, New Zealand, Niue, Northern Mariana Islands, Palau, Papua New Guinea, Pitcairn Islands, Samoa, Solomon Islands, Tokelau, Tonga, Tuvalu, Vanuatu, and Wallis and Futuna Islands.

South America includes Argentina, Bolivia, Brazil, Chile, Colombia, Ecuador, Falkland Islands, French Guiana, Guyana, Paraguay, Peru, Suriname, Uruguay, and Venezuela.

Explanatory Notes

The tables presented in this compendium make use of the following symbols:

NA Not available.

X Not applicable.

D Data withheld to limit disclosure.

– Represents zero.

For More Information

The *2013 Yearbook* data tables are also available in Excel format on the Department of Homeland Security website at http://www.dhs.gov/immigration-statistics.

Lawful Permanent Residents

Table 1.
PERSONS OBTAINING LAWFUL PERMANENT RESIDENT STATUS: FISCAL YEARS 1820 TO 2013

Year	Number	Year	Number	Year	Number	Year	Number
1820.	8,385	1870.	387,203	1920.	430,001	1970.	373,326
1821.	9,127	1871.	321,350	1921.	805,228	1971.	370,478
1822.	6,911	1872.	404,806	1922.	309,556	1972.	384,685
1823.	6,354	1873.	459,803	1923.	522,919	1973.	398,515
1824.	7,912	1874.	313,339	1924.	706,896	1974.	393,919
1825.	10,199	1875.	227,498	1925.	294,314	1975.	385,378
1826.	10,837	1876.	169,986	1926.	304,488	1976 [1]	499,093
1827.	18,875	1877.	141,857	1927.	335,175	1977.	458,755
1828.	27,382	1878.	138,469	1928.	307,255	1978.	589,810
1829.	22,520	1879.	177,826	1929.	279,678	1979.	394,244
1830.	23,322	1880.	457,257	1930.	241,700	1980.	524,295
1831.	22,633	1881.	669,431	1931.	97,139	1981.	595,014
1832.	60,482	1882.	788,992	1932.	35,576	1982.	533,624
1833.	58,640	1883.	603,322	1933.	23,068	1983.	550,052
1834.	65,365	1884.	518,592	1934.	29,470	1984.	541,811
1835.	45,374	1885.	395,346	1935.	34,956	1985.	568,149
1836.	76,242	1886.	334,203	1936.	36,329	1986.	600,027
1837.	79,340	1887.	490,109	1937.	50,244	1987.	599,889
1838.	38,914	1888.	546,889	1938.	67,895	1988.	641,346
1839.	68,069	1889.	444,427	1939.	82,998	1989.	1,090,172
1840.	84,066	1890.	455,302	1940.	70,756	1990.	1,535,872
1841.	80,289	1891.	560,319	1941.	51,776	1991.	1,826,595
1842.	104,565	1892.	579,663	1942.	28,781	1992.	973,445
1843.	52,496	1893.	439,730	1943.	23,725	1993.	903,916
1844.	78,615	1894.	285,631	1944.	28,551	1994.	803,993
1845.	114,371	1895.	258,536	1945.	38,119	1995.	720,177
1846.	154,416	1896.	343,267	1946.	108,721	1996.	915,560
1847.	234,968	1897.	230,832	1947.	147,292	1997.	797,847
1848.	226,527	1898.	229,299	1948.	170,570	1998.	653,206
1849.	297,024	1899.	311,715	1949.	188,317	1999.	644,787
1850.	369,980	1900.	448,572	1950.	249,187	2000.	841,002
1851.	379,466	1901.	487,918	1951.	205,717	2001.	1,058,902
1852.	371,603	1902.	648,743	1952.	265,520	2002.	1,059,356
1853.	368,645	1903.	857,046	1953.	170,434	2003.	703,542
1854.	427,833	1904.	812,870	1954.	208,177	2004.	957,883
1855.	200,877	1905.	1,026,499	1955.	237,790	2005.	1,122,257
1856.	200,436	1906.	1,100,735	1956.	321,625	2006.	1,266,129
1857.	251,306	1907.	1,285,349	1957.	326,867	2007.	1,052,415
1858.	123,126	1908.	782,870	1958.	253,265	2008.	1,107,126
1859.	121,282	1909.	751,786	1959.	260,686	2009.	1,130,818
1860.	153,640	1910.	1,041,570	1960.	265,398	2010.	1,042,625
1861.	91,918	1911.	878,587	1961.	271,344	2011.	1,062,040
1862.	91,985	1912.	838,172	1962.	283,763	2012.	1,031,631
1863.	176,282	1913.	1,197,892	1963.	306,260	2013.	990,553
1864.	193,418	1914.	1,218,480	1964.	292,248		
1865.	248,120	1915.	326,700	1965.	296,697		
1866.	318,568	1916.	298,826	1966.	323,040		
1867.	315,722	1917.	295,403	1967.	361,972		
1868.	138,840	1918.	110,618	1968.	454,448		
1869.	352,768	1919.	141,132	1969.	358,579		

[1] Includes the 15 months from July 1, 1975 to September 30, 1976 because the end date of fiscal years was changed from June 30 to September 30.

Source: U.S. Department of Homeland Security.

Table 2.
PERSONS OBTAINING LAWFUL PERMANENT RESIDENT STATUS BY REGION AND SELECTED COUNTRY OF LAST RESIDENCE: FISCAL YEARS 1820 TO 2013

Region and country of last residence [1]	1820 to 1829	1830 to 1839	1840 to 1849	1850 to 1859	1860 to 1869	1870 to 1879	1880 to 1889	1890 to 1899	1900 to 1909
Total.	128,502	538,381	1,427,337	2,814,554	2,081,261	2,742,137	5,248,568	3,694,294	8,202,388
Europe	99,618	422,853	1,369,423	2,622,617	1,880,389	2,252,050	4,638,684	3,576,411	7,572,569
Austria-Hungary [2,3]	-	-	-	-	3,375	60,127	314,787	534,059	2,001,376
Austria [2,3]	-	-	-	-	2,700	54,529	204,805	268,218	532,416
Hungary [2,3]	-	-	-	-	483	5,598	109,982	203,350	685,567
Belgium.	28	20	3,996	5,765	5,785	6,991	18,738	19,642	37,429
Bulgaria [4]	-	-	-	-	-	-	-	52	34,651
Czechoslovakia [5]	-	-	-	-	-	-	-	-	-
Denmark	173	927	671	3,227	13,553	29,278	85,342	56,671	61,227
Finland [6]	-	-	-	-	3	286	9,617	36,719	
France.	7,694	39,330	75,300	81,778	35,938	71,901	48,193	35,616	67,735
Germany [3]	5,753	124,726	385,434	976,072	723,734	751,769	1,445,181	579,072	328,722
Greece	17	49	17	32	51	209	1,807	12,732	145,402
Ireland [7].	51,617	170,672	656,145	1,029,486	427,419	422,264	674,061	405,710	344,940
Italy.	430	2,225	1,476	8,643	9,853	46,296	267,660	603,761	1,930,475
Netherlands.	1,105	1,377	7,624	11,122	8,387	14,267	52,715	29,349	42,463
Norway-Sweden [8]	91	1,149	12,389	22,202	82,937	178,823	586,441	334,058	426,981
Norway [8]	-	-	-	-	-	88,644	185,111	96,810	182,542
Sweden [8].	-	-	-	-	-	90,179	401,330	237,248	244,439
Poland [3].	19	366	105	1,087	1,886	11,016	42,910	107,793	-
Portugal [9].	252	896	359	4,218	4,741	13,990	15,189	25,874	65,154
Romania	-	-	-	-	-	-	5,842	6,808	57,322
Russia [3,6,10].	86	280	520	423	1,667	34,977	173,081	413,382	1,501,301
Spain	2,866	2,016	1,917	8,803	6,970	5,571	3,999	9,189	24,818
Switzerland	3,148	4,430	4,819	24,423	21,124	25,212	81,151	37,020	32,541
United Kingdom [11]	26,336	74,350	218,572	445,322	532,956	578,447	810,900	328,759	469,518
Yugoslavia [12]	-	-	-	-	-	-	-	-	-
Other Europe	3	40	79	14	10	626	1,070	145	514
Asia	34	55	121	36,080	54,408	134,071	71,152	61,304	300,441
China	3	8	32	35,933	54,028	133,139	65,797	15,268	19,884
Hong Kong	-	-	-	-	-	-	-	-	-
India	9	38	33	42	50	166	247	102	3,026
Iran	-	-	7	-	4	17	18	26	-
Israel.	-	-	-	-	-	-	-	-	-
Japan	-	-	-	-	138	193	1,583	13,998	139,712
Jordan.	-	-	-	-	-	-	-	-	-
Korea [13]	-	-	-	-	-	-	-	-	-
Philippines.	-	-	-	-	-	4	1	19	605
Syria [14]	-	-	-	-	2	7	140	-	-
Taiwan.	-	-	-	-	-	-	-	-	-
Turkey	19	8	45	94	129	382	2,478	27,510	127,999
Vietnam.	-	-	-	-	-	-	-	-	-
Other Asia	3	1	4	11	57	163	888	4,381	9,215
America.	9,656	31,911	50,527	84,201	130,427	345,889	529,845	38,756	277,882
Canada and Newfoundland [15,16,17]	2,297	11,875	34,285	64,171	117,975	323,974	492,508	2,668	123,067
Mexico [16,17]	3,835	7,187	3,069	3,446	1,957	5,133	2,405	734	31,188
Caribbean	3,061	11,792	11,803	12,447	8,809	14,592	27,600	31,885	100,960
Cuba.	-	-	-	-	3,420	8,705	20,134	23,669	-
Dominican Republic	-	-	-	-	-	-	-	-	-
Haiti	-	-	-	-	78	149	124	101	-
Jamaica [18]	-	-	-	-	61	257	355	223	-
Other Caribbean [18]	3,061	11,792	11,803	12,447	5,250	5,481	6,987	7,892	100,960
Central America	57	94	297	512	70	202	359	674	7,341
Belize	-	-	-	-	9	26	80	25	583
Costa Rica.	-	-	-	-	2	4	1	4	-
El Salvador	-	-	-	-	-	3	-	7	-
Guatemala	-	-	-	-	1	10	3	9	-
Honduras	-	-	-	-	-	11	4	4	-
Nicaragua	-	-	-	-	-	1	1	3	-
Panama [19]	-	-	-	-	-	-	-	-	-
Other Central America	57	94	297	512	58	147	270	622	6,758

See footnotes at end of table.

Table 2.
PERSONS OBTAINING LAWFUL PERMANENT RESIDENT STATUS BY REGION AND SELECTED COUNTRY OF LAST RESIDENCE: FISCAL YEARS 1820 TO 2013 – *Continued*

Region and country of last residence [1]	1820 to 1829	1830 to 1839	1840 to 1849	1850 to 1859	1860 to 1869	1870 to 1879	1880 to 1889	1890 to 1899	1900 to 1909
South America	405	957	1,062	3,569	1,536	1,109	1,954	1,389	15,253
Argentina.	-	-	-	-	7	58	64	36	-
Bolivia.	-	-	-	-	-	5	-	-	-
Brazil	-	-	-	-	32	219	199	92	-
Chile.	-	-	-	-	25	92	44	66	-
Colombia.	-	-	-	-	2	196	1,210	607	-
Ecuador.	-	-	-	-	-	7	14	33	-
Guyana	-	-	-	-	41	95	68	27	-
Paraguay.	-	-	-	-	-	2	-	-	-
Peru	-	-	-	-	35	127	25	79	-
Suriname	-	-	-	-	-	-	-	-	-
Uruguay.	-	-	-	-	-	22	4	144	-
Venezuela	-	-	-	-	36	190	248	-	-
Other South America	405	957	1,062	3,569	1,358	96	78	305	15,253
Other America	1	6	11	56	80	879	5,019	1,406	73
Africa	19	66	67	104	458	441	768	432	6,326
Egypt.	-	-	-	5	8	29	145	51	-
Ethiopia.	-	-	-	-	-	-	-	-	-
Liberia.	1	8	5	7	43	52	21	9	-
Morocco	-	4	1	-	-	15	12	9	-
South Africa.	-	-	-	-	79	48	23	9	-
Other Africa	18	54	61	92	328	297	567	354	6,326
Oceania.	2	1	3	110	107	9,094	7,341	3,279	11,677
Australia	2	1	2	104	96	8,933	7,250	3,098	11,191
New Zealand [20].	-	-	-	2	6	39	21	12	-
Other Oceania	-	-	1	4	5	122	70	169	486
Not Specified [21]	19,173	83,495	7,196	71,442	15,472	592	778	14,112	33,493

See footnotes at end of table.

Table 2.
PERSONS OBTAINING LAWFUL PERMANENT RESIDENT STATUS BY REGION AND SELECTED COUNTRY OF LAST RESIDENCE: FISCAL YEARS 1820 TO 2013 – *Continued*

Region and country of last residence [1]	1910 to 1919	1920 to 1929	1930 to 1939	1940 to 1949	1950 to 1959	1960 to 1969	1970 to 1979	1980 to 1989	1990 to 1999
Total	6,347,380	4,295,510	699,375	856,608	2,499,268	3,213,749	4,248,203	6,244,379	9,775,398
Europe	4,985,411	2,560,340	444,404	472,524	1,404,973	1,133,443	826,327	669,694	1,349,219
Austria-Hungary [2,3]	1,154,727	60,891	13,902	13,677	113,015	27,590	20,387	20,437	27,529
Austria [2,3]	589,174	31,392	6,678	8,496	81,354	17,571	14,239	15,374	18,234
Hungary [2,3]	565,553	29,499	7,224	5,181	31,661	10,019	6,148	5,063	9,295
Belgium	32,574	21,511	4,013	12,473	18,885	9,647	5,413	7,028	7,077
Bulgaria [4]	27,180	2,824	1,062	449	97	598	1,011	1,124	16,948
Czechoslovakia [5]	-	101,182	17,757	8,475	1,624	2,758	5,654	5,678	8,970
Denmark	45,830	34,406	3,470	4,549	10,918	9,797	4,405	4,847	6,189
Finland [6]	-	16,922	2,438	2,230	4,923	4,310	2,829	2,569	3,970
France	60,335	54,842	13,761	36,954	50,113	46,975	27,018	32,894	36,552
Germany [3]	174,227	386,634	117,736	119,403	576,905	209,616	77,142	85,752	92,207
Greece	198,108	60,774	10,599	8,605	45,153	74,173	102,370	37,729	25,403
Ireland [7]	166,445	201,644	28,195	15,701	47,189	37,788	11,461	22,210	65,384
Italy	1,229,916	528,133	85,053	50,509	189,061	200,111	150,031	55,562	75,992
Netherlands	46,065	29,397	7,791	13,877	46,703	37,918	10,373	11,234	13,345
Norway-Sweden [8]	192,445	170,329	13,452	17,326	44,231	36,150	10,298	13,941	17,825
Norway [8]	79,488	70,327	6,901	8,326	22,813	17,371	3,927	3,835	5,211
Sweden [8]	112,957	100,002	6,551	9,000	21,418	18,779	6,371	10,106	12,614
Poland [3]	-	224,420	26,460	7,774	6,498	55,773	33,699	63,483	172,249
Portugal [9]	82,489	44,829	3,518	6,765	13,928	70,568	104,754	42,685	25,497
Romania	13,566	67,810	5,264	1,254	914	2,339	10,774	24,753	48,136
Russia [3,6,10]	1,106,998	61,604	2,473	605	453	2,329	28,132	33,311	433,427
Spain	53,262	47,109	3,669	2,774	6,880	40,793	41,718	22,783	18,443
Switzerland	22,839	31,772	5,990	9,904	17,577	19,193	8,536	8,316	11,768
United Kingdom [11]	371,878	342,762	61,813	131,794	195,709	220,213	133,218	153,644	156,182
Yugoslavia [12]	-	49,215	6,920	2,039	6,966	17,990	31,862	16,267	57,039
Other Europe	6,527	21,330	9,068	5,387	7,231	6,814	5,242	3,447	29,087
Asia	269,736	126,740	19,292	34,532	135,844	358,563	1,406,526	2,391,356	2,859,899
China	20,916	30,648	5,874	16,072	8,836	14,060	17,627	170,897	342,058
Hong Kong	-	-	-	-	13,781	67,047	117,350	112,132	116,894
India	3,478	2,076	554	1,692	1,922	18,638	148,018	231,649	352,528
Iran	-	208	198	1,144	3,195	9,059	33,763	98,141	76,899
Israel	-	-	-	98	21,376	30,911	36,306	43,669	41,340
Japan	77,125	42,057	2,683	1,557	41,968	40,956	52,812	44,150	66,582
Jordan	-	-	-	3	4,919	9,230	25,541	28,928	42,755
Korea [13]	-	-	-	83	4,845	27,048	241,192	322,708	179,770
Philippines	-	-	457	4,099	17,245	70,660	337,726	502,056	534,338
Syria [14]	-	5,307	2,188	1,179	1,091	2,432	8,086	14,534	22,906
Taiwan	-	-	-	-	721	15,657	83,155	119,051	132,647
Turkey	160,717	40,374	1,314	754	2,980	9,464	12,209	19,208	38,687
Vietnam	-	-	-	-	290	2,949	121,716	200,632	275,379
Other Asia	7,500	6,070	6,024	7,851	12,675	40,452	171,025	483,601	637,116
America	1,070,539	1,591,278	230,319	328,435	921,644	1,674,185	1,903,636	2,694,504	5,137,142
Canada and Newfoundland [15,16,17]	708,715	949,286	162,703	160,911	353,169	433,128	179,267	156,313	194,788
Mexico [16,17]	185,334	498,945	32,709	56,158	273,847	441,824	621,218	1,009,586	2,757,418
Caribbean	120,860	83,482	18,052	46,285	115,869	427,843	708,643	789,343	1,004,114
Cuba	-	12,769	10,641	25,976	73,221	202,030	256,497	132,552	159,037
Dominican Republic	-	-	1,165	4,802	10,219	83,552	139,249	221,552	359,818
Haiti	-	-	207	823	3,787	28,992	55,166	121,406	177,446
Jamaica [18]	-	-	-	-	7,397	62,218	130,226	193,874	177,143
Other Caribbean [18]	120,860	70,713	6,039	14,684	21,245	51,051	127,505	119,959	130,670
Central America	15,692	16,511	6,840	20,135	40,201	98,569	120,376	339,376	610,189
Belize	40	285	193	433	1,133	4,185	6,747	14,964	12,600
Costa Rica	-	-	580	1,965	4,044	17,975	12,405	25,017	17,054
El Salvador	-	-	712	4,885	5,094	14,405	29,428	137,418	273,017
Guatemala	-	-	632	1,303	4,197	14,357	23,837	58,847	126,043
Honduras	-	-	809	1,874	5,320	15,087	15,653	39,071	72,880
Nicaragua	-	-	564	4,393	7,812	10,383	10,911	31,102	80,446
Panama [19]	-	-	1,774	5,282	12,601	22,177	21,395	32,957	28,149
Other Central America	15,652	16,226	1,576	-	-	-	-	-	-

See footnotes at end of table.

Table 2.
PERSONS OBTAINING LAWFUL PERMANENT RESIDENT STATUS BY REGION AND SELECTED COUNTRY OF LAST RESIDENCE: FISCAL YEARS 1820 TO 2013 – *Continued*

Region and country of last residence [1]	1910 to 1919	1920 to 1929	1930 to 1939	1940 to 1949	1950 to 1959	1960 to 1969	1970 to 1979	1980 to 1989	1990 to 1999
South America	39,938	43,025	9,990	19,662	78,418	250,754	273,529	399,803	570,596
Argentina.	-	-	1,397	3,108	16,346	49,384	30,303	23,442	30,065
Bolivia.	-	-	77	893	2,759	6,205	5,635	9,798	18,111
Brazil	-	4,627	1,468	3,653	11,547	29,238	18,600	22,944	50,744
Chile.	-	-	568	1,320	4,669	12,384	15,032	19,749	18,200
Colombia.	-	-	1,278	3,454	15,567	68,371	71,265	105,494	137,985
Ecuador.	-	-	320	2,207	8,574	34,107	47,464	48,015	81,358
Guyana	-	-	193	596	1,131	4,546	38,278	85,886	74,407
Paraguay.	-	-	36	85	576	1,249	1,486	3,518	6,082
Peru	-	-	460	1,273	5,980	19,783	25,311	49,958	110,117
Suriname	-	-	33	130	299	612	714	1,357	2,285
Uruguay.	-	-	153	754	1,026	4,089	8,416	7,235	6,062
Venezuela	-	-	1,360	2,182	9,927	20,758	11,007	22,405	35,180
Other South America	39,938	38,398	2,647	7	17	28	18	2	-
Other America	-	29	25	25,284	60,140	22,076	603	83	37
Africa	8,867	6,362	2,120	6,720	13,016	23,780	71,405	141,987	346,410
Egypt.	-	1,063	781	1,613	1,996	5,581	23,543	26,744	44,604
Ethiopia.	-	-	10	28	302	804	2,588	12,927	40,097
Liberia.	-	-	35	37	289	841	2,391	6,420	13,587
Morocco	-	-	110	1,463	3,293	2,880	1,967	3,471	15,768
South Africa.	-	-	312	1,022	2,278	4,360	10,002	15,505	21,964
Other Africa	8,867	5,299	872	2,557	4,858	9,314	30,914	76,920	210,390
Oceania.	12,339	9,860	3,240	14,262	11,319	23,659	39,983	41,432	56,800
Australia	11,280	8,404	2,260	11,201	8,275	14,986	18,708	16,901	24,288
New Zealand [20].	-	935	790	2,351	1,799	3,775	5,018	6,129	8,600
Other Oceania	1,059	521	190	710	1,245	4,898	16,257	18,402	23,912
Not Specified [21]	488	930	-	135	12,472	119	326	305,406	25,928

See footnotes at end of table.

Table 2.
PERSONS OBTAINING LAWFUL PERMANENT RESIDENT STATUS BY REGION AND SELECTED COUNTRY OF LAST RESIDENCE: FISCAL YEARS 1820 TO 2013 – *Continued*

Region and country of last residence [1]	2000 to 2009	2010	2011	2012	2013
Total.	10,299,430	1,042,625	1,062,040	1,031,631	990,553
Europe	1,349,609	95,429	90,712	86,956	91,095
Austria-Hungary [2,3]	33,929	4,325	4,703	3,208	2,061
Austria [2,3]	21,151	3,319	3,654	2,199	1,053
Hungary [2,3]	12,778	1,006	1,049	1,009	1,008
Belgium.	8,157	732	700	698	803
Bulgaria [4].	40,003	2,465	2,549	2,322	2,720
Czechoslovakia [5]	18,691	1,510	1,374	1,316	1,258
Denmark	6,049	545	473	492	546
Finland [6]	3,970	414	398	373	360
France.	45,637	4,339	3,967	4,201	4,668
Germany [3]	122,373	7,929	7,072	6,732	6,880
Greece	16,841	966	1,196	1,264	1,526
Ireland [7].	15,642	1,610	1,533	1,694	1,765
Italy.	28,329	2,956	2,670	2,946	3,233
Netherlands.	17,351	1,520	1,258	1,294	1,376
Norway-Sweden [8]	19,382	1,662	1,530	1,441	1,665
Norway [8]	4,599	363	405	314	389
Sweden [8].	14,783	1,299	1,125	1,127	1,276
Poland [3].	117,921	7,391	6,634	6,024	6,073
Portugal [9].	11,479	759	878	837	917
Romania	52,154	3,735	3,679	3,477	3,475
Russia [3,6,10].	167,152	7,502	8,548	10,114	10,154
Spain	17,695	2,040	2,319	2,316	2,970
Switzerland	12,173	868	861	916	1,040
United Kingdom [11]	171,979	14,781	13,443	13,938	15,321
Yugoslavia [12]	131,831	4,772	4,611	4,488	4,445
Other Europe	290,871	22,608	20,316	16,865	17,839
Asia	3,470,835	410,209	438,580	416,488	389,301
China	591,711	67,634	83,603	78,184	68,410
Hong Kong	57,583	3,263	3,149	2,642	2,614
India.	590,464	66,185	66,331	63,320	65,506
Iran.	76,755	9,078	9,015	8,955	9,658
Israel.	54,081	5,172	4,389	4,640	4,555
Japan	84,552	7,100	6,751	6,581	6,383
Jordan.	53,550	9,327	8,211	7,014	5,949
Korea [13].	209,758	22,022	22,748	20,802	22,937
Philippines.	545,463	56,399	55,251	55,441	52,955
Syria [14]	30,807	7,424	7,983	6,674	3,999
Taiwan.	92,657	6,785	6,206	5,295	5,336
Turkey.	48,394	7,435	9,040	7,362	7,189
Vietnam.	289,616	30,065	33,486	27,578	26,578
Other Asia	745,444	112,320	122,417	122,000	107,232
America.	4,441,529	426,981	423,277	409,664	399,380
Canada and Newfoundland [15,16,17]	236,349	19,491	19,506	20,138	20,489
Mexico [16,17]	1,704,166	138,717	142,823	145,326	134,198
Caribbean	1,053,357	139,389	133,012	126,615	121,349
Cuba.	271,742	33,372	36,261	32,551	31,343
Dominican Republic	291,492	53,890	46,036	41,535	41,487
Haiti	203,827	22,336	21,802	22,446	20,083
Jamaica [18].	172,523	19,439	19,298	20,300	19,052
Other Caribbean [18]	113,773	10,352	9,615	9,783	9,384
Central America	591,130	43,597	43,249	39,837	44,056
Belize	9,682	997	933	875	969
Costa Rica.	21,571	2,306	2,230	2,152	2,232
El Salvador	251,237	18,547	18,477	15,874	18,015
Guatemala	156,992	10,263	10,795	9,857	9,829
Honduras	63,513	6,381	6,053	6,773	8,795
Nicaragua	70,015	3,476	3,314	2,943	2,940
Panama [19]	18,120	1,627	1,447	1,363	1,276
Other Central America	-	-	-	-	-

See footnotes at end of table.

Table 2.
PERSONS OBTAINING LAWFUL PERMANENT RESIDENT STATUS BY REGION AND SELECTED COUNTRY OF LAST RESIDENCE: FISCAL YEARS 1820 TO 2013 – *Continued*

Region and country of last residence [1]	2000 to 2009	2010	2011	2012	2013
South America	856,508	85,783	84,687	77,748	79,287
Argentina.	47,955	4,312	4,335	4,218	4,227
Bolivia.	21,921	2,211	2,113	1,920	2,005
Brazil	115,404	12,057	11,643	11,248	10,772
Chile.	19,792	1,940	1,854	1,628	1,751
Colombia.	236,570	21,861	22,130	20,272	20,611
Ecuador.	107,977	11,463	11,068	9,284	10,553
Guyana	70,373	6,441	6,288	5,282	5,564
Paraguay	4,623	449	501	454	437
Peru	137,614	14,063	13,836	12,414	12,370
Suriname	2,363	202	167	216	170
Uruguay.	9,827	1,286	1,521	1,348	1,314
Venezuela	82,087	9,497	9,229	9,464	9,512
Other South America	2	1	2	-	1
Other America	19	4	-	-	1
Africa	759,734	98,246	97,429	103,685	94,589
Egypt.	81,564	9,822	9,096	10,172	10,719
Ethiopia.	87,207	13,853	13,985	15,400	13,484
Liberia.	23,316	2,924	3,117	3,451	3,036
Morocco	40,844	4,847	4,249	3,534	3,202
South Africa.	32,221	2,705	2,754	2,960	2,693
Other Africa	494,582	64,095	64,228	68,168	61,455
Oceania.	65,793	5,946	5,825	5,573	6,061
Australia	32,728	3,077	3,062	3,146	3,529
New Zealand [20].	12,495	1,046	1,006	980	1,027
Other Oceania	20,570	1,823	1,757	1,447	1,505
Not Specified [21]	211,930	5,814	6,217	9,265	10,127

- Represents zero or not available.

[1] Prior to 1906 refers to country of origin; from 1906 to 2013 refers to country of last residence. Because of changes in country boundaries, data for a particular country may not necessarily refer to the same geographic area over time.

[2] Austria and Hungary not reported separately for all years during 1860 to 1869, 1890 to 1899, and 1900 to 1909.

[3] Poland included in Austria, Germany, Hungary, and Russia from 1899 to 1919.

[4] Bulgaria included Serbia and Montenegro from 1899 to 1919.

[5] Includes Czech Republic, Czechoslovakia (former), and Slovakia.

[6] Finland included in Russia from 1899 to 1919.

[7] Northern Ireland included in Ireland prior to 1925.

[8] Norway and Sweden not reported separately until 1861.

[9] Cape Verde included in Portugal from 1892 to 1952.

[10] Refers to the Russian Empire from 1820 to 1920. Between 1920 and 1990 refers to the Soviet Union. From 1991 to 1999, refers to Russia, Armenia, Azerbaijan, Belarus, Georgia, Kazakhstan, Kyrgyzstan, Moldova, Tajikistan, Turkmenistan, Ukraine, and Uzbekistan. Beginning in 2000, refers to Russia only.

[11] United Kingdom refers to England, Scotland, Wales and Northern Ireland since 1925.

[12] Includes Bosnia-Herzegovina, Croatia, Kosovo, Macedonia, Montenegro, Serbia, Serbia and Montenegro, and Slovenia.

[13] Includes both North and South Korea.

[14] Syria included in Turkey from 1886 to 1923.

[15] Includes British North America and Canadian provinces.

[16] Land arrivals not completely enumerated until 1908.

[17] No data available for Canada or Mexico from 1886 to 1893.

[18] Jamaica included in British West Indies from 1892 to 1952.

[19] Panama Canal Zone included in Panama from 1932 to 1972.

[20] New Zealand included in Australia from 1892 to 1924.

[21] Includes 32,897 persons returning in 1906 to their homes in the United States.

Note: Official recording of immigration to the United States began in 1820 after the passage of the Act of March 2, 1819. From 1820 to 1867, figures represent alien passenger arrivals at seaports; from 1868 to 1891 and 1895 to 1897, immigrant alien arrivals; from 1892 to 1894 and 1898 to 2013, immigrant aliens admitted for permanent residence; from 1892 to 1903, aliens entering by cabin class were not counted as immigrants. Land arrivals were not completely enumerated until 1908. For this table, Fiscal Year 1843 covers 9 months ending September 30, 1843; Fiscal Years 1832 and 1850 cover 15 months ending December 31 of the respective years; and Fiscal Year 1868 covers 6 months ending June 30, 1868; and Fiscal Year 1976 covers 15 months ending September 30, 1976.

Source: U.S. Department of Homeland Security.

Table 3.
PERSONS OBTAINING LAWFUL PERMANENT RESIDENT STATUS BY REGION AND COUNTRY OF BIRTH: FISCAL YEARS 2004 TO 2013

Region and country of birth	2004	2005	2006	2007	2008	2009	2010	2011	2012	2013
REGION										
Total....................	957,883	1,122,257	1,266,129	1,052,415	1,107,126	1,130,818	1,042,625	1,062,040	1,031,631	990,553
Africa	66,417	85,094	117,421	94,710	105,915	127,046	101,355	100,374	107,241	98,304
Asia	342,930	411,722	440,335	397,834	399,027	413,312	422,063	451,593	429,599	400,548
Europe	124,884	164,989	146,292	106,566	103,782	105,476	88,801	83,850	81,671	86,556
North America	342,383	345,476	413,992	339,294	393,196	375,180	336,553	333,902	327,771	315,660
Oceania................	5,985	6,546	7,384	6,101	5,263	5,578	5,345	4,980	4,742	5,277
South America	72,057	103,127	137,971	106,516	98,549	102,860	87,178	86,096	79,401	80,945
Unknown	3,227	5,303	2,734	1,394	1,394	1,366	1,330	1,245	1,206	3,263
COUNTRY										
Total....................	957,883	1,122,257	1,266,129	1,052,415	1,107,126	1,130,818	1,042,625	1,062,040	1,031,631	990,553
Afghanistan	2,137	4,749	3,417	1,753	2,813	3,165	2,017	1,648	1,617	2,196
Albania	3,840	5,947	7,914	5,737	5,754	5,137	4,711	3,612	3,364	3,186
Algeria................	805	1,115	1,300	1,036	1,037	1,485	1,305	1,364	1,369	1,241
American Samoa	12	15	28	11	14	19	14	D	-	D
Angola.................	107	188	272	199	221	173	148	148	187	143
Anguilla...............	22	35	32	25	22	21	19	25	23	22
Antigua-Barbuda........	414	440	570	415	444	437	359	368	337	344
Argentina..............	4,805	7,081	7,327	5,645	5,353	5,780	4,399	4,473	4,359	4,372
Armenia................	1,833	2,591	6,317	4,351	3,586	3,442	2,979	2,983	2,681	2,722
Aruba	31	42	51	55	36	38	49	39	54	45
Australia	2,604	3,193	3,249	2,518	2,464	2,622	2,512	2,343	2,414	2,759
Austria	402	532	524	485	443	512	442	424	407	415
Azerbaijan	969	1,523	2,371	1,166	1,071	834	781	728	663	637
Bahamas...............	586	698	847	738	682	751	652	668	619	630
Bahrain	116	140	148	133	96	120	104	119	104	115
Bangladesh	8,061	11,487	14,644	12,074	11,753	16,651	14,819	16,707	14,705	12,099
Barbados..............	630	846	959	689	585	603	465	455	460	428
Belarus	2,255	3,503	3,086	2,328	2,390	2,407	2,038	1,964	1,659	1,970
Belgium................	638	859	716	638	642	686	592	567	574	675
Belize	871	876	1,252	1,073	1,077	1,041	965	905	847	946
Benin	185	193	275	258	317	401	486	462	415	342
Bermuda	100	116	160	108	92	108	72	71	85	88
Bhutan	17	30	78	52	42	594	6,109	10,137	10,198	8,954
Bolivia	1,768	2,197	4,025	2,590	2,436	2,837	2,253	2,173	1,948	2,071
Bosnia-Herzegovina	10,552	14,074	3,789	1,569	1,491	1,501	946	878	815	697
Botswana	34	54	53	49	41	55	66	76	80	53
Brazil.................	10,556	16,662	17,903	14,295	12,195	14,701	12,258	11,763	11,441	11,033
British Virgin Islands........	35	41	47	40	53	46	46	37	39	45
Brunei.................	22	49	25	32	18	26	20	25	19	21
Bulgaria...............	4,253	5,635	4,828	3,981	2,960	3,133	2,570	2,661	2,440	2,844
Burkina Faso	103	128	221	238	238	416	377	433	558	585
Burma.................	1,379	2,095	4,562	3,130	3,403	13,621	12,925	16,518	17,383	12,565
Burundi	100	186	320	257	255	1,505	841	593	535	260
Cambodia	3,553	4,022	5,773	4,246	3,713	3,771	2,986	2,745	2,473	2,624
Cameroon	1,309	1,458	2,919	3,392	3,771	3,463	4,161	4,754	3,815	3,908
Canada	15,569	21,878	18,207	15,495	15,109	16,140	13,328	12,800	12,932	13,181
Cape Verde	1,015	1,225	1,780	2,048	1,916	2,238	1,668	1,808	1,684	1,673
Cayman Islands	38	37	65	40	37	45	52	41	44	44
Central African Republic	17	24	51	52	88	107	101	134	116	213
Chad..................	23	31	73	74	96	102	120	171	155	111
Chile..................	1,810	2,404	2,774	2,274	2,017	2,250	1,950	1,853	1,673	1,736
China, People's Republic	55,494	69,933	87,307	76,655	80,271	64,238	70,863	87,016	81,784	71,798
Colombia...............	18,846	25,566	43,144	33,187	30,213	27,849	22,406	22,635	20,931	21,131
Comoros	4	6	7	7	D	D	D	8	10	3
Congo, Democratic Republic	155	260	738	1,129	1,261	2,122	1,764	2,424	3,731	2,792
Congo, Republic..............	670	1,064	1,600	972	950	1,563	968	1,371	1,461	1,059
Costa Rica..............	1,755	2,278	3,109	2,540	2,090	2,384	2,164	2,135	2,020	2,114
Cote d'Ivoire	666	930	2,067	1,193	1,645	2,159	1,621	1,302	1,760	1,486
Croatia	1,511	1,780	945	482	455	496	357	349	336	353
Cuba..................	20,488	36,261	45,614	29,104	49,500	38,954	33,573	36,452	32,820	32,219

See footnotes at end of table.

Table 3.
PERSONS OBTAINING LAWFUL PERMANENT RESIDENT STATUS BY REGION AND COUNTRY OF BIRTH:
FISCAL YEARS 2004 TO 2013 – *Continued*

Region and country of birth	2004	2005	2006	2007	2008	2009	2010	2011	2012	2013
Cyprus.	143	196	180	137	141	142	122	101	107	126
Czech Republic	457	476	344	287	227	146	190	303	677	676
Czechoslovakia (former)	673	784	1,442	927	862	865	750	466	159	74
Denmark	566	718	699	517	498	603	518	459	459	506
Djibouti	37	50	34	23	39	54	37	56	106	90
Dominica	132	198	471	428	454	484	366	287	125	244
Dominican Republic	30,506	27,503	38,068	28,024	31,879	49,414	53,870	46,109	41,566	41,311
Ecuador.	8,626	11,608	17,489	12,248	11,663	12,128	11,492	11,103	9,342	10,591
Egypt.	5,522	7,905	10,500	9,267	8,712	8,844	8,978	7,778	8,988	10,294
El Salvador	29,807	21,359	31,782	21,127	19,659	19,909	18,806	18,667	16,256	18,260
Equatorial Guinea.	13	10	13	4	16	32	12	13	20	18
Eritrea	675	796	1,593	1,081	1,270	1,928	1,656	2,102	2,643	2,138
Estonia	322	438	423	368	287	282	260	191	227	211
Ethiopia.	8,286	10,571	16,152	12,786	12,917	15,462	14,266	13,793	14,544	13,097
Fiji.	1,593	1,422	2,115	1,637	1,176	1,194	1,201	1,041	853	895
Finland	388	574	542	426	302	423	397	363	348	331
France.	3,688	4,496	4,357	3,494	4,935	4,569	3,919	3,653	3,862	4,425
French Polynesia	13	19	37	27	26	30	16	21	30	-
Gabon.	50	66	85	95	82	171	138	204	197	127
Gambia	422	581	897	826	739	978	859	972	1,159	1,018
Georgia	964	1,389	2,003	1,554	1,620	1,578	1,518	1,490	1,341	1,368
Germany	7,099	9,264	8,436	7,582	7,091	7,583	6,888	6,125	5,812	6,032
Ghana	5,337	6,491	9,367	7,610	8,195	8,401	7,429	8,798	10,592	10,265
Greece	769	1,070	1,124	882	769	798	745	949	1,054	1,361
Grenada	609	840	1,068	751	784	748	664	579	671	687
Guatemala.	18,920	16,818	24,133	17,908	16,182	12,187	10,467	11,092	10,341	10,224
Guinea	347	495	1,110	1,088	1,735	1,725	1,379	1,555	1,656	1,518
Guinea-Bissau	5	26	25	25	17	20	30	29	47	43
Guyana	6,351	9,317	9,552	5,726	6,823	6,670	6,749	6,599	5,683	5,897
Haiti	14,191	14,524	22,226	30,405	26,007	24,280	22,582	22,111	22,818	20,351
Honduras.	5,508	7,012	8,177	7,646	6,540	6,404	6,448	6,133	6,884	8,898
Hong Kong.	3,951	3,705	3,256	3,527	3,373	2,651	2,432	2,306	2,104	2,226
Hungary.	1,272	1,567	1,704	1,266	1,127	1,314	1,022	1,044	1,054	1,052
Iceland	105	135	145	95	122	131	105	90	103	139
India	70,151	84,680	61,369	65,353	63,352	57,304	69,162	69,013	66,434	68,458
Indonesia	2,419	3,924	4,868	3,716	3,606	3,679	3,032	2,856	2,603	2,731
Iran.	10,434	13,887	13,947	10,460	13,852	18,553	14,182	14,822	12,916	12,863
Iraq.	3,494	4,077	4,337	3,765	4,795	12,110	19,855	21,133	20,369	9,552
Ireland.	1,531	2,088	1,906	1,503	1,465	1,637	1,507	1,371	1,514	1,626
Israel	4,160	5,755	5,943	4,496	5,851	5,612	4,515	3,826	4,153	3,996
Italy.	2,346	3,066	3,215	2,569	2,514	2,892	2,579	2,443	2,673	2,960
Jamaica.	14,430	18,345	24,976	19,375	18,477	21,783	19,825	19,662	20,705	19,400
Japan	7,697	8,768	8,265	6,748	6,821	7,690	6,264	6,161	6,061	5,925
Jordan.	3,431	3,748	4,038	3,917	3,936	4,282	3,868	3,876	4,099	4,188
Kazakhstan	1,906	2,223	2,073	1,604	1,630	1,562	1,282	1,235	1,202	1,241
Kenya	5,335	5,347	8,779	7,030	6,998	9,880	7,421	7,762	7,043	6,123
Kiribati	D	4	8	10	4	10	6	D	6	3
Korea, North	NA	NA	NA	NA	NA	67	35	36	49	48
Korea, South [1]	19,766	26,562	24,386	22,405	26,666	25,859	22,227	22,824	20,846	23,166
Kosovo	X	X	X	X	-	-	355	670	782	839
Kuwait.	1,091	1,152	1,230	1,017	1,104	1,124	1,037	973	1,044	937
Kyrgyzstan	439	656	785	597	632	574	507	542	648	652
Laos	1,147	1,242	2,892	2,575	2,198	1,688	1,200	956	949	923
Latvia	605	768	892	568	455	444	435	426	436	424
Lebanon	3,818	4,282	4,083	4,267	4,254	3,831	3,487	3,295	2,879	2,783
Lesotho.	14	12	18	14	16	14	23	25	17	20
Liberia.	2,757	4,880	6,887	4,102	7,193	7,641	4,837	4,151	4,109	3,334
Libya	185	223	271	186	285	296	355	357	315	376
Lithuania	2,480	2,417	1,885	1,361	967	1,069	985	936	924	854
Luxembourg.	13	35	28	39	28	30	22	24	19	40
Macau.	192	133	189	178	205	158	143	130	120	106
Macedonia.	775	1,070	1,317	1,227	1,107	1,128	963	1,078	906	895

See footnotes at end of table.

Table 3.
PERSONS OBTAINING LAWFUL PERMANENT RESIDENT STATUS BY REGION AND COUNTRY OF BIRTH: FISCAL YEARS 2004 TO 2013 – *Continued*

Region and country of birth	2004	2005	2006	2007	2008	2009	2010	2011	2012	2013
Madagascar	54	60	72	53	77	71	80	83	79	95
Malawi	83	131	131	123	133	164	164	123	192	159
Malaysia	1,987	2,632	2,281	2,149	1,945	2,014	1,714	2,273	2,605	2,477
Mali	163	277	408	412	523	576	528	629	734	667
Malta	57	74	70	53	66	58	74	51	62	43
Marshall Islands	48	32	53	48	39	48	37	38	50	46
Mauritania	170	275	720	651	844	597	495	393	410	354
Mauritius	65	99	108	88	83	110	84	101	77	83
Mexico	175,411	161,445	173,749	148,640	189,989	164,920	139,120	143,446	146,406	135,028
Micronesia, Federated States	5	6	12	7	13	16	10	9	13	4
Moldova	1,507	3,506	3,036	1,356	1,692	2,295	1,981	2,258	2,021	2,485
Monaco	7	7	4	6	7	4	12	6	5	8
Mongolia	229	323	497	530	659	831	594	774	691	729
Montenegro	X	X	X	-	-	-	120	204	265	265
Montserrat	33	50	90	66	61	43	27	30	27	-
Morocco	4,128	4,411	4,949	4,513	4,425	5,447	5,013	4,399	3,656	3,336
Mozambique	59	54	78	81	69	66	53	60	94	73
Namibia	40	63	56	57	46	53	60	43	59	57
Nepal	2,878	3,158	3,733	3,472	4,093	4,514	7,115	10,166	11,312	13,046
Netherlands	1,303	1,815	1,651	1,368	1,240	1,499	1,321	1,085	1,091	1,142
Netherlands Antilles	72	116	100	93	78	97	77	86	106	128
New Caledonia	D	5	7	5	5	5	13	6	5	D	6
New Zealand	1,131	1,293	1,100	1,047	893	947	919	803	814	921
Nicaragua	4,009	3,305	4,145	3,716	3,614	4,137	3,565	3,401	3,046	3,048
Niger	62	126	116	97	107	183	96	96	48	37
Nigeria	9,374	10,597	13,459	12,448	12,475	15,253	13,376	11,824	13,575	13,840
Norway	405	423	481	343	350	407	334	339	276	335
Oman	122	101	155	103	70	74	63	60	74	73
Pakistan	12,086	14,926	17,418	13,492	19,719	21,555	18,258	15,546	14,740	13,251
Palau	6	8	8	11	6	16	18	7	10	16
Panama	1,417	1,815	2,418	1,916	1,678	1,806	1,536	1,374	1,281	1,234
Papua New Guinea	19	44	30	31	15	19	30	20	21	27
Paraguay	328	516	719	545	481	530	467	500	467	448
Peru	11,794	15,676	21,718	17,699	15,184	16,957	14,247	14,064	12,609	12,564
Philippines	57,846	60,746	74,606	72,596	54,030	60,029	58,173	57,011	57,327	54,446
Poland	14,326	15,351	17,051	10,355	8,354	8,754	7,643	6,863	6,300	6,430
Portugal	1,069	1,125	1,409	1,019	772	946	755	821	811	918
Qatar	125	174	226	138	151	134	148	193	141	191
Romania	4,571	7,103	7,137	5,802	4,930	4,910	4,003	3,882	3,748	3,773
Russia	17,410	18,055	13,159	9,426	11,695	8,238	6,718	7,944	9,969	9,753
Rwanda	163	276	502	357	378	952	489	520	592	540
Saint Kitts-Nevis	299	342	458	347	363	310	339	350	311	259
Saint Lucia	616	832	1,212	928	946	1,027	872	785	919	853
Saint Vincent and the Grenadines	400	625	756	567	568	591	576	468	503	529
Samoa	203	173	283	290	227	250	219	267	238	237
Sao Tome and Principe	9	8	6	7	7	11	10	9	12	6
Saudi Arabia	906	1,210	1,542	1,171	1,194	1,418	1,263	1,396	1,343	1,463
Senegal	769	913	1,367	1,024	1,149	1,524	1,285	1,424	1,615	1,340
Serbia	X	X	X	-	-	-	20	244	704	866
Serbia and Montenegro	3,331	5,202	5,891	3,586	3,255	3,166	2,196	1,398	801	653
Seychelles	25	16	15	7	16	10	8	15	7	6
Sierra Leone	1,596	2,731	3,572	1,999	2,795	2,687	2,011	1,985	1,688	1,651
Singapore	966	1,204	997	985	922	832	774	690	712	835
Slovakia	800	965	1,111	763	653	706	538	594	528	507
Slovenia	88	114	115	87	79	108	74	69	86	62
Solomon Islands	6	3	5	10	7	D	6	D	D	3
Somalia	3,929	5,829	9,462	6,251	10,745	13,390	4,558	4,451	5,204	3,764
South Africa	3,370	4,536	3,201	2,988	2,723	3,171	2,758	2,649	2,781	2,629
South Sudan	X	X	X	X	X	X	X	-	17	59
Soviet Union (former)	929	2,899	6,229	5,090	5,270	5,911	4,978	3,687	1,296	1,264

See footnotes at end of table.

Table 3.
PERSONS OBTAINING LAWFUL PERMANENT RESIDENT STATUS BY REGION AND COUNTRY OF BIRTH: FISCAL YEARS 2004 TO 2013 – *Continued*

Region and country of birth	2004	2005	2006	2007	2008	2009	2010	2011	2012	2013
Spain	1,339	1,888	1,971	1,578	1,621	1,769	1,684	1,890	1,842	2,480
Sri Lanka	1,431	1,894	2,191	1,831	1,935	2,009	2,036	2,053	1,994	1,847
Sudan	3,211	5,231	5,504	2,930	3,598	3,577	2,397	2,628	2,471	1,945
Suriname	166	300	314	197	218	227	216	196	187	178
Swaziland	15	16	11	13	18	42	22	19	24	15
Sweden	1,270	1,517	1,376	1,145	1,019	1,138	1,097	979	968	1,106
Switzerland	855	1,092	983	705	720	798	675	615	635	697
Syria	2,256	2,831	2,918	2,385	2,641	2,442	2,555	2,785	3,014	3,366
Taiwan	9,005	9,196	8,086	8,990	9,073	8,038	6,732	6,154	5,331	5,385
Tajikistan	167	207	239	172	231	265	299	382	411	550
Tanzania	747	829	949	832	838	2,773	1,850	1,427	1,516	837
Thailand	4,318	5,505	11,749	8,751	6,637	10,444	9,384	9,962	9,459	7,583
Togo	2,041	1,523	1,720	1,565	1,661	1,680	1,563	1,506	1,756	1,257
Tonga	327	309	437	438	365	379	343	408	276	348
Trinidad and Tobago	5,384	6,568	8,854	6,829	5,937	6,256	5,435	5,023	5,214	4,724
Tunisia	457	495	510	417	410	416	418	440	422	445
Turkey	3,835	4,614	4,941	4,425	4,210	4,958	4,483	4,403	4,162	4,144
Turkmenistan	117	148	248	217	274	290	224	260	223	210
Turks and Caicos Islands	28	34	52	31	35	31	29	33	30	50
U.S. Virgin Islands	13	8	7	3	D	3	D	D	D	D
Uganda	721	858	1,372	1,122	1,174	1,364	1,085	1,239	1,340	1,350
Ukraine	14,156	22,745	17,140	11,001	10,813	11,223	8,477	8,292	7,642	8,193
United Arab Emirates	586	812	1,006	758	693	697	779	707	854	910
United Kingdom	14,915	19,800	17,207	14,545	14,348	15,748	12,792	11,572	12,014	12,984
United States	57	183	333	171	216	181	201	269	279	319
Uruguay	787	1,154	1,664	1,418	1,451	1,775	1,331	1,553	1,374	1,352
Uzbekistan	1,995	2,887	4,015	4,665	6,375	5,467	4,770	5,056	4,726	4,382
Venezuela	6,220	10,645	11,341	10,692	10,514	11,154	9,409	9,183	9,387	9,572
Vietnam	31,524	32,784	30,691	28,691	31,497	29,234	30,632	34,157	28,304	27,101
Yemen	1,760	3,366	4,308	2,396	1,872	3,134	3,591	3,361	2,620	3,532
Zambia	359	499	672	576	613	704	628	652	643	505
Zimbabwe	628	923	1,049	1,057	953	983	1,274	1,016	914	924
All other countries	31	48	34	29	24	39	29	28	26	30
Unknown	3,227	5,303	2,734	1,394	1,394	1,366	1,330	1,245	1,206	3,263

NA Not available.

X Not applicable.

D Data withheld to limit disclosure.

- Represents zero.

[1] Data for South Korea prior to Fiscal Year 2009 include a small number of cases from North Korea.

Source: U.S. Department of Homeland Security.

Table 4.
PERSONS OBTAINING LAWFUL PERMANENT RESIDENT STATUS BY STATE OR TERRITORY OF RESIDENCE: FISCAL YEARS 2004 TO 2013

State or territory of residence	2004	2005	2006	2007	2008	2009	2010	2011	2012	2013
Total....................	957,883	1,122,257	1,266,129	1,052,415	1,107,126	1,130,818	1,042,625	1,062,040	1,031,631	990,553
Alabama..................	2,247	4,200	4,277	3,393	3,877	3,891	3,740	4,063	3,873	3,848
Alaska....................	1,261	1,524	1,554	1,617	1,534	1,608	1,703	1,799	1,612	1,460
Arizona..................	19,507	18,986	21,529	17,528	20,638	20,997	18,243	20,333	18,434	16,097
Arkansas.................	2,288	2,698	2,924	2,722	2,997	2,942	2,684	2,874	2,795	2,900
California................	253,858	232,014	264,667	228,941	238,444	227,876	208,446	210,591	196,622	191,806
Colorado.................	11,255	11,975	12,713	11,039	12,741	12,841	12,489	13,547	13,327	11,108
Connecticut...............	12,335	15,334	18,697	12,932	12,190	13,632	12,222	12,577	12,237	10,985
Delaware.................	1,705	2,991	2,263	2,085	2,295	2,184	2,198	2,355	2,208	2,325
District of Columbia.......	2,148	2,457	3,775	2,541	2,652	2,934	2,897	2,724	2,811	2,981
Florida...................	76,178	122,915	155,986	126,277	133,445	127,006	107,276	109,229	103,047	102,939
Georgia..................	16,681	31,527	32,202	27,353	27,769	28,396	24,833	27,015	26,134	24,387
Guam....................	1,275	1,436	1,716	1,438	1,305	1,427	1,383	1,313	1,430	1,210
Hawaii...................	6,405	6,480	7,499	7,236	6,572	6,929	7,037	7,296	6,764	6,226
Idaho....................	2,299	2,768	2,377	2,044	2,766	3,120	2,556	2,602	2,428	2,120
Illinois..................	46,896	52,415	52,452	41,971	42,723	41,889	37,909	38,325	38,373	35,988
Indiana..................	6,262	6,913	8,122	6,639	8,028	9,087	8,539	8,262	8,359	7,668
Iowa....................	4,067	4,535	4,085	3,103	3,696	3,963	4,245	4,624	4,679	4,105
Kansas..................	4,139	4,512	4,277	4,141	5,344	5,319	5,501	5,086	4,980	5,000
Kentucky.................	3,820	5,265	5,504	4,340	5,315	5,260	4,930	5,403	5,243	5,159
Louisiana................	3,095	3,776	2,693	3,475	4,011	4,299	4,397	4,226	4,454	4,355
Maine...................	1,322	1,907	1,717	1,488	1,617	1,675	1,349	1,467	1,497	1,208
Maryland.................	20,549	22,868	30,199	24,255	27,062	26,722	26,450	25,778	24,971	25,361
Massachusetts............	28,067	34,232	35,558	30,555	30,369	32,607	31,069	32,236	31,392	29,482
Michigan.................	18,851	23,591	20,907	18,727	17,947	18,919	18,579	18,347	17,494	16,952
Minnesota................	12,097	15,449	18,249	13,814	15,832	18,020	12,408	12,389	12,999	12,781
Mississippi...............	1,312	1,829	1,480	1,593	1,679	1,652	1,709	1,666	1,583	1,716
Missouri.................	7,050	8,742	6,852	6,459	7,078	7,142	7,151	7,048	6,635	6,345
Montana.................	452	589	505	575	543	553	457	511	503	445
Nebraska.................	3,002	2,996	3,795	3,066	3,668	3,989	4,400	4,535	4,384	4,141
Nevada..................	8,798	9,823	14,713	12,308	11,768	12,334	10,803	10,449	10,343	9,886
New Hampshire...........	2,280	3,298	2,987	2,272	2,466	2,483	2,556	2,478	2,466	2,227
New Jersey...............	50,699	56,176	65,931	55,834	53,997	58,879	56,920	55,547	50,790	53,082
New Mexico..............	3,076	3,513	3,805	3,112	3,509	3,887	3,528	3,767	3,714	3,664
New York................	103,151	136,815	180,157	136,739	143,679	150,722	147,999	148,426	149,505	133,601
North Carolina...........	11,036	16,710	18,987	15,469	15,174	18,562	16,112	17,571	17,487	16,798
North Dakota.............	591	864	649	496	662	843	1,058	948	1,144	1,234
Ohio....................	12,072	16,892	16,585	14,078	14,595	15,375	13,585	13,857	13,948	13,819
Oklahoma................	3,578	4,702	4,590	4,269	4,306	5,007	4,627	4,503	4,646	4,648
Oregon..................	8,540	9,623	9,188	7,905	9,028	9,026	7,997	7,694	7,791	7,171
Pennsylvania.............	18,813	28,902	25,950	22,811	23,646	24,105	24,130	25,397	25,032	24,720
Puerto Rico..............	4,760	3,623	4,093	2,917	3,287	4,084	4,283	3,288	3,106	2,942
Rhode Island.............	3,740	3,852	4,778	3,354	3,735	4,156	4,027	3,681	3,798	3,337
South Carolina...........	2,672	5,028	5,291	4,788	4,241	4,747	4,401	4,216	3,924	4,266
South Dakota.............	747	881	1,013	668	773	1,271	987	1,337	1,521	1,231
Tennessee...............	5,844	8,960	10,037	8,942	8,348	9,042	8,156	8,279	8,573	8,380
Texas...................	92,440	95,951	89,027	77,278	89,811	95,384	87,750	94,481	95,557	92,674
Utah....................	4,346	5,082	5,749	5,168	6,087	6,466	6,085	6,426	5,932	5,503
Vermont.................	814	1,042	894	791	771	792	867	943	877	838
Virginia.................	22,104	27,095	38,483	29,682	30,257	29,825	28,607	27,767	28,227	27,861
Washington..............	19,758	26,480	23,803	22,657	23,170	27,562	22,283	23,789	23,060	22,994
West Virginia.............	634	847	763	721	798	734	729	830	779	760
Wisconsin...............	5,580	7,907	8,339	7,381	7,306	6,727	6,189	6,245	6,049	5,918
Wyoming................	304	321	376	380	458	429	452	420	427	522
Other [1]................	1,077	937	1,366	1,047	1,117	1,495	1,694	1,480	1,667	1,379
Unknown................	6	9	1	1	-	2	-	-	-	-

- Represents zero.

[1] Includes U.S. territories and armed forces posts.

Source: U.S. Department of Homeland Security.

Table 5.
PERSONS OBTAINING LAWFUL PERMANENT RESIDENT STATUS BY CORE BASED STATISTICAL AREA (CBSA) OF RESIDENCE: FISCAL YEARS 2004 TO 2013 (Ranked by 2013 LPR Flow)

Geographic area	2004	2005	2006	2007	2008	2009	2010	2011	2012	2013
Total..............................	957,883	1,122,257	1,266,129	1,052,415	1,107,126	1,130,818	1,042,625	1,062,040	1,031,631	990,553
New York-Northern New Jersey-Long Island, NY-NJ-PA	138,568	172,832	224,408	175,735	179,971	189,849	186,084	183,681	179,011	167,393
Los Angeles-Long Beach-Santa Ana, CA	110,821	98,235	120,875	95,410	96,492	97,538	87,443	86,161	81,508	79,893
Miami-Fort Lauderdale-Pompano Beach, FL...	49,802	79,550	98,911	78,170	87,786	83,936	69,420	71,775	66,153	66,636
Washington-Arlington-Alexandria, DC-VA-MD-WV.....................	32,274	37,142	54,543	40,703	42,832	42,567	41,322	39,365	38,518	39,170
Chicago-Joliet-Naperville, IL-IN-WI..........	43,826	49,014	49,746	39,504	39,826	38,840	35,109	35,039	34,898	32,819
Houston-Sugar Land-Baytown, TX..........	34,995	34,788	31,555	26,842	30,510	32,021	30,844	31,136	31,738	31,953
San Francisco-Oakland-Fremont, CA........	37,225	33,873	38,340	35,640	36,114	32,302	31,761	32,433	29,583	30,600
Dallas-Fort Worth-Arlington, TX.............	25,231	28,955	26,623	23,263	26,441	29,020	26,003	28,090	28,010	26,760
Boston-Cambridge-Quincy, MA-NH	22,712	27,133	28,468	24,676	24,687	26,346	24,969	25,909	25,042	23,867
Atlanta-Sandy Springs-Marietta, GA	12,970	25,345	25,269	22,054	22,329	23,343	20,445	22,035	21,289	20,054
Philadelphia-Camden-Wilmington, PA-NJ-DE-MD	14,699	22,674	20,754	18,455	18,913	18,932	18,253	18,925	17,903	18,121
Seattle-Tacoma-Bellevue, WA..............	13,825	18,939	17,094	16,862	17,090	20,712	16,866	17,823	17,644	17,865
San Jose-Sunnyvale-Santa Clara, CA	21,210	19,557	18,258	19,255	21,022	18,677	18,619	18,554	16,937	17,292
San Diego-Carlsbad-San Marcos, CA	20,031	19,299	17,270	18,288	20,491	20,779	19,769	21,556	18,893	16,567
Riverside-San Bernardino-Ontario, CA.......	17,473	15,519	19,466	16,779	17,792	17,010	14,926	14,885	14,547	14,026
Detroit-Warren-Livonia, MI	12,665	15,862	14,040	12,875	11,801	12,856	12,682	12,198	11,597	11,131
Phoenix-Mesa-Glendale, AZ	12,254	12,971	14,593	11,355	13,525	13,700	12,240	14,013	12,805	11,025
Minneapolis-St. Paul-Bloomington, MN-WI....	10,181	12,954	15,861	11,903	13,406	14,958	10,434	10,175	10,673	10,478
Orlando-Kissimmee-Sanford, FL...........	6,018	10,427	17,409	14,618	13,956	11,408	10,676	10,204	10,229	10,200
Baltimore-Towson, MD	5,852	6,959	8,627	6,896	8,214	8,268	8,207	8,229	8,608	8,599
Las Vegas-Paradise, NV	7,010	7,826	12,705	10,373	9,507	10,307	9,004	8,719	8,785	8,381
Tampa-St. Petersburg-Clearwater, FL........	7,238	11,841	13,542	10,730	10,089	10,296	8,818	8,996	8,700	8,360
Sacramento–Arden-Arcade–Roseville, CA	9,124	12,366	12,751	9,755	9,434	9,358	8,047	8,469	7,975	7,504
Denver-Aurora-Broomfield, CO	7,311	7,807	8,401	7,384	8,408	8,468	8,215	9,189	8,967	7,498
Austin-Round Rock-San Marcos, TX	4,275	5,424	4,974	4,551	5,799	5,698	5,434	6,068	5,897	6,015
Portland-Vancouver-Hillsboro, OR-WA	7,340	8,927	8,209	6,882	7,611	7,844	6,730	6,469	6,352	5,934
El Paso, TX	4,157	3,736	4,295	4,004	4,746	4,593	4,646	5,640	5,436	5,261
San Antonio-New Braunfels, TX	3,683	4,584	4,346	4,143	4,872	4,917	4,740	5,422	5,712	5,082
Charlotte-Gastonia-Rock Hill, NC-SC........	2,744	4,312	4,851	4,103	4,262	4,844	4,178	5,010	5,400	5,053
Columbus, OH	3,703	5,040	5,568	4,769	5,402	6,006	4,460	4,955	5,129	4,868
Honolulu, HI........................	4,907	4,955	5,727	5,507	5,022	4,999	5,169	5,550	5,020	4,656
Bridgeport-Stamford-Norwalk, CT	4,735	6,187	7,654	5,149	4,660	5,334	4,587	4,651	4,640	4,468
Nashville-Davidson-Murfreesboro-Franklin, TN ..	2,415	3,997	4,939	4,226	3,871	4,498	3,897	4,149	4,285	4,275
Providence-New Bedford-Fall River, RI-MA	4,637	4,973	5,933	4,426	4,689	5,187	4,912	4,675	4,787	4,263
Indianapolis-Carmel, IN.................	2,364	2,529	3,152	2,721	3,386	4,108	3,606	3,900	4,336	3,944
Raleigh-Cary, NC.....................	2,621	3,634	3,910	3,435	3,432	4,072	3,909	3,793	3,746	3,798
Kansas City, MO-KS	3,492	3,640	3,551	3,146	3,773	4,085	4,299	4,104	3,838	3,696
Salt Lake City, UT....................	2,703	3,254	3,566	3,052	3,668	4,241	3,879	4,360	3,811	3,403
Hartford-West Hartford-East Hartford, CT	4,080	4,730	5,498	3,901	3,754	4,216	3,869	4,090	4,059	3,373
McAllen-Edinburg-Mission, TX	5,378	4,013	3,549	2,576	3,229	3,143	2,654	3,409	3,617	3,267
St. Louis, MO-IL	4,198	5,830	3,793	3,615	3,799	3,792	3,553	3,553	3,408	3,187
Jacksonville, FL	2,841	4,464	3,877	3,656	3,475	3,659	3,503	3,453	3,365	3,170
Cleveland-Elyria-Mentor, OH..............	3,214	4,547	3,773	3,135	3,084	3,081	3,111	2,883	3,111	3,076
Fresno, CA.........................	4,873	3,969	4,772	4,124	4,472	3,567	3,010	3,073	2,894	2,853
Worcester, MA	2,844	3,616	3,678	2,964	2,935	3,146	3,283	3,312	3,201	2,853
Oxnard-Thousand Oaks-Ventura, CA	4,519	3,621	4,093	3,818	3,884	3,535	3,104	3,112	2,792	2,801
Cincinnati-Middletown, OH-KY-IN	2,423	3,163	3,383	3,096	2,877	2,977	2,813	2,850	2,697	2,762
San Juan-Caguas-Guaynabo, PR...........	4,324	3,323	3,703	2,581	2,949	3,740	3,894	2,940	2,842	2,706
Milwaukee-Waukesha-West Allis, WI	2,320	3,520	3,058	2,813	2,949	2,893	2,569	2,885	2,767	2,686
Pittsburgh, PA	2,090	3,189	2,169	2,114	2,256	2,354	2,319	2,732	2,607	2,645
Other CBSAs	174,644	212,807	224,457	192,547	207,159	213,644	196,675	204,036	202,309	191,377
Other metropolitan areas	149,049	182,804	191,572	164,500	176,213	181,358	167,930	174,076	172,557	163,284
Other micropolitan areas.............	25,595	30,003	32,885	28,047	30,946	32,286	28,745	29,960	29,752	28,093
Non-CBSA	13,029	14,382	16,115	13,810	14,453	15,140	13,655	13,398	13,557	12,844
Unknown	15	23	27	26	22	14	11	9	3	45

Source: U.S. Department of Homeland Security.

Table 6.
PERSONS OBTAINING LAWFUL PERMANENT RESIDENT STATUS BY TYPE AND MAJOR CLASS OF ADMISSION: FISCAL YEARS 2004 TO 2013

Type and class of admission	2004	2005	2006	2007	2008	2009	2010	2011	2012	2013
TOTAL										
Total	957,883	1,122,257	1,266,129	1,052,415	1,107,126	1,130,818	1,042,625	1,062,040	1,031,631	990,553
Family-sponsored preferences	214,355	212,970	222,229	194,900	227,761	211,859	214,589	234,931	202,019	210,303
First: Unmarried sons/daughters of U.S. citizens and their children	26,380	24,729	25,432	22,858	26,173	23,965	26,998	27,299	20,660	24,358
Second: Spouses, children, and unmarried sons/daughters of alien residents	93,609	100,139	112,051	86,151	103,456	98,567	92,088	108,618	99,709	99,115
Third: Married sons/daughters of U.S. citizens and their spouses and children	28,695	22,953	21,491	20,611	29,273	25,930	32,817	27,704	21,752	21,294
Fourth: Brothers/sisters of U.S. citizens (at least 21 years of age) and their spouses and children	65,671	65,149	63,255	65,280	68,859	63,397	62,686	71,310	59,898	65,536
Immediate relatives of U.S. citizens	417,815	436,115	580,348	494,920	488,483	535,554	476,414	453,158	478,780	439,460
Spouses	252,193	259,144	339,843	274,358	265,671	317,129	271,909	258,320	273,429	248,332
Children [1]	88,088	94,858	120,064	103,828	101,342	98,270	88,297	80,311	81,121	71,382
Parents	77,534	82,113	120,441	116,734	121,470	120,155	116,208	114,527	124,230	119,746
Employment-based preferences	155,317	246,865	159,075	161,733	164,741	140,903	148,343	139,339	143,998	161,110
First: Priority workers	31,291	64,731	36,960	26,697	36,678	40,924	41,055	25,251	39,316	38,978
Second: Professionals with advanced degrees or aliens of exceptional ability	32,534	42,597	21,911	44,162	70,046	45,552	53,946	66,831	50,959	63,026
Third: Skilled workers, professionals, and unskilled workers	85,969	129,070	89,922	85,030	48,903	40,398	39,762	37,216	39,229	43,632
Fourth: Certain special immigrants	5,394	10,121	9,533	5,038	7,754	10,341	11,100	6,701	7,866	6,931
Fifth: Employment creation (investors)	129	346	749	806	1,360	3,688	2,480	3,340	6,628	8,543
Diversity	50,084	46,234	44,471	42,127	41,761	47,879	49,763	50,103	40,320	45,618
Refugees	61,013	112,676	99,609	54,942	90,030	118,836	92,741	113,045	105,528	77,395
Asylees	10,217	30,286	116,845	81,183	76,362	58,532	43,550	55,415	45,086	42,235
Parolees	7,121	7,715	4,569	1,999	1,172	2,385	1,592	1,147	758	556
Children born abroad to alien residents	707	571	623	597	637	587	716	633	643	643
Nicaraguan Adjustment and Central American Relief Act (NACARA)	2,292	1,155	661	340	296	296	248	158	183	138
Cancellation of removal	32,702	20,785	29,516	14,927	11,128	8,156	8,180	7,430	6,818	5,763
Haitian Refugee Immigration Fairness Act (HRIFA)	2,451	2,820	3,375	2,448	1,580	552	386	154	93	62
Other	3,809	4,065	4,808	2,299	3,175	5,279	6,103	6,527	7,405	7,270
ADJUSTMENTS OF STATUS										
Total	583,921	738,302	819,248	621,047	640,568	667,776	566,576	580,092	547,559	530,802
Family-sponsored preferences	64,427	70,459	79,709	52,059	56,899	39,787	26,279	28,346	18,560	26,415
First: Unmarried sons/daughters of U.S. citizens and their children	7,782	6,389	8,275	7,358	5,650	5,112	3,922	3,343	2,750	2,538
Second: Spouses, children, and unmarried sons/daughters of alien residents	45,669	55,362	62,507	37,046	41,881	24,597	11,716	11,985	8,692	6,520
Third: Married sons/daughters of U.S. citizens and their spouses and children	4,672	4,164	3,954	3,126	3,811	3,306	4,465	3,085	2,453	1,829
Fourth: Brothers/sisters of U.S. citizens (at least 21 years of age) and their spouses and children	6,304	4,544	4,973	4,529	5,557	6,772	6,176	9,933	4,665	15,528
Immediate relatives of U.S. citizens	269,964	266,851	357,127	277,188	251,090	309,073	252,842	243,174	239,986	232,105
Spouses	209,358	208,758	275,676	211,843	191,197	242,123	189,460	178,868	182,276	167,211
Children [1]	30,706	30,738	43,826	31,351	25,465	28,586	22,750	20,288	18,285	16,519
Parents	29,900	27,355	37,625	33,994	34,428	38,364	40,632	44,018	39,425	48,375
Employment-based preferences	128,232	219,987	121,586	133,082	149,527	127,121	136,010	124,384	126,016	140,009
First: Priority workers	27,060	60,240	32,060	23,802	35,082	39,420	39,070	23,605	37,799	37,283
Second: Professionals with advanced degrees or aliens of exceptional ability	31,134	41,109	20,939	42,991	68,832	44,336	52,388	65,140	49,414	60,956
Third: Skilled workers, professionals, and unskilled workers	65,875	109,713	60,390	62,642	38,981	33,525	34,433	29,757	31,208	34,937
Fourth: Certain special immigrants	4,094	8,737	7,917	3,332	6,301	8,855	9,384	5,306	6,644	5,602
Fifth: Employment creation (investors)	69	188	280	315	331	985	735	576	951	1,231

See footnotes at end of table.

Table 6.
PERSONS OBTAINING LAWFUL PERMANENT RESIDENT STATUS BY TYPE AND MAJOR CLASS OF ADMISSION: FISCAL YEARS 2004 TO 2013 – *Continued*

Type and class of admission	2004	2005	2006	2007	2008	2009	2010	2011	2012	2013
Diversity	2,031	1,850	1,853	1,360	1,440	1,277	1,571	1,617	1,356	1,505
Refugees.........................	61,013	112,676	99,609	54,942	90,030	118,836	92,741	113,045	105,528	77,395
Asylees..........................	10,217	30,286	116,845	81,183	76,362	58,532	43,550	55,415	45,086	42,235
Parolees	7,121	7,715	4,569	1,999	1,172	2,385	1,592	1,147	758	556
Children born abroad to alien residents	-	-	-	-	-	-	-	-	-	-
Nicaraguan Adjustment and Central American Relief Act (NACARA)	2,292	1,155	661	340	296	296	248	158	183	138
Cancellation of removal	32,702	20,785	29,516	14,927	11,128	8,156	8,180	7,430	6,818	5,763
Haitian Refugee Immigration Fairness Act (HRIFA)	2,451	2,820	3,375	2,448	1,580	552	386	154	93	62
Other............................	3,471	3,718	4,398	1,519	1,044	1,761	3,177	5,222	3,175	4,619
NEW ARRIVALS										
Total	373,962	383,955	446,881	431,368	466,558	463,042	476,049	481,948	484,072	459,751
Family-sponsored preferences	149,928	142,511	142,520	142,841	170,862	172,072	188,310	206,585	183,459	183,888
First: Unmarried sons/daughters of U.S. citizens and their children	18,598	18,340	17,157	15,500	20,523	18,853	23,076	23,956	17,910	21,820
Second: Spouses, children, and unmarried sons/daughters of alien residents	47,940	44,777	49,544	49,105	61,575	73,970	80,372	96,633	91,017	92,595
Third: Married sons/daughters of U.S. citizens and their spouses and children...	24,023	18,789	17,537	17,485	25,462	22,624	28,352	24,619	19,299	19,465
Fourth: Brothers/sisters of U.S. citizens (at least 21 years of age) and their spouses and children................	59,367	60,605	58,282	60,751	63,302	56,625	56,510	61,377	55,233	50,008
Immediate relatives of U.S. citizens........	147,851	169,264	223,221	217,732	237,393	226,481	223,572	209,984	238,794	207,355
Spouses........................	42,835	50,386	64,167	62,515	74,474	75,006	82,449	79,452	91,153	81,121
Children [1]	57,382	64,120	76,238	72,477	75,877	69,684	65,547	60,023	62,836	54,863
Parents........................	47,634	54,758	82,816	82,740	87,042	81,791	75,576	70,509	84,805	71,371
Employment-based preferences...........	27,085	26,878	37,489	28,651	15,214	13,782	12,333	14,955	17,982	21,101
First: Priority workers.................	4,231	4,491	4,900	2,895	1,596	1,504	1,985	1,646	1,517	1,695
Second: Professionals with advanced degrees or aliens of exceptional ability ...	1,400	1,488	972	1,171	1,214	1,216	1,558	1,691	1,545	2,070
Third: Skilled workers, professionals, and unskilled workers	20,094	19,357	29,532	22,388	9,922	6,873	5,329	7,459	8,021	8,695
Fourth: Certain special immigrants	1,300	1,384	1,616	1,706	1,453	1,486	1,716	1,395	1,222	1,329
Fifth: Employment creation (investors).....	60	158	469	491	1,029	2,703	1,745	2,764	5,677	7,312
Diversity	48,053	44,384	42,618	40,767	40,321	46,602	48,192	48,486	38,964	44,113
Refugees..........................	-	-	-	-	-	-	-	-	-	-
Asylees...........................	-	-	-	-	-	-	-	-	-	-
Parolees	-	-	-	-	-	-	-	-	-	-
Children born abroad to alien residents	707	571	623	597	637	587	716	633	643	643
Nicaraguan Adjustment and Central American Relief Act (NACARA)	-	-	-	-	-	-	-	-	-	-
Cancellation of removal	-	-	-	-	-	-	-	-	-	-
Haitian Refugee Immigration Fairness Act (HRIFA)	-	-	-	-	-	-	-	-	-	-
Other............................	338	347	410	780	2,131	3,518	2,926	1,305	4,230	2,651

- Represents zero.

[1] Includes orphans.

Source: U.S. Department of Homeland Security.

Table 7.
PERSONS OBTAINING LAWFUL PERMANENT RESIDENT STATUS BY TYPE AND DETAILED CLASS OF ADMISSION: FISCAL YEAR 2013

Type and class of admission	Total	Adjustments of status	New arrivals
Total, all immigrants....................	990,553	530,802	459,751
Family-sponsored preferences....................	210,303	26,415	183,888
First: Unmarried sons/daughters of U.S. citizens and their children	24,358	2,538	21,820
Unmarried sons/daughters of U.S. citizens, new arrivals (F11)....................	13,239	-	13,239
Unmarried sons/daughters of U.S. citizens, adjustments (F16)....................	2,370	2,370	-
Unmarried sons/daughters of U.S. citizens, new arrivals, self petitioning (B11)....................	D	-	D
Unmarried sons/daughters of U.S. citizens, adjustments, self petitioning (B16)	D	D	-
Children of F11 or F16, new arrivals (F12)	D	-	D
Children of F11 or F16, adjustments (F17)	D	D	-
Second: Spouses, children, and unmarried sons/daughters of alien residents....................	99,115	6,520	92,595
Spouses of alien residents, subject to country limits, new arrivals (F21)....................	8,979	-	8,979
Spouses of alien residents, subject to country limits, adjustments (F26)	1,564	1,564	-
Spouses of alien residents, subject to country limits, new arrivals, self petitioning (B21)....................	17	-	17
Spouses of alien residents, subject to country limits, adjustments, self petitioning (B26)	433	433	-
Spouses of alien residents, subject to country limits, adjustments, conditional (C26)	D	D	-
Spouses of alien residents, exempt from country limits, new arrivals (FX1)....................	18,477	-	18,477
Spouses of alien residents, exempt from country limits, adjustments (FX6)....................	898	898	-
Spouses of alien residents, exempt from country limits, new arrivals, self petitioning (BX1)....................	4	-	4
Spouses of alien residents, exempt from country limits, adjustments, self petitioning (BX6)....................	207	207	-
Spouses of alien residents, exempt from country limits, new arrivals, conditional (CX1)....................	3	-	3
Spouses of alien residents, exempt from country limits, adjustments, conditional (CX6)	D	D	-
Children of alien residents, subject to country limits, new arrivals (F22)	9,272	-	9,272
Children of alien residents, subject to country limits, adjustments (F27)....................	769	769	-
Children of alien residents, subject to country limits, new arrivals, self petitioning (B22)	11	-	11
Children of alien residents, subject to country limits, adjustments, self petitioning (B27)	72	72	-
Children of B21, B22, B26, or B27, subject to country limits, new arrivals (B23)	11	-	11
Children of B21, B22, B26, or B27, subject to country limits, adjustments (B28)....................	67	67	-
Children of F21, F22, F26, or F27, subject to country limits, new arrivals (F23)	4,332	-	4,332
Children of F21, F22, F26, or F27, subject to country limits, adjustments (F28)....................	44	44	-
Children of C24 or C29, subject to country limits, adjustments, conditional (C20)	6	6	-
Children of B24 or B29, subject to country limits, new arrivals (B25)	D	-	D
Children of B24 or B29, subject to country limits, adjustments (B20)....................	5	5	-
Children of F24 or F29, subject to country limits, new arrivals (F25)	9,433	-	9,433
Children of F24 or F29, subject to country limits, adjustments (F20)....................	101	101	-
Children of alien residents, exempt from country limits, new arrivals (FX2)	25,046	-	25,046
Children of alien residents, exempt from country limits, adjustments (FX7)....................	457	457	-
Children of alien residents, exempt from country limits, adjustments, self petitioning (BX7)	42	42	-
Children of BX1, BX2, BX6, or BX7, exempt from country limits, new arrivals (BX3)	D	-	D
Children of BX1, BX2, BX6, or BX7, exempt from country limits, adjustments (BX8)	37	37	-
Children of FX1, FX2, FX7, or FX8, exempt from country limits, new arrivals (FX3)....................	5,909	-	5,909
Children of FX1, FX2, FX7, or FX8, exempt from country limits, adjustments (FX8)	41	41	-
Step-children of alien residents, exempt from country limits, adjustments, conditional (CX7)	D	D	-
Unmarried sons/daughters of alien residents, subject to country limits, new arrivals (F24)	11,094	-	11,094
Unmarried sons/daughters of alien residents, subject to country limits, adjustments (F29)	1,762	1,762	-
Unmarried sons/daughters of alien residents, subject to country limits, new arrivals, self petitioning (B24)....................	4	-	4
Unmarried sons/daughters of alien residents, subject to country limits, adjustments, self petitioning (B29)	10	10	-
Third: Married sons/daughters of U.S. citizens and their spouses and children	21,294	1,829	19,465
Married sons/daughters of U.S. citizens, new arrivals (F31)....................	5,551	-	5,551
Married Amerasian sons/daughters of U.S. citizens, adjustments (A36)....................	D	D	-
Married sons/daughters of U.S. citizens, adjustments (F36)	840	840	-
Spouses of married sons/daughters of U.S. citizens, new arrivals (F32)....................	4,877	-	4,877
Spouses of married sons/daughters of U.S. citizens, adjustments (F37)	698	698	-
Spouses of married sons/daughters of U.S. citizens, adjustments, conditional (C37)	D	D	-
Children of married sons/daughters of U.S. citizens, new arrivals (F33)....................	9,037	-	9,037
Children of married sons/daughters of U.S. citizens, adjustments (F38)....................	D	D	-
Fourth: Brothers/sisters of U.S. citizens (at least 21 years of age) and their spouses and children....................	65,536	15,528	50,008
Brothers/sisters of U.S. citizens, new arrivals (F41)	17,593	-	17,593
Brothers/sisters of U.S. citizens, adjustments (F46)....................	9,429	9,429	-
Spouses of brothers/sisters of U.S. citizens, new arrivals (F42)....................	11,437	-	11,437
Spouses of brothers/sisters of U.S. citizens, adjustments (F47)	3,454	3,454	-
Children of brothers/sisters of U.S. citizens, new arrivals (F43)	20,978	-	20,978
Children of brothers/sisters of U.S. citizens, adjustments (F48)....................	2,645	2,645	-

See footnotes at end of table.

Table 7.
PERSONS OBTAINING LAWFUL PERMANENT RESIDENT STATUS BY TYPE AND DETAILED CLASS OF ADMISSION: FISCAL YEAR 2013 – *Continued*

Type and class of admission	Total	Adjustments of status	New arrivals
Immediate relatives of U.S. citizens.	439,460	232,105	207,355
Spouses, new arrivals (IR1)	42,556	-	42,556
Spouses, adjustments (IR6)	37,496	37,496	-
Spouses, new arrivals, conditional (CR1)	38,151	-	38,151
Spouses, adjustments, conditional (CR6)	101,842	101,842	-
Spouses, new arrivals, self petitioning (IB1)	130	-	130
Spouses, adjustments, self petitioning (IB6)	2,527	2,527	-
Spouses, widows or widowers, new arrivals (IW1)	284	-	284
Spouses, widows or widowers, adjustments (IW6)	407	407	-
Spouses, entered as fiancé(e), adjustments, conditional (CF1)	24,341	24,341	-
Spouses, entered as fiancé(e), adjustments (IF1)	598	598	-
Children, new arrivals (IR2)	41,617	-	41,617
Children, adjustments (IR7)	8,046	8,046	-
Children, new arrivals, conditional (CR2)	6,316	-	6,316
Children, adjustments, conditional (CR7)	4,992	4,992	-
Children, new arrivals, self petitioning (IB2)	D	-	D
Children, adjustments, self petitioning (IB7)	278	278	-
Children of IB1 or IB6, new arrivals (IB3)	190	-	190
Children of IB1 or IB6, adjustments (IB8)	213	213	-
Children of IW1 or IW6, new arrivals (IW2)	102	-	102
Children of IW1 or IW6, adjustments (IW7)	63	63	-
Step-children of CF1, adjustments (CF2)	2,650	2,650	-
Children of IF1, adjustments (IF2)	243	243	-
Children adopted abroad under the Hague Convention, new arrivals (IH3)	2,341	-	2,341
Children to be adopted under the Hague Convention, new arrivals (IH4)	244	-	244
Orphans adopted abroad, new arrivals (IR3)	2,961	-	2,961
Orphans adopted abroad, adjustments (IR8)	17	17	-
Orphans to be adopted, new arrivals (IR4)	994	-	994
Orphans to be adopted, adjustments (IR9)	17	17	-
Parents of adult U.S. citizens, new arrivals (IR5)	71,370	-	71,370
Parents of adult U.S. citizens, adjustments (IRO)	48,358	48,358	-
Parents battered or abused, of U.S. citizens, new arrivals, self petitioning (IB5)	D	-	D
Parents battered or abused, of U.S. citizens, adjustments, self petitioning (IBO)	17	17	-
Employment-based preferences	161,110	140,009	21,101
First: Priority workers	38,978	37,283	1,695
Aliens with extraordinary ability, new arrivals (E11)	461	-	461
Aliens with extraordinary ability, adjustments (E16)	3,603	3,603	-
Outstanding professors or researchers, new arrivals (E12)	19	-	19
Outstanding professors or researchers, adjustments (E17)	3,098	3,098	-
Multinational executives or managers, new arrivals (E13)	129	-	129
Multinational executives or managers, adjustments (E18)	8,915	8,915	-
Spouses of E11, E12, E13, E16, E17, or E18, new arrivals (E14)	445	-	445
Spouses of E11, E12, E13, E16, E17, or E18, adjustments (E19)	11,999	11,999	-
Children of E11, E12, E13, E16, E17, or E18, new arrivals (E15)	641	-	641
Children of E11, E12, E13, E16, E17, or E18, adjustments (E10)	9,668	9,668	-
Second: Professionals with advanced degrees or aliens of exceptional ability	63,026	60,956	2,070
Professionals holding advanced degrees, new arrivals (E21)	646	-	646
Professionals holding advanced degrees, adjustments (E26)	30,484	30,484	-
Spouses of E21 or E26, new arrivals (E22)	616	-	616
Spouses of E21 or E26, adjustments (E27)	21,045	21,045	-
Children of E21 or E26, new arrivals (E23)	808	-	808
Children of E21 or E26, adjustments (E28)	9,427	9,427	-
Third: Skilled workers, professionals, and needed unskilled workers	43,632	34,937	8,695
Schedule—A worker, new arrivals (EX1)	D	-	D
Schedule—A worker, adjustments (EX6)	D	D	-
Skilled workers, new arrivals (E31)	1,366	-	1,366
Skilled workers, adjustments (E36)	7,219	7,219	-
Professionals with baccalaureate degrees, new arrivals (E32)	729	-	729
Professionals with baccalaureate degrees, adjustments (E37)	9,377	9,377	-
Needed unskilled workers, new arrivals (EW3)	621	-	621
Needed unskilled workers, adjustments (EW8)	722	722	-

See footnotes at end of table.

Table 7.
PERSONS OBTAINING LAWFUL PERMANENT RESIDENT STATUS BY TYPE AND DETAILED CLASS OF ADMISSION:
FISCAL YEAR 2013 – Continued

Type and class of admission	Total	Adjustments of status	New arrivals
Chinese Student Protection Act (CSPA) principals, adjustments (EC6)	D	D	-
Spouses of E31, E32, E36, or E37, new arrivals (E34)	1,706	-	1,706
Spouses of E31, E32, E36, or E37, adjustments (E39)	10,797	10,797	-
Spouses of EW3 or EW8, new arrivals (EW4)	D	-	D
Spouses of EW3 or EW8, adjustments (EW9)	409	409	-
Spouses of EC6, adjustments (EC7)	D	D	-
Children of E31, E32, E36, or E37, new arrivals (E35)	3,098	-	3,098
Children of E31, E32, E36, or E37, adjustments (E30)	6,197	6,197	-
Children of EW3 or EW8, new arrivals (EW5)	724	-	724
Children of EW3 or EW8, adjustments (EW0)	D	D	-
Fourth: Certain special immigrants	6,931	5,602	1,329
Broadcast (IBCB of BBG) employees, new arrivals (BC1)	14	-	14
Broadcast (IBCG of BBG) employees, adjustments (BC6)	22	22	-
Ministers, new arrivals (SD1)	64	-	64
Ministers, adjustments (SD6)	793	793	-
Employees of U.S. government abroad, new arrivals (SE1)	284	-	284
Employees of U.S. government abroad, adjustments (SE6)	9	9	-
Former employees of the Panama Canal Company or Canal Zone Government, new arrivals (SF1)	D	-	D
Former employees of the Panama Canal Company or Canal Zone Government, adjustments (SF6)	D	D	-
Retired employees of international organizations, new arrivals (SK1)	D	-	D
Retired employees of international organizations, adjustments (SK6)	188	188	-
Juvenile court dependents, new arrivals (SL1)	29	-	29
Juvenile court dependents, adjustments (SL6)	2,735	2,735	-
Retired NATO-6 civilian employees, adjustments (SN6)	D	D	-
Religious workers, new arrivals (SR1)	35	-	35
Religious workers, adjustments (SR6)	500	500	-
Spouses of BC1 or BC6, new arrivals (BC2)	7	-	7
Spouses of BC1 or BC6, adjustments (BC7)	9	9	-
Spouses of SD1 or SD6, new arrivals (SD2)	67	-	67
Spouses of SD1 or SD6, adjustments (SD7)	336	336	-
Spouses of SE1 or SE6, new arrivals (SE2)	204	-	204
Spouses of SE1 or SE6, adjustments (SE7)	3	3	-
Spouses or children of SG1 or SG6, adjustments (SG7)	D	D	-
Spouses of SK1 or SK6, adjustments (SK7)	39	39	-
Spouses of SN1 of SN6, adjustments (SN7)	D	D	-
Spouses of SR1 or SR6, new arrivals (SR2)	17	-	17
Spouses of SR1 or SR6, adjustments (SR7)	127	127	-
Children of BC1 or BC6, new arrivals (BC3)	15	-	15
Children of BC1 or BC6, adjustments (BC8)	6	6	-
Children of SD1 or SD6, new arrivals (SD3)	117	-	117
Children of SD1 or SD6, adjustments (SD8)	419	419	-
Children of SE1 or SE6, new arrivals (SE3)	437	-	437
Children of SE1 or SE6, adjustments (SE8)	11	11	-
Certain unmarried children of SK1 or SK6, new arrivals (SK3)	D	-	D
Certain unmarried children of SK1 or SK6, adjustments (SK8)	247	247	-
Children of SR1 or SR6, new arrivals (SR3)	33	-	33
Children of SR1 or SR6, adjustments (SR8)	149	149	-
Certain unmarried sons/daughters of SN1 or SN6, adjustments (SN8)	3	3	-
Fifth: Employment creation (investors)	8,543	1,231	7,312
Employment creation, not in targeted area, new arrivals, conditional (C51)	32	-	32
Employment creation, not in targeted area, adjustments, conditional (C56)	56	56	-
Employment creation, targeted area, pilot program, new arrivals, conditional (I51)	2,455	-	2,455
Employment creation, targeted area, pilot program, adjustments, conditional (I56)	480	480	-
Employment creation, targeted area, new arrivals, conditional (T51)	23	-	23
Employment creation, targeted area, adjustments, conditional (T56)	56	56	-
Investor pilot program, not targeted, new arrivals, conditional (R51)	D	-	D
Investor pilot program, not targeted, adjustments, conditional (R56)	D	D	-
Spouses of C51 or C56, new arrivals, conditional (C52)	29	-	29
Spouses of C51 or C56, adjustments, conditional (C57)	D	D	-
Spouses of I51 or I56, new arrivals, conditional (I52)	1,776	-	1,776
Spouses of I51 or I56, adjustments, conditional (I57)	200	200	-
Spouses of T51 or T56, new arrivals, conditional (T52)	22	-	22
Spouses of T51 or T56, adjustments, conditional (T57)	31	31	-
Spouses of R51 or R56, adjustments, conditional (R57)	D	D	-

See footnotes at end of table.

Table 7.

PERSONS OBTAINING LAWFUL PERMANENT RESIDENT STATUS BY TYPE AND DETAILED CLASS OF ADMISSION: FISCAL YEAR 2013 – *Continued*

Type and class of admission	Total	Adjustments of status	New arrivals
Children of C51 or C56, new arrivals, conditional (C53)	46	-	46
Children of C51 or C56, adjustments, conditional (C58)	55	55	-
Children of I51 or I56, new arrivals, conditional (I53)	2,894	-	2,894
Children of I51 or I56, adjustments, conditional (I58)	262	262	-
Children of T51 or T56, new arrivals, conditional (T53)	30	-	30
Children of T51 or T56, adjustments, conditional (T58)	61	61	-
Children of R51 or R56, new arrivals, conditional (R53)	D	-	D
Diversity	45,618	1,505	44,113
Principals, new arrivals (DV1)	23,483	-	23,483
Principals, adjustments (DV6)	938	938	-
Spouses of DV1 or DV6, new arrivals (DV2)	10,034	-	10,034
Spouses of DV1 or DV6, adjustments (DV7)	365	365	-
Children of DV1 or DV6, new arrivals (DV3)	10,596	-	10,596
Children of DV1 or DV6, adjustments (DV8)	202	202	-
Refugees and asylees	119,630	119,630	-
Refugees	77,395	77,395	-
Cuban refugees (P.L. 89-732 of 1966) (CU6)	24,632	24,632	-
Non-Cuban spouses or children of Cuban refugees (CU7)	2,772	2,772	-
Indochinese refugees (P.L. 95-145 of 1977) (IC6)	D	D	-
Spouses or children of Indochinese refugees not qualified as refugees on their own (IC7)	D	D	-
Refugee parolees (P.L. 95-412 of 1978) (R86)	D	D	-
Other refugees (P.L. 96-212 Refugee Act of 1980) (RE6)	21,993	21,993	-
Spouses of RE6 (RE7)	8,548	8,548	-
Children of RE6 (RE8)	19,441	19,441	-
Other relatives (RE9)	3	3	-
Asylees	42,235	42,235	-
Asylees (AS6)	22,679	22,679	-
Iraqi asylees (GA6)	D	D	-
Spouses of AS6 (AS7)	D	D	-
Children of AS6 (AS8)	11,631	11,631	-
Parolees	556	556	-
Parolees, Polish/Hungarian (PH6)	D	D	-
Parolees, Soviet/Indochinese (LA6)	529	529	-
Parolees, Indochinese (ID6)	D	D	-
Children born abroad to alien residents (NA3)	643	-	643
Nicaraguan and Central American Relief Act (NACARA Section 202, P.L. 105-100)	138	138	-
Principals (NC6)	104	104	-
Spouses of NC6 (NC7)	16	16	-
Children of NC6 (NC8)	14	14	-
Unmarried sons/daughters of NC6 (NC9)	4	4	-
Cancellation of removal	5,763	5,763	-
Sec. 244, P.L. 89-236, subject to 4,000 annual limit (Z13)	4,069	4,069	-
Battered spouses or children (Violence Against Women Act), P.L. 103-322 of 1994, subject to 4,000 annual limit (Z14)	D	D	-
Salvadoran, Guatemalan and former Soviet bloc country nationals (NACARA Section 203, P.L. 105-100 of 1997) (Z15)	1,606	1,606	-
Crewmen who entered on or before June 30, 1964 and are immediate relatives of U.S. citizens or special immigrants (Z56)	D	D	-
Haitian Refugee Immigration Fairness Act (HRIFA, P.L. 105-277)	62	62	-
Haitian asylum applicants (HA6)	26	26	-
Haitian parolees (HB6)	6	6	-
Haitian children without parents (HC6)	D	D	-
Spouses of HA6 (HA7)	D	D	-
Spouses of HB6 (HB7)	3	3	-
Children of HA6 (HA8)	16	16	-
Children of HB6 (HB8)	4	4	-
Unmarried sons/daughters of HA6 (HA9)	4	4	-
IRCA legalization	40	40	-
Entered without inspection before 1/1/82 (W16)	20	20	-
Entered as nonimmigrant and overstayed visa before 1/1/82 (W26)	D	D	-
Seasonal Agricultural Workers (SAW), worked at least 90 days during each year ending May 1, 1984, 1985, and 1986 (S16)	D	D	-
Seasonal Agricultural Workers (SAW), worked at least 90 days during the year ending on May 1, 1986 (S26)	14	14	-
IRCA legalization dependents	8	4	4
Spouses of legalized aliens, new arrivals (LB1)	D	-	D
Spouses of legalized aliens, new arrivals, conditional (CB1)	D	-	D
Spouses of legalized aliens, adjustments (LB6)	D	D	-

See footnotes at end of table.

Table 7.
PERSONS OBTAINING LAWFUL PERMANENT RESIDENT STATUS BY TYPE AND DETAILED CLASS OF ADMISSION: FISCAL YEAR 2013 – *Continued*

Type and class of admission	Total	Adjustments of status	New arrivals
Children of LB1 or LB6, new arrivals (LB2)	D	-	D
Children of LB1 or LB6, adjustments (LB7)	D	D	-
Other	7,222	4,575	2,647
Amerasians, born in Vietnam between 1/1/62-1/1/76, new arrivals (AM1)	6	-	6
Spouses or children of AM1 or AM6, new arrivals (AM2)	11	-	11
Spouses or children of AM1 or AM6, adjustments (AM7)	D	D	-
Mothers, guardians, or next of kin of AM1 or AM6, new arrivals (AM3)	D	-	D
Individuals born under diplomatic status, adjustments, (DS1)	21	21	-
Parolees adjusting under the Help HAITI Act of 2010, adjustments (HH6)	99	99	-
Cuban Haitian entrants, adjustments (P.L. 99-603) (CH6)	D	D	-
American Indians born in Canada, new arrivals (S13)	214	-	214
Special immigrant interpreters who are nationals of Iraq or Afghanistan, new arrivals (SI1)	25	-	25
Special immigrant interpreters who are nationals of Iraq or Afghanistan, adjustments (SI6)	3	3	-
Spouses of SI1 or SI6, new arrivals (SI2)	18	-	18
Children of SI1 or SI6, new arrivals (SI3)	51	-	51
Certain Iraqis employed by US Government, new arrivals (SQ1)	866	-	866
Certain Iraqis employed by US Government, adjustments (SQ6)	5	5	-
Spouses of SQ1 or SQ6, new arrivals (SQ2)	464	-	464
Spouses of SQ1 or SQ6, adjustments (SQ7)	D	D	-
Children of SQ1 or SQ6, new arrivals (SQ3)	859	-	859
Adjustment of T1 nonimmigrant (ST6)	297	297	-
Adjustment of T2 nonimmigrant (ST7)	91	91	-
Adjustment of T3 nonimmigrant (ST8)	194	194	-
Adjustment of T4 nonimmigrant (ST0)	11	11	-
Adjustment of T5 nonimmigrant (ST9)	15	15	-
Spouses of SU6, new arrivals (SU2)	D	-	D
Children of SU6, new arrivals (SU3)	42	-	42
Parents of SU6, new arrivals (SU5)	D	-	D
Adjustment of U1 nonimmigrant (SU6)	2,371	2,371	-
Adjustment of U2 nonimmigrant (SU7)	211	211	-
Adjustment of U3 nonimmigrant (SU8)	795	795	-
Adjustment of U4 nonimmigrant (SU0)	231	231	-
Adjustment of U5 nonimmigrant (SU9)	104	104	-
Late amnesty applicants (Immigration Reform and Control Act) (W46)	6	6	-
Children born subsequent to issuance of parent's employment-based preference visa, new arrivals (XE3)	D	-	D
Children born subsequent to issuance of parent's family-sponsored preference visa, new arrivals (XF3)	34	-	34
Children born subsequent to issuance of parent's immediate relative of U.S. citizen visa, new arrivals (XR3)	15	-	15
Children born subsequent to issuance of parent's visa other, new arrivals (XN3)	36	-	36
Entered before 7/1/24, Section 249, P.L. 89-236, adjustments (Z33)	D	D	-
Entered 7/1/24-6/28/40, Section 249, P.L. 89-236, adjustments (Z03)	D	D	-
Entered 6/29/40-1/1/72, Section 249, P.L. 89-236, adjustments (Z66)	104	104	-
Foreign government official who is immediate relative of U.S. citizen or special immigrant (Z83)	10	10	-

D Data withheld to limit disclosure.

- Represents zero.

Source: U.S. Department of Homeland Security.

Table 8.
PERSONS OBTAINING LAWFUL PERMANENT RESIDENT STATUS BY SEX, AGE, MARITAL STATUS, AND OCCUPATION: FISCAL YEAR 2013

Characteristic	Total	Sex Male	Sex Female	Sex Unknown
AGE				
Total . . .	990,553	434,284	513,736	42,533
Under 1 year . . .	3,507	1,719	1,691	97
1 to 4 years . . .	30,243	14,714	15,002	527
5 to 9 years . . .	46,203	23,244	22,207	752
10 to 14 years . . .	56,988	28,491	27,387	1,110
15 to 19 years . . .	75,497	37,703	36,467	1,327
20 to 24 years . . .	90,396	39,234	50,105	1,057
25 to 29 years . . .	112,244	47,571	63,886	787
30 to 34 years . . .	122,446	56,069	65,609	768
35 to 39 years . . .	104,210	50,575	53,071	564
40 to 44 years . . .	81,892	37,794	43,564	534
45 to 49 years . . .	63,818	27,903	35,427	488
50 to 54 years . . .	50,001	20,872	28,726	403
55 to 59 years . . .	40,195	16,096	23,654	445
60 to 64 years . . .	31,529	12,584	18,539	406
65 to 74 years . . .	36,117	14,658	20,903	556
75 years and over . . .	12,758	5,049	7,493	216
Unknown . . .	32,509	8	5	32,496
BROAD AGE GROUPS				
Total . . .	990,553	434,284	513,736	42,533
Under 16 years . . .	150,511	74,975	72,817	2,719
16 to 20 years . . .	80,199	39,575	39,213	1,411
21 years and over . . .	727,334	319,726	401,701	5,907
Unknown . . .	32,509	8	5	32,496
MARITAL STATUS				
Total . . .	990,553	434,284	513,736	42,533
Single . . .	355,199	177,516	163,544	14,139
Married . . .	579,295	244,100	309,961	25,234
Widowed . . .	25,564	2,820	20,765	1,979
Divorced/separated . . .	26,107	7,666	17,265	1,176
Unknown . . .	4,388	2,182	2,201	5
OCCUPATION				
Total . . .	990,553	434,284	513,736	42,533
Management, professional, and related occupations . . .	117,974	71,952	41,529	4,493
Service occupations . . .	46,841	25,137	19,091	2,613
Sales and office occupations . . .	29,767	12,301	15,148	2,318
Farming, fishing, and forestry occupations . . .	11,589	8,672	2,071	846
Construction, extraction, maintenance, and repair occupations . . .	6,538	6,321	135	82
Production, transportation, and material moving occupations . . .	40,153	29,563	9,140	1,450
Military . . .	46	38	8	-
No occupation/not working outside home . . .	471,041	162,159	283,733	25,149
Homemakers . . .	130,162	4,735	114,407	11,020
Students or children . . .	249,910	120,224	119,489	10,197
Retirees . . .	9,330	3,980	5,277	73
Unemployed . . .	81,639	33,220	44,560	3,859
Unknown . . .	266,604	118,141	142,881	5,582

- Represents zero.

Source: U.S. Department of Homeland Security.

Table 9.
PERSONS OBTAINING LAWFUL PERMANENT RESIDENT STATUS BY BROAD CLASS OF ADMISSION AND SELECTED DEMOGRAPHIC CHARACTERISTICS: FISCAL YEAR 2013

Characteristic	Total	Family-sponsored preferences	Employment-based preferences	Immediate relatives of U.S. citizens	Diversity	Refugees and asylees	Other
SEX							
Total	990,553	210,303	161,110	439,460	45,618	119,630	14,432
Male	434,284	92,857	81,638	167,980	23,099	61,693	7,017
Female	513,736	101,165	78,003	251,004	18,220	57,937	7,407
Unknown	42,533	16,281	1,469	20,476	4,299	-	8
AGE							
Total	990,553	210,303	161,110	439,460	45,618	119,630	14,432
Under 1 year	3,507	1,191	160	741	724	-	691
1 to 4 years	30,243	10,113	3,438	9,121	2,868	4,152	551
5 to 9 years	46,203	15,277	8,253	11,553	2,647	8,002	471
10 to 14 years	56,988	19,111	9,779	16,773	1,830	8,980	515
15 to 19 years	75,497	26,344	11,189	25,261	1,990	9,968	745
20 to 24 years	90,396	21,610	5,470	42,524	5,810	13,930	1,052
25 to 29 years	112,244	13,063	8,756	63,837	8,410	16,686	1,492
30 to 34 years	122,446	15,758	32,591	51,925	6,713	13,449	2,010
35 to 39 years	104,210	16,869	35,346	34,161	4,307	11,244	2,283
40 to 44 years	81,892	16,630	22,064	28,045	2,610	10,439	2,104
45 to 49 years	63,818	15,155	12,482	25,229	1,686	8,001	1,265
50 to 54 years	50,001	12,070	6,143	24,798	1,069	5,241	680
55 to 59 years	40,195	8,316	2,616	25,112	638	3,217	296
60 to 64 years	31,529	4,457	1,135	23,156	307	2,342	132
65 to 74 years	36,117	2,553	480	29,949	178	2,839	118
75 years and over	12,758	293	39	11,249	14	1,140	23
Unknown	32,509	11,493	1,169	16,026	3,817	-	4
BROAD AGE GROUPS							
Total	990,553	210,303	161,110	439,460	45,618	119,630	14,432
Under 16 years	150,511	50,490	23,844	42,340	8,432	23,030	2,375
16 to 20 years	80,199	28,072	10,847	27,675	2,508	10,311	786
21 years and over	727,334	120,248	125,250	353,419	30,861	86,289	11,267
Unknown	32,509	11,493	1,169	16,026	3,817	-	4
MARITAL STATUS							
Total	990,553	210,303	161,110	439,460	45,618	119,630	14,432
Single	355,199	128,357	55,197	82,455	23,042	59,888	6,260
Married	579,295	75,222	102,911	321,509	21,832	51,521	6,300
Widowed	25,564	1,469	191	21,163	138	2,478	125
Divorced/separated	26,107	5,008	2,121	12,582	594	5,001	801
Unknown	4,388	247	690	1,751	12	742	946
OCCUPATION							
Total	990,553	210,303	161,110	439,460	45,618	119,630	14,432
Management, professional, and related occupations	117,974	14,270	61,067	26,563	11,530	4,206	338
Service occupations	46,841	13,067	2,613	18,273	4,036	8,588	264
Sales and office occupations	29,767	9,914	2,993	12,330	2,530	1,830	170
Farming, fishing, and forestry occupations	11,589	4,870	221	6,061	D	D	91
Construction, extraction, maintenance, and repair occupations	6,538	1,241	522	3,813	28	805	129
Production, transportation, and material moving occupations	40,153	10,235	2,651	16,162	754	10,070	281
Military	46	6	9	23	D	D	-
No occupation/not working outside home	471,041	127,996	57,934	213,151	19,506	48,843	3,611
Homemakers	130,162	28,909	15,973	77,611	1,738	5,452	479
Students or children	249,910	88,254	36,145	74,715	15,672	32,338	2,786
Retirees	9,330	160	230	8,238	19	660	23
Unemployed	81,639	10,673	5,586	52,587	2,077	10,393	323
Unknown	266,604	28,704	33,100	143,084	7,085	45,083	9,548

D Data withheld to limit disclosure.

- Represents zero.

Source: U.S. Department of Homeland Security.

Table 10.
PERSONS OBTAINING LAWFUL PERMANENT RESIDENT STATUS BY BROAD CLASS OF ADMISSION AND REGION
AND COUNTRY OF BIRTH: FISCAL YEAR 2013

Region and country of birth	Total	Family-sponsored preferences	Employment-based preferences	Immediate relatives of U.S. citizens	Diversity	Refugees and asylees	Other
REGION							
Total..	990,553	210,303	161,110	439,460	45,618	119,630	14,432
Africa..	98,304	9,603	5,605	43,550	18,560	20,577	409
Asia..	400,548	78,708	101,860	141,880	14,958	59,649	3,493
Europe..	86,556	5,145	21,806	44,319	10,143	4,338	805
North America..	315,660	96,178	18,676	160,598	468	30,854	8,886
Oceania..	5,277	447	1,201	2,850	715	40	24
South America..	80,945	19,247	11,833	44,314	662	4,101	788
Unknown..	3,263	975	129	1,949	112	71	27
COUNTRY							
Total..	990,553	210,303	161,110	439,460	45,618	119,630	14,432
Afghanistan..	2,196	271	66	699	64	520	576
Albania..	3,186	359	92	1,565	938	227	5
Algeria..	1,241	75	65	423	628	45	5
Angola..	143	23	6	69	14	31	-
Anguilla..	22	12	D	D	-	-	1
Antigua-Barbuda..	344	144	6	180	9	4	1
Argentina..	4,372	314	1,296	2,414	38	245	65
Armenia..	2,722	238	121	1,165	803	387	8
Aruba..	45	6	10	29	-	-	-
Australia..	2,759	56	868	1,451	368	D	D
Austria..	415	13	143	209	38	5	7
Azerbaijan..	637	54	54	283	131	109	6
Bahamas..	630	73	61	458	15	13	10
Bahrain..	115	12	47	32	12	12	-
Bangladesh..	12,099	6,272	740	4,701	92	245	49
Barbados..	428	140	D	246	-	D	-
Belarus..	1,970	97	188	656	682	335	12
Belgium..	675	20	298	292	50	10	5
Belize..	946	299	53	561	10	8	15
Benin..	342	15	4	183	117	18	5
Bermuda..	88	13	17	55	-	-	3
Bhutan..	8,954	5	9	24	4	8,911	1
Bolivia..	2,071	485	326	1,129	30	72	29
Bosnia-Herzegovina..	697	37	61	449	39	111	-
Botswana..	53	D	18	27	D	5	-
Brazil..	11,033	549	2,801	7,273	9	265	136
British Virgin Islands..	45	16	3	26	-	-	-
Brunei..	21	D	13	4	D	-	-
Bulgaria..	2,844	122	404	1,454	798	58	8
Burkina Faso..	585	20	24	288	115	134	4
Burma..	12,565	476	101	687	190	11,110	1
Burundi..	260	9	8	39	20	184	-
Cambodia..	2,624	381	50	1,782	340	60	11
Cameroon..	3,908	253	119	1,212	1,153	1,165	6
Canada..	13,181	608	6,120	6,088	61	26	278
Cape Verde..	1,673	871	8	787	3	-	4
Cayman Islands..	44	9	3	28	D	D	-
Central African Republic..	213	9	4	18	D	179	D
Chad..	111	7	D	23	6	72	D
Chile..	1,736	208	381	1,067	14	49	17
China, People's Republic..	71,798	13,109	20,245	24,135	26	14,146	137
Colombia..	21,131	5,322	1,812	12,709	8	1,170	110
Congo, Democratic Republic..	2,792	68	35	421	1,076	1,190	2
Congo, Republic..	1,059	38	12	201	509	294	5
Costa Rica..	2,114	249	211	1,564	21	47	22
Cote d'Ivoire..	1,486	131	62	642	235	379	37
Croatia..	353	16	78	219	16	23	1

See footnotes at end of table.

Table 10.
PERSONS OBTAINING LAWFUL PERMANENT RESIDENT STATUS BY BROAD CLASS OF ADMISSION AND REGION AND COUNTRY OF BIRTH: FISCAL YEAR 2013 – *Continued*

Region and country of birth	Total	Family-sponsored preferences	Employment-based preferences	Immediate relatives of U.S. citizens	Diversity	Refugees and asylees	Other
Cuba	32,219	2,492	12	3,110	194	26,407	4
Cyprus	126	D	54	58	7	D	1
Czech Republic	676	23	132	475	28	8	10
Czechoslovakia (former)	74	4	33	31	D	-	D
Denmark	506	17	239	237	9	D	D
Djibouti	90	D	D	20	7	58	-
Dominica	244	155	6	76	6	-	1
Dominican Republic	41,311	22,147	380	18,568	26	90	100
Ecuador	10,591	4,095	927	5,173	D	158	D
Egypt	10,294	813	814	3,218	3,101	2,321	27
El Salvador	18,260	8,232	813	7,449	-	425	1,341
Equatorial Guinea	18	D	D	12	-	3	-
Eritrea	2,138	139	31	501	163	1,303	1
Estonia	211	15	36	133	16	10	1
Ethiopia	13,097	1,390	251	5,331	2,255	3,858	12
Fiji	895	225	29	375	226	36	4
Finland	331	5	161	137	23	D	D
France	4,425	153	2,086	1,896	250	27	13
Gabon	127	3	6	77	7	33	1
Gambia	1,018	76	24	644	4	237	33
Georgia	1,368	75	92	734	354	96	17
Germany	6,032	141	1,927	3,331	558	50	25
Ghana	10,265	1,324	451	6,407	1,989	73	21
Greece	1,361	65	288	914	73	18	3
Grenada	687	235	30	413	D	D	6
Guatemala	10,224	3,700	778	3,945	D	734	D
Guinea	1,518	77	25	423	174	780	39
Guinea-Bissau	43	D	4	29	5	D	1
Guyana	5,897	3,569	132	2,164	12	9	11
Haiti	20,351	9,908	113	8,142	-	1,997	191
Honduras	8,898	3,133	623	4,591	29	243	279
Hong Kong	2,226	768	738	671	31	12	6
Hungary	1,052	39	253	640	106	10	4
Iceland	139	D	77	49	10	-	D
India	68,458	11,943	35,720	19,756	39	754	246
Indonesia	2,731	265	657	1,340	112	338	19
Iran	12,863	2,272	1,584	3,054	3,447	2,481	25
Iraq	9,552	266	96	668	39	6,804	1,679
Ireland	1,626	36	614	920	50	D	D
Israel	3,996	212	1,509	2,078	124	38	35
Italy	2,960	111	1,038	1,564	168	69	10
Jamaica	19,400	6,095	679	12,510	D	64	D
Japan	5,925	140	2,343	3,115	294	10	23
Jordan	4,188	1,255	282	2,393	77	167	14
Kazakhstan	1,241	47	145	601	271	164	13
Kenya	6,123	379	586	2,927	903	1,307	21
Korea, North	48	7	17	12	-	12	-
Korea, South	23,166	1,795	14,300	6,978	16	19	58
Kosovo	839	92	23	436	122	166	-
Kuwait	937	207	214	371	74	66	5
Kyrgyzstan	652	16	40	214	175	199	8
Laos	923	88	26	681	D	124	D
Latvia	424	23	53	287	45	11	5
Lebanon	2,783	777	455	1,372	69	97	13
Lesotho	20	-	5	9	D	D	-
Liberia	3,334	397	34	1,238	896	761	8
Libya	376	21	45	173	46	91	-
Lithuania	854	58	88	553	138	14	3

See footnotes at end of table.

Table 10.
PERSONS OBTAINING LAWFUL PERMANENT RESIDENT STATUS BY BROAD CLASS OF ADMISSION AND REGION AND COUNTRY OF BIRTH: FISCAL YEAR 2013 – *Continued*

Region and country of birth	Total	Family-sponsored preferences	Employment-based preferences	Immediate relatives of U.S. citizens	Diversity	Refugees and asylees	Other
Luxembourg	40	D	11	21	5	D	-
Macau	106	49	24	D	D	-	-
Macedonia	895	113	57	560	128	32	5
Madagascar	95	D	21	49	18	D	-
Malawi	159	8	32	103	7	7	2
Malaysia	2,477	186	771	609	30	874	7
Mali	667	39	25	369	17	182	35
Malta	43	7	D	22	D	7	-
Marshall Islands	46	-	D	D	-	-	-
Mauritania	354	26	3	73	5	247	-
Mauritius	83	6	29	40	D	D	1
Mexico	135,028	35,528	8,066	85,476	7	597	5,354
Moldova	2,485	80	77	733	883	579	133
Mongolia	729	18	149	278	98	177	9
Montenegro	265	32	4	206	D	20	D
Morocco	3,336	325	135	2,241	606	19	10
Mozambique	73	3	11	34	3	22	-
Namibia	57	-	11	37	3	4	2
Nepal	13,046	492	1,362	1,822	3,210	6,137	23
Netherlands	1,142	33	560	514	27	4	4
Netherlands Antilles	128	31	18	73	D	D	1
New Zealand	921	40	287	484	104	D	D
Nicaragua	3,048	868	73	1,874	18	127	88
Niger	37	8	-	24	5	-	-
Nigeria	13,840	2,059	900	7,957	2,778	115	31
Norway	335	10	117	192	D	D	-
Oman	73	9	32	25	3	4	-
Pakistan	13,251	3,966	2,553	5,956	14	696	66
Palau	16	D	D	12	-	-	-
Panama	1,234	251	96	845	9	23	10
Papua New Guinea	27	D	5	15	D	-	-
Paraguay	448	66	59	292	3	26	2
Peru	12,564	3,770	918	7,420	4	328	124
Philippines	54,446	15,170	10,482	28,653	D	33	D
Poland	6,430	1,215	1,111	3,403	645	15	41
Portugal	918	80	188	627	14	7	2
Qatar	191	43	43	66	25	12	2
Romania	3,773	292	891	2,112	401	55	22
Russia	9,753	458	1,509	5,411	1,452	836	87
Rwanda	540	16	9	79	97	335	4
Saint Kitts-Nevis	259	115	8	126	5	-	5
Saint Lucia	853	238	27	572	9	3	4
Saint Vincent and the Grenadines	529	168	23	328	7	-	3
Samoa	237	12	-	225	-	-	-
Saudi Arabia	1,463	224	270	695	148	117	9
Senegal	1,340	153	72	897	75	95	48
Serbia	866	39	111	611	73	32	-
Serbia and Montenegro	653	68	74	276	79	138	18
Sierra Leone	1,651	198	30	836	377	204	6
Singapore	835	59	501	241	16	15	3
Slovakia	507	28	132	309	31	3	4
Slovenia	62	-	10	46	D	D	-
Somalia	3,764	115	11	851	19	2,766	2
South Africa	2,629	84	1,042	1,164	267	64	8
South Sudan	59	-	-	43	-	16	-
Soviet Union (former)	1,264	25	152	580	8	488	11
Spain	2,480	74	985	1,120	115	182	4
Sri Lanka	1,847	164	586	555	210	327	5

See footnotes at end of table.

Table 10.
PERSONS OBTAINING LAWFUL PERMANENT RESIDENT STATUS BY BROAD CLASS OF ADMISSION AND REGION AND COUNTRY OF BIRTH: FISCAL YEAR 2013 – *Continued*

Region and country of birth	Total	Family-sponsored preferences	Employment-based preferences	Immediate relatives of U.S. citizens	Diversity	Refugees and asylees	Other
Sudan	1,945	80	46	612	250	956	1
Suriname	178	39	18	110	5	D	D
Swaziland	15	D	D	7	-	D	-
Sweden	1,106	34	443	543	70	7	9
Switzerland	697	13	313	314	40	9	8
Syria	3,366	1,047	285	1,673	70	277	14
Taiwan	5,385	837	2,353	2,007	170	4	14
Tajikistan	550	40	50	189	205	66	-
Tanzania	837	49	108	435	50	194	1
Thailand	7,583	371	451	3,491	33	3,076	161
Togo	1,257	101	10	638	273	230	5
Tonga	348	112	-	225	9	-	2
Trinidad and Tobago	4,724	1,288	366	2,994	31	13	32
Tunisia	445	8	66	330	31	9	1
Turkey	4,144	198	1,292	1,785	730	116	23
Turkmenistan	210	8	14	78	58	52	-
Turks and Caicos Islands	50	9	D	36	-	D	-
Uganda	1,350	110	83	700	166	281	10
Ukraine	8,193	578	790	3,960	1,847	738	280
United Arab Emirates	910	172	315	268	82	61	12
United Kingdom	12,984	518	5,948	6,303	144	24	47
United States	319	16	35	221	D	25	D
Uruguay	1,352	86	163	956	D	130	D
Uzbekistan	4,382	220	111	743	2,944	337	27
Venezuela	9,572	744	3,000	3,607	537	1,647	37
Vietnam	27,101	13,847	458	12,528	4	214	50
Yemen	3,532	631	37	2,575	108	172	9
Zambia	505	27	100	309	28	40	1
Zimbabwe	924	38	206	372	44	257	7
All other countries	72	5	17	45	D	D	-
Unknown	3,263	975	129	1,949	112	71	27

D Data withheld to limit disclosure.

- Represents zero.

Source: U.S. Department of Homeland Security.

Table 11.
PERSONS OBTAINING LAWFUL PERMANENT RESIDENT STATUS BY BROAD CLASS OF ADMISSION AND REGION AND COUNTRY OF LAST RESIDENCE: FISCAL YEAR 2013

Region and country of last residence	Total	Family-sponsored preferences	Employment-based preferences	Immediate relatives of U.S. citizens	Diversity	Refugees and asylees	Other
REGION							
Total.........................	990,553	210,303	161,110	439,460	45,618	119,630	14,432
Africa	94,589	9,502	4,612	42,612	18,012	19,463	388
Asia	389,301	77,288	95,975	140,097	14,749	57,753	3,439
Europe	91,095	5,934	22,729	45,339	10,563	5,733	797
North America	320,093	97,485	22,975	161,162	771	30,120	7,580
Oceania.....................	6,061	586	1,598	3,032	770	50	25
South America	79,287	19,003	11,052	43,772	620	4,113	727
Unknown....................	10,127	505	2,169	3,446	133	2,398	1,476
COUNTRY							
Total.........................	990,553	210,303	161,110	439,460	45,618	119,630	14,432
Afghanistan	1,624	182	46	580	53	196	567
Albania	2,926	317	70	1,483	837	215	4
Algeria......................	1,162	71	28	415	602	42	4
Angola......................	141	16	13	61	17	34	-
Anguilla	32	19	D	D	-	-	1
Antigua-Barbuda.............	407	170	9	210	11	6	1
Argentina....................	4,227	321	1,158	2,404	32	247	65
Armenia.....................	2,769	249	114	1,280	775	344	7
Aruba	51	6	10	35	-	-	-
Australia	3,529	180	1,245	1,638	440	11	15
Austria	1,053	23	162	218	38	607	5
Azerbaijan	447	19	51	188	101	84	4
Bahamas....................	691	86	77	483	19	21	5
Bahrain	167	18	46	79	7	17	-
Bangladesh	11,819	6,208	579	4,666	91	227	48
Barbados....................	477	158	44	270	D	D	-
Belarus	1,989	89	167	649	697	375	12
Belgium.....................	803	25	385	317	61	11	4
Belize	969	306	64	562	11	11	15
Benin	373	21	D	183	129	34	D
Bermuda	121	16	34	65	3	-	3
Bhutan	159	3	8	23	4	120	1
Bolivia......................	2,005	474	298	1,104	28	73	28
Bosnia-Herzegovina	591	37	40	422	33	59	-
Botswana	101	-	34	33	8	26	-
Brazil.......................	10,772	556	2,636	7,205	3	259	113
British Virgin Islands.........	89	30	6	47	6	-	-
Brunei......................	30	3	10	14	3	-	-
Bulgaria.....................	2,720	115	340	1,422	780	54	9
Burkina Faso	618	21	22	298	128	145	4
Burma......................	2,064	413	62	647	165	776	1
Burundi	172	D	D	30	14	118	-
Cambodia	2,525	363	45	1,721	335	56	5
Cameroon	3,777	236	90	1,167	1,096	1,181	7
Canada	20,489	1,848	10,528	7,416	345	77	275
Cape Verde	1,669	876	8	777	3	D	D
Cayman Islands	97	14	17	57	5	4	-
Central African Republic	94	7	D	17	D	66	1
Chad........................	190	7	4	22	3	153	1
Chile.......................	1,751	205	398	1,061	15	58	14
China, People's Republic......	68,410	12,688	18,507	23,623	33	13,421	138
Colombia....................	20,611	5,271	1,667	12,467	9	1,089	108
Congo, Democratic Republic ...	1,804	57	21	384	1,025	316	1
Congo, Republic.............	932	30	11	194	503	191	3
Costa Rica...................	2,232	267	224	1,620	17	83	21
Cote d'Ivoire	1,357	119	49	587	193	375	34
Croatia	316	9	59	199	19	29	1
Cuba.......................	31,343	2,468	6	3,048	186	25,631	4

See footnotes at end of table.

Table 11.
PERSONS OBTAINING LAWFUL PERMANENT RESIDENT STATUS BY BROAD CLASS OF ADMISSION AND REGION AND COUNTRY OF LAST RESIDENCE: FISCAL YEAR 2013 – *Continued*

Region and country of last residence	Total	Family-sponsored preferences	Employment-based preferences	Immediate relatives of U.S. citizens	Diversity	Refugees and asylees	Other
Cyprus	174	8	77	64	15	9	1
Czech Republic	665	23	137	462	28	7	8
Czechoslovakia (former)	90	4	43	31	3	3	6
Denmark	546	28	249	239	19	8	3
Djibouti	122	3	3	19	3	94	-
Dominica	226	143	6	70	D	-	D
Dominican Republic	41,487	22,291	390	18,578	28	106	94
Ecuador	10,553	4,055	886	5,140	D	242	D
Egypt	10,719	869	783	3,301	3,028	2,700	38
El Salvador	18,015	8,226	793	7,412	-	401	1,183
Equatorial Guinea	23	D	D	11	D	D	-
Eritrea	929	66	10	275	44	533	1
Estonia	198	12	24	133	13	15	1
Ethiopia	13,484	1,400	211	5,536	2,299	4,026	12
Fiji	825	205	21	350	211	34	4
Finland	360	7	164	148	36	D	D
France	4,668	214	2,114	1,992	280	52	16
Gabon	153	D	8	74	5	63	D
Gambia	1,035	78	35	646	7	237	32
Georgia	1,213	63	78	656	326	73	17
Germany	6,880	246	2,118	3,792	599	100	25
Ghana	10,379	1,341	390	6,398	1,968	262	20
Greece	1,526	82	272	990	146	33	3
Grenada	676	235	35	395	4	D	D
Guatemala	9,829	3,692	740	3,918	D	622	D
Guinea	1,614	90	23	422	180	862	37
Guinea-Bissau	29	D	D	22	3	D	-
Guyana	5,564	3,403	90	2,042	8	11	10
Haiti	20,083	9,849	98	7,957	D	1,985	D
Honduras	8,795	3,133	591	4,551	27	236	257
Hong Kong	2,614	1,098	588	856	45	22	5
Hungary	1,008	37	229	619	107	12	4
Iceland	147	D	82	51	11	-	D
India	65,506	11,446	33,687	19,101	70	961	241
Indonesia	2,483	239	557	1,262	93	313	19
Iran	9,658	1,953	1,088	2,796	3,126	667	28
Iraq	3,882	151	31	527	20	1,569	1,584
Ireland	1,765	46	711	924	77	D	D
Israel	4,555	313	1,714	2,204	229	58	37
Italy	3,233	177	992	1,731	223	101	9
Jamaica	19,052	5,960	640	12,351	D	62	D
Japan	6,383	157	2,532	3,337	300	34	23
Jordan	5,949	1,393	337	2,657	98	1,425	39
Kazakhstan	1,025	27	79	526	216	164	13
Kenya	8,253	453	539	3,235	890	3,119	17
Korea, North	110	21	37	45	D	D	-
Korea, South	22,827	1,745	13,772	7,183	42	27	58
Kosovo	901	97	21	447	127	209	-
Kuwait	701	127	107	318	94	53	2
Kyrgyzstan	609	16	27	202	150	205	9
Laos	807	69	19	670	D	45	D
Latvia	408	24	42	302	26	9	5
Lebanon	3,417	812	415	1,352	42	783	13
Lesotho	24	-	4	8	7	5	-
Liberia	3,036	383	31	1,246	920	448	8
Libya	287	15	10	162	34	66	-
Lithuania	801	55	68	538	120	17	3

See footnotes at end of table.

Table 11.
PERSONS OBTAINING LAWFUL PERMANENT RESIDENT STATUS BY BROAD CLASS OF ADMISSION AND REGION AND COUNTRY OF LAST RESIDENCE: FISCAL YEAR 2013 – *Continued*

Region and country of last residence	Total	Family-sponsored preferences	Employment-based preferences	Immediate relatives of U.S. citizens	Diversity	Refugees and asylees	Other
Luxembourg.	41	-	16	19	3	3	-
Macau.	169	91	D	44	D	-	-
Macedonia.	905	114	51	565	128	41	6
Madagascar.	89	D	16	47	18	D	-
Malawi	172	8	32	106	10	14	2
Malaysia	8,311	205	681	600	87	6,729	9
Mali	695	41	31	358	8	222	35
Malta	256	7	4	20	6	219	-
Marshall Islands	47	-	4	43	-	-	-
Mauritania.	263	11	3	61	4	184	-
Mauritius.	63	D	12	37	7	D	1
Mexico	134,198	35,626	8,065	85,307	17	695	4,488
Moldova	2,428	67	53	703	843	630	132
Monaco.	16	-	11	D	D	-	-
Mongolia.	679	17	136	272	89	156	9
Montenegro.	252	32	4	186	3	27	-
Morocco.	3,202	319	80	2,178	591	24	10
Mozambique.	128	3	8	26	6	85	-
Namibia.	68	-	20	35	D	10	D
Nepal	21,681	481	1,287	1,805	3,120	14,968	20
Netherlands.	1,376	64	702	545	39	22	4
Netherlands Antilles.	144	35	20	75	11	3	-
New Zealand	1,027	82	321	515	101	4	4
Nicaragua	2,940	840	57	1,820	16	125	82
Niger.	49	D	D	28	11	-	-
Nigeria	13,258	2,025	648	7,749	2,725	91	20
Norway	389	23	129	215	18	4	-
Oman	130	15	44	49	12	4	6
Pakistan	12,653	3,827	2,175	5,989	16	579	67
Palau.	16	-	D	13	-	D	-
Panama.	1,276	262	109	855	13	27	10
Papua New Guinea.	26	-	5	15	6	-	-
Paraguay	437	71	51	283	D	28	D
Peru	12,370	3,755	856	7,335	4	318	102
Philippines.	52,955	15,143	9,850	27,826	6	29	101
Poland.	6,073	1,193	963	3,260	603	13	41
Portugal.	917	101	167	626	13	9	1
Qatar.	413	99	63	158	81	10	2
Romania.	3,475	285	684	1,982	357	145	22
Russia.	10,154	477	1,473	5,313	1,519	1,287	85
Rwanda.	673	16	8	79	93	472	5
Saint Kitts-Nevis.	266	113	15	127	6	-	5
Saint Lucia	843	234	28	568	6	3	4
Saint Vincent and the Grenadines	488	152	16	314	3	-	3
Samoa	226	12	-	214	-	-	-
Saudi Arabia	1,592	218	256	758	200	155	5
Senegal.	1,385	166	56	907	64	146	46
Serbia.	867	46	91	622	68	39	1
Serbia and Montenegro	552	60	56	267	76	77	16
Sierra Leone	1,500	184	18	799	345	148	6
Singapore	1,645	83	1,152	329	48	30	3
Slovakia	503	29	103	295	31	41	4
Slovenia	61	-	14	43	4	-	-
Somalia.	606	27	D	198	7	371	D
South Africa.	2,693	94	886	1,163	309	234	7
South Sudan	24	D	-	12	D	8	-
Soviet Union (former)	562	22	11	470	7	43	9
Spain	2,970	180	1,039	1,293	157	297	4

See footnotes at end of table.

Table 11.
PERSONS OBTAINING LAWFUL PERMANENT RESIDENT STATUS BY BROAD CLASS OF ADMISSION AND REGION AND COUNTRY OF LAST RESIDENCE: FISCAL YEAR 2013 – *Continued*

Region and country of last residence	Total	Family-sponsored preferences	Employment-based preferences	Immediate relatives of U.S. citizens	Diversity	Refugees and asylees	Other
Sri Lanka	1,680	152	486	516	178	344	4
Sudan	1,421	90	34	518	182	595	2
Suriname	170	43	13	106	D	D	4
Swaziland	29	D	12	10	D	D	-
Sweden	1,276	70	477	593	100	23	13
Switzerland	1,040	23	572	361	61	15	8
Syria	3,999	925	236	1,456	34	1,339	9
Taiwan	5,336	870	2,235	2,044	168	5	14
Tajikistan	464	16	37	169	170	72	-
Tanzania	981	52	83	420	47	378	1
Thailand	12,027	373	449	3,428	37	7,574	166
Togo	1,216	100	10	615	268	218	5
Tonga	338	107	-	220	9	-	2
Trinidad and Tobago	4,721	1,299	346	2,999	30	16	31
Tunisia	479	9	41	324	22	82	1
Turkey	7,189	195	1,251	1,792	728	3,202	21
Turkmenistan	168	5	11	65	52	35	-
Turks and Caicos Islands	55	7	D	40	-	D	-
Uganda	1,781	115	78	768	139	672	9
Ukraine	8,057	564	614	3,966	1,807	830	276
United Arab Emirates	2,002	387	539	578	294	148	56
United Kingdom	15,321	904	7,005	6,879	439	47	47
Uruguay	1,314	83	134	952	-	129	16
Uzbekistan	4,139	197	71	687	2,882	275	27
Venezuela	9,512	765	2,865	3,673	515	1,657	37
Vietnam	26,578	13,595	336	12,397	4	198	48
Yemen	3,553	607	31	2,554	104	247	10
Zambia	489	24	53	300	17	94	1
Zimbabwe	835	27	144	344	23	293	4
All other countries	63	12	7	39	D	D	-
Unknown	10,127	505	2,169	3,446	133	2,398	1,476

D Data withheld to limit disclosure.

- Represents zero.

Source: U.S. Department of Homeland Security.

Table 12.
IMMIGRANT ORPHANS ADOPTED BY U.S. CITIZENS BY SEX, AGE, AND REGION AND COUNTRY OF BIRTH: FISCAL YEAR 2013

Region and country of birth	Total	Sex			Age			
		Male	Female	Unknown	Under 1 year	1 to 4 years	5 years and over	Unknown
REGION								
Total	6,574	2,972	3,599	3	508	3,738	2,326	2
Africa	1,872	954	918	-	313	919	640	-
Asia	2,986	1,212	1,774	-	127	2,145	714	-
Europe	888	436	452	-	17	375	496	-
North America	569	257	309	3	10	221	336	2
Oceania	34	13	21	-	20	7	7	-
South America	225	100	125	-	21	71	133	-
COUNTRY								
Total	6,574	2,972	3,599	3	508	3,738	2,326	2
Armenia	13	5	8	-	3	6	4	-
Bangladesh	16	6	10	-	7	D	D	-
Belize	12	7	5	-	-	4	8	-
Brazil	17	9	8	-	-	4	13	-
Bulgaria	150	65	85	-	-	66	84	-
China, People's Republic	2,268	825	1,443	-	45	1,751	472	-
Colombia	142	62	80	-	18	46	78	-
Congo, Democratic Republic	195	85	110	-	38	125	32	-
Congo, Republic	77	40	37	-	12	59	6	-
Costa Rica	10	D	D	-	-	-	10	-
Dominican Republic	14	6	8	-	-	9	5	-
Ecuador	11	4	7	-	-	4	7	-
Ethiopia	910	486	424	-	217	401	292	-
Ghana	157	77	80	-	D	D	78	-
Guatemala	21	8	13	-	-	-	21	-
Guyana	36	15	21	-	3	11	22	-
Haiti	327	159	168	-	-	166	161	-
Honduras	15	7	8	-	-	6	9	-
Hong Kong	17	9	8	-	-	10	7	-
Hungary	23	11	12	-	-	6	17	-
India	112	36	76	-	D	D	34	-
Jamaica	70	29	38	3	-	4	64	2
Japan	21	17	4	-	D	D	D	-
Korea, South	176	132	44	-	8	159	9	-
Latvia	65	35	30	-	-	5	60	-
Liberia	11	D	D	-	-	3	8	-
Lithuania	11	7	4	-	-	3	8	-
Marshall Islands	18	8	10	-	18	-	-	-
Mexico	20	7	13	-	-	D	D	-
Morocco	21	13	8	-	8	10	3	-
Nicaragua	35	9	26	-	3	14	18	-
Nigeria	144	62	82	-	16	76	52	-
Pakistan	47	29	18	-	17	13	17	-
Peru	18	9	9	-	-	6	12	-
Philippines	166	79	87	-	-	51	115	-
Poland	49	24	25	-	-	19	30	-
Russia	248	129	119	-	5	201	42	-
Saint Vincent and the Grenadines	18	10	8	-	6	9	3	-
Sierra Leone	24	10	14	-	-	3	21	-
South Africa	17	10	7	-	-	11	6	-
Taiwan	86	48	38	-	24	39	23	-
Thailand	34	14	20	-	-	22	12	-
Uganda	260	139	121	-	16	133	111	-
Ukraine	320	154	166	-	11	65	244	-
All other countries	152	70	82	-	11	59	82	-

D Data withheld to limit disclosure.

- Represents zero.

Source: U.S. Department of Homeland Security.

Refugees and Asylees

Table 13.
REFUGEE ARRIVALS: FISCAL YEARS 1980 TO 2013

Year	Number	Year	Number	Year	Number
1980.	207,116	1992.	115,548	2004.	52,840
1981.	159,252	1993.	114,181	2005.	53,738
1982.	98,096	1994.	111,680	2006.	41,094
1983.	61,218	1995.	98,973	2007.	48,218
1984.	70,393	1996.	75,421	2008.	60,107
1985.	67,704	1997.	69,653	2009.	74,602
1986.	62,146	1998.	76,712	2010.	73,293
1987.	64,528	1999.	85,285	2011.	56,384
1988.	76,483	2000.	72,143	2012.	58,179
1989.	107,070	2001.	68,925	2013.	69,909
1990.	122,066	2002.	26,788		
1991.	113,389	2003.	28,286		

Note: Data series began following the Refugee Act of 1980. Excludes Amerasian immigrants except in Fiscal Years 1989 to 1991.

Source: U.S. Department of State, Bureau of Population, Refugees, and Migration (PRM), Worldwide Refugee Admissions Processing System (WRAPS), Fiscal Years 1980 to 2013.

Table 14.
REFUGEE ARRIVALS BY REGION AND COUNTRY OF NATIONALITY: FISCAL YEARS 2004 TO 2013

Region and country of nationality	2004	2005	2006	2007	2008	2009	2010	2011	2012	2013
REGION										
Total..........................	52,840	53,738	41,094	48,218	60,107	74,602	73,293	56,384	58,179	69,909
Africa	29,108	20,746	18,129	17,486	8,943	9,678	13,325	7,693	10,629	15,984
Asia	12,276	15,769	10,086	23,564	44,819	58,309	52,695	44,583	44,416	48,840
Europe	7,879	10,524	9,615	4,192	2,059	1,693	1,238	996	908	482
North America	2,998	6,368	3,145	2,922	4,177	4,800	4,856	2,930	1,948	4,206
Oceania........................	-	-	-	-	-	-	-	-	-	-
South America	579	331	119	54	100	57	126	46	130	233
Unknown	-	-	-	-	9	65	1,053	136	148	164
COUNTRY										
Total..........................	52,840	53,738	41,094	48,218	60,107	74,602	73,293	56,384	58,179	69,909
Afghanistan	959	902	651	441	576	349	515	428	481	661
Angola.........................	20	21	13	4	-	8	-	D	-	6
Armenia........................	88	86	87	29	9	4	D	15	8	3
Azerbaijan	407	299	77	78	30	38	18	16	10	3
Belarus	659	445	350	219	111	146	103	66	83	10
Bhutan	-	-	3	-	5,320	13,452	12,363	14,999	15,070	9,134
Bosnia-Herzegovina	244	61	16	D	-	-	-	-	-	-
Burma.........................	1,056	1,447	1,612	13,896	18,139	18,202	16,693	16,972	14,160	16,299
Burundi........................	276	214	466	4,545	2,889	762	530	110	186	193
Cambodia	3	9	9	15	8	15	9	5	6	30
Cameroon	D	6	29	5	D	4	6	-	7	-
Central African Republic	24	-	23	15	56	59	45	182	136	318
Chad...........................	4	-	4	10	23	6	28	25	12	32
China, People's Republic........	3	13	21	27	50	54	72	28	54	101
Colombia.......................	577	323	115	54	94	57	123	46	126	230
Congo, Democratic Republic	569	424	405	848	727	1,135	3,174	977	1,863	2,563
Congo, Republic.................	73	43	66	206	197	293	154	27	102	161
Cote d'Ivoire	-	5	23	11	30	9	4	7	33	20
Croatia	92	39	D	-	-	-	-	-	-	-
Cuba...........................	2,980	6,360	3,143	2,922	4,177	4,800	4,818	2,920	1,948	4,205
Egypt..........................	3	-	D	3	5	7	15	6	13	3
Equatorial Guinea...............	-	25	11	14	-	9	9	-	-	-
Eritrea.........................	128	327	538	963	251	1,571	2,570	2,032	1,346	1,824
Estonia	27	17	7	6	6	D	-	-	D	-
Ethiopia........................	2,689	1,663	1,271	1,028	299	321	668	560	620	765
Gambia	3	-	6	13	6	10	10	7	D	11
Georgia	33	11	4	7	20	4	4	20	7	D
Haiti	17	8	-	-	-	-	18	-	-	-
Honduras.......................	-	-	-	-	-	-	20	5	-	-
Indonesia	5	6	10	-	-	-	-	D	-	-
Iran...........................	1,786	1,856	2,792	5,482	5,270	5,381	3,543	2,032	1,758	2,579
Iraq...........................	66	198	202	1,608	13,822	18,838	18,016	9,388	12,163	19,487
Jordan.........................	-	-	-	3	-	-	7	3	3	13
Kazakhstan	312	80	124	45	62	52	46	53	7	11
Kenya	-	D	5	-	-	D	-	D	23	5
Korea, North	-	-	9	22	37	25	8	23	22	17
Kuwait.........................	14	-	-	24	D	7	40	5	3	12
Kyrgyzstan.....................	100	38	15	17	25	46	27	30	49	19
Laos...........................	6,005	8,517	830	117	59	14	36	211	21	-
Latvia	52	25	21	17	6	D	-	4	-	-
Liberia.........................	7,140	4,289	2,346	1,606	992	385	244	121	69	94
Lithuania	13	9	-	4	-	-	4	-	-	-
Mauritania	-	3	88	62	26	16	74	3	-	-
Moldova	1,711	1,016	721	565	487	445	356	331	255	119
Nepal	D	-	D	3	4	7	-	10	47	34
Nigeria	34	11	15	20	76	3	D	D	D	D
Pakistan	11	9	20	30	104	67	59	54	274	158
Russia.........................	1,446	5,982	6,003	1,773	426	495	326	165	197	125
Rwanda........................	176	183	112	202	108	111	230	74	157	139
Serbia and Montenegro	151	38	11	-	D	-	-	-	-	-
Sierra Leone	1,084	829	439	166	99	51	54	28	D	4
Somalia........................	13,331	10,405	10,357	6,969	2,523	4,189	4,884	3,161	4,911	7,608

See footnotes at end of table.

Table 14.
REFUGEE ARRIVALS BY REGION AND COUNTRY OF NATIONALITY: FISCAL YEARS 2004 TO 2013 – *Continued*

Region and country of nationality	2004	2005	2006	2007	2008	2009	2010	2011	2012	2013
South Sudan	X	X	X	X	X	X	X	-	D	17
Sri Lanka	D	-	6	D	D	33	118	69	55	92
Sudan	3,500	2,205	1,848	705	375	683	558	334	1,077	2,160
Syria	-	7	27	17	24	25	25	29	31	36
Togo	35	72	18	40	204	14	9	5	26	18
Uganda	8	10	20	38	42	8	30	10	18	15
Ukraine	3,482	2,889	2,483	1,605	1,022	601	449	428	372	227
Uzbekistan	426	271	527	190	134	152	185	96	140	51
Vietnam	979	2,009	3,039	1,500	1,112	1,486	873	79	41	69
Yemen	8	D	11	6	-	47	15	-	-	12
Zimbabwe	D	D	13	D	3	10	7	8	3	12
All other countries	26	29	28	18	28	26	45	36	31	37
Unknown[1]	-	-	-	-	9	65	1,053	136	148	164

X Not applicable.

D Data withheld to limit disclosure.

- Represents zero.

[1] Includes admissions from Palestinian Territory.

Note: Excludes Amerasian immigrants.

Source: U.S. Department of State, Bureau of Population, Refugees, and Migration (PRM), Worldwide Refugee Admissions Processing System (WRAPS), Fiscal Years 2004 to 2013.

Table 15.
REFUGEE ARRIVALS BY RELATIONSHIP TO PRINCIPAL APPLICANT AND SEX, AGE, AND MARITAL STATUS: FISCAL YEAR 2013

Characteristic	Total	Principal applicants	Dependents Spouses	Dependents Children
SEX				
Total.	69,909	31,698	11,278	26,933
Male	37,792	21,891	1,731	14,170
Female	32,117	9,807	9,547	12,763
AGE				
Total.	69,909	31,698	11,278	26,933
Under 1 year	180	D	-	D
1 to 4 years.	6,313	75	-	6,238
5 to 9 years.	7,145	111	-	7,034
10 to 14 years.	6,331	270	-	6,061
15 to 19 years.	6,347	901	61	5,385
20 to 24 years.	7,730	4,808	958	1,964
25 to 29 years.	8,402	6,395	1,964	43
30 to 34 years.	6,926	4,943	1,970	13
35 to 39 years.	5,166	3,530	1,627	9
40 to 44 years.	4,377	2,902	1,472	3
45 to 49 years.	3,108	2,083	D	D
50 to 54 years.	2,396	1,623	D	D
55 to 59 years.	1,751	1,200	551	-
60 to 64 years.	1,347	938	409	-
65 to 74 years.	1,762	1,384	D	D
75 years and over	628	D	D	-
BROAD AGE GROUPS				
Total.	69,909	31,698	11,278	26,933
Under 16 years	21,177	538	D	D
16 to 20 years	6,710	1,417	D	D
21 years and over	42,022	29,743	11,125	1,154
MARITAL STATUS				
Total.	69,909	31,698	11,278	26,933
Single	39,392	12,494	D	D
Married	26,789	15,502	D	D
Widowed	1,933	D	-	D
Divorced/separated	1,761	1,756	-	5
Unknown	34	D	-	D

D Data withheld to limit disclosure.

- Represents zero.

Note: Excludes Amerasian immigrants.

Source: U.S. Department of State, Bureau of Population, Refugees, and Migration (PRM), Worldwide Refugee Admissions Processing System (WRAPS).

Table 16.
INDIVIDUALS GRANTED ASYLUM AFFIRMATIVELY OR DEFENSIVELY: FISCAL YEARS 1990 TO 2013

Year	Total	Affirmative	Defensive
1990.	8,472	5,672	2,800
1991.	5,035	2,908	2,127
1992.	6,307	4,123	2,184
1993.	9,543	7,509	2,034
1994.	13,828	11,775	2,053
1995.	20,703	17,573	3,130
1996.	23,532	18,624	4,908
1997.	22,939	16,380	6,559
1998.	20,507	13,216	7,291
1999.	26,571	18,150	8,421
2000.	32,514	23,278	9,236
2001.	39,148	29,147	10,001
2002.	36,937	25,960	10,977
2003.	28,743	15,367	13,376
2004.	27,376	14,354	13,022
2005.	25,274	13,517	11,757
2006.	26,289	12,985	13,304
2007.	25,234	12,375	12,859
2008.	22,976	12,084	10,892
2009.	22,236	11,936	10,300
2010.	21,106	11,202	9,904
2011.	24,904	13,376	11,528
2012.	29,367	17,389	11,978
2013.	25,199	15,266	9,933

Source: U.S. Department of Homeland Security, U.S. Citizenship and Immigration Service (USCIS), Refugee, Asylum, and Parole System (RAPS) and the U.S. Department of Justice (DOJ), Executive Office for Immigration Review (EOIR).

Table 17.
INDIVIDUALS GRANTED ASYLUM AFFIRMATIVELY BY REGION AND COUNTRY OF NATIONALITY: FISCAL YEARS 2004 TO 2013

Region and country of nationality	2004	2005	2006	2007	2008	2009	2010	2011	2012	2013
REGION										
Total..............................	14,354	13,517	12,985	12,375	12,084	11,936	11,202	13,376	17,389	15,266
Africa	3,858	2,695	2,062	2,518	2,651	2,828	2,644	3,029	5,022	4,844
Asia	3,040	3,870	3,333	4,425	4,841	5,546	5,414	6,459	8,022	7,579
Europe	864	676	550	675	753	811	728	962	1,211	779
North America	2,206	2,909	3,598	2,239	1,750	1,479	1,427	1,534	1,651	1,152
Oceania............................	65	23	18	27	23	17	8	19	20	10
South America	4,264	3,308	3,383	2,438	1,974	1,126	928	1,327	1,425	862
Unknown	57	36	41	53	92	129	53	46	38	40
COUNTRY										
Total..............................	14,354	13,517	12,985	12,375	12,084	11,936	11,202	13,376	17,389	15,266
Afghanistan	35	14	9	43	45	81	114	119	158	97
Albania	178	92	43	33	31	33	26	18	20	12
Algeria.............................	10	6	5	3	8	5	9	8	12	3
Angola.............................	6	5	3	5	4	3	D	15	9	8
Armenia............................	250	162	155	203	105	85	85	47	36	77
Azerbaijan	89	34	28	16	10	23	21	18	28	23
Bahrain	-	-	-	-	-	-	D	4	22	4
Bangladesh	41	37	36	29	32	46	35	30	29	45
Belarus	145	112	100	86	78	113	65	115	200	106
Bhutan	D	D	8	13	4	8	-	D	-	-
Bolivia	5	3	D	3	8	10	15	19	21	8
Bosnia-Herzegovina	13	25	17	13	9	5	7	5	8	5
Brazil..............................	24	28	36	43	38	51	46	38	46	27
Bulgaria............................	42	43	34	37	48	24	17	13	19	14
Burkina Faso	7	9	13	31	17	21	41	55	58	66
Burma..............................	190	98	94	125	153	168	158	143	98	55
Burundi	25	17	29	25	28	21	21	20	20	25
Cambodia	42	23	13	11	5	5	8	-	D	D
Cameroon	599	391	235	299	286	223	183	225	251	147
Central African Republic	7	17	5	6	12	15	13	6	9	10
Chad...............................	20	13	19	31	35	37	18	8	12	5
China, People's Republic............	930	2,234	1,550	1,828	2,037	2,716	2,898	3,887	4,738	4,072
Colombia...........................	2,899	2,214	2,178	1,491	1,113	637	358	325	337	187
Congo, Democratic Republic	70	54	47	36	38	31	30	49	71	50
Congo, Republic....................	93	60	58	72	53	42	64	88	79	68
Cote d'Ivoire	86	94	73	53	43	38	37	104	110	55
Cuba...............................	26	71	50	43	64	27	24	20	24	24
Djibouti	-	-	-	D	D	7	16	46	15	12
Dominican Republic	D	-	D	3	D	D	D	4	16	4
Ecuador............................	9	7	10	14	11	8	9	5	18	13
Egypt..............................	143	142	176	194	234	308	315	752	2,570	3,102
El Salvador	119	183	498	416	314	202	157	97	135	76
Eritrea.............................	132	141	112	152	181	237	179	155	121	85
Estonia	10	10	-	3	D	5	-	-	-	-
Ethiopia............................	755	469	440	510	587	700	681	564	663	494
Fiji................................	65	23	18	27	23	16	8	18	17	10
Gambia	31	28	37	43	50	49	53	69	109	57
Georgia	57	37	14	13	20	21	17	9	11	12
Ghana..............................	10	4	5	8	6	9	6	5	8	5
Guatemala..........................	206	247	474	539	378	347	293	281	313	230
Guinea	157	127	95	123	119	121	126	74	59	26
Guinea-Bissau	11	D	-	-	-	D	-	D	-	D
Haiti...............................	1,781	2,282	2,423	1,062	729	595	667	816	632	443
Honduras...........................	5	16	26	19	22	38	51	59	138	109
India...............................	144	72	52	75	102	147	102	101	94	94
Indonesia	100	99	431	567	383	177	70	84	88	44
Iran................................	203	147	139	171	328	257	396	366	607	612
Iraq................................	161	192	180	391	586	544	276	262	314	408
Israel	4	7	4	10	13	17	7	5	5	4
Jamaica............................	D	9	7	12	19	42	49	49	48	36

See footnotes at end of table.

Table 17.
INDIVIDUALS GRANTED ASYLUM AFFIRMATIVELY BY REGION AND COUNTRY OF NATIONALITY: FISCAL YEARS 2004 TO 2013 – *Continued*

Region and country of nationality	2004	2005	2006	2007	2008	2009	2010	2011	2012	2013
Jordan	19	28	17	25	23	19	7	11	48	26
Kazakhstan	24	10	15	23	18	26	33	54	88	67
Kenya	188	131	84	181	215	234	179	107	126	90
Kosovo	X	X	X	X	-	5	23	18	28	18
Kyrgyzstan	18	13	9	22	26	31	50	147	127	79
Laos	26	12	13	33	15	13	16	4	3	D
Latvia	14	8	4	5	D	3	-	4	3	-
Lebanon	30	25	10	50	44	37	21	19	22	14
Liberia	332	128	65	55	63	47	36	23	15	33
Libya	3	-	3	-	3	D	11	66	43	30
Macedonia	7	D	8	-	3	4	4	3	D	11
Madagascar	-	-	-	-	D	-	11	5	5	-
Malaysia	11	6	4	5	7	6	D	10	7	8
Mali	18	25	28	51	35	54	77	58	59	61
Mauritania	59	44	17	12	5	17	34	29	28	25
Mexico	53	85	84	103	176	190	136	173	305	209
Moldova	11	16	12	35	49	114	81	133	172	97
Mongolia	60	72	56	103	77	49	103	96	80	40
Morocco	5	6	3	D	D	4	D	12	9	4
Nepal	163	237	211	281	347	493	408	417	572	473
Nicaragua	D	8	20	20	28	20	20	13	21	6
Niger	22	9	8	4	11	4	8	D	D	4
Nigeria	31	31	23	28	36	38	31	31	64	63
Pakistan	182	123	93	132	163	197	201	255	234	271
Peru	108	92	59	44	43	18	21	33	27	13
Philippines	24	12	8	20	16	16	12	3	14	9
Romania	68	16	16	26	10	6	3	14	8	4
Russia	231	236	231	287	372	365	390	466	542	347
Rwanda	31	51	64	70	75	59	96	70	85	58
Saudi Arabia	4	5	7	D	8	7	16	10	17	43
Senegal	18	9	7	11	9	23	10	15	16	8
Serbia and Montenegro	57	26	30	65	52	37	18	16	34	20
Sierra Leone	62	44	23	20	20	35	22	14	14	6
Somalia	156	74	57	75	70	95	62	29	50	20
South Africa	4	11	5	4	4	5	3	6	9	5
Sri Lanka	18	16	15	34	39	126	107	50	34	34
Sudan	84	59	47	84	86	73	70	99	122	83
Syria	26	19	12	8	23	8	12	46	327	763
Tajikistan	7	-	-	3	10	14	23	36	24	25
Tanzania	11	19	4	6	8	6	7	10	12	3
Togo	349	199	87	60	39	35	15	17	20	22
Turkey	24	16	9	16	34	25	47	31	31	25
Turkmenistan	20	21	26	15	13	7	11	17	9	6
Uganda	59	46	31	78	55	56	88	89	87	49
Ukraine	49	62	40	64	64	73	67	133	152	121
Uzbekistan	111	74	88	109	105	99	78	111	83	63
Venezuela	1,198	952	1,080	834	753	393	467	898	960	608
Vietnam	6	8	15	11	21	35	22	18	15	8
Yemen	5	D	7	26	18	25	43	34	31	44
Zambia	14	13	6	9	9	D	6	8	D	D
Zimbabwe	238	203	141	159	194	153	61	79	56	38
All other countries	98	75	58	82	81	87	102	86	110	96
Unknown	57	36	41	53	92	129	53	46	38	40

X Not applicable.

D Data withheld to limit disclosure.

- Represents zero.

Source: U.S. Department of Homeland Security, U.S. Citizenship and Immigration Services (USCIS), Refugee, Asylum, and Parole System (RAPS).

Table 18.
INDIVIDUALS GRANTED ASYLUM AFFIRMATIVELY BY RELATIONSHIP TO PRINCIPAL APPLICANT AND SEX, AGE, AND MARITAL STATUS: FISCAL YEAR 2013

Characteristic	Total	Principal applicants	Dependents Spouses	Children
SEX				
Total	15,266	10,574	2,030	2,662
Male	7,748	5,253	1,099	1,396
Female	7,518	5,321	931	1,266
AGE				
Total	15,266	10,574	2,030	2,662
Under 1 year	10	-	-	10
1 to 4 years	542	3	-	539
5 to 9 years	820	4	-	816
10 to 14 years	720	24	-	696
15 to 19 years	868	360	D	D
20 to 24 years	1,918	1,695	D	D
25 to 29 years	2,687	2,304	383	-
30 to 34 years	2,351	1,898	453	-
35 to 39 years	1,720	1,378	342	-
40 to 44 years	1,448	1,165	283	-
45 to 49 years	1,001	792	209	-
50 to 54 years	513	413	100	-
55 to 59 years	292	241	51	-
60 to 64 years	145	112	33	-
65 to 74 years	162	127	35	-
75 years and over	69	58	11	-
BROAD AGE GROUPS				
Total	15,266	10,574	2,030	2,662
Under 16 years	2,373	65	-	2,308
16 to 20 years	845	514	7	324
21 years and over	12,048	9,995	2,023	30
MARITAL STATUS				
Total	15,266	10,574	2,030	2,662
Single	7,178	4,516	-	2,662
Married	7,277	5,247	2,030	-
Widowed	230	230	-	-
Divorced/separated	576	576	-	-
Unknown	5	5	-	-

D Data withheld to limit disclosure.

- Represents zero.

Note: Data not available for individuals granted asylum defensively.

Source: U.S. Department of Homeland Security, U.S. Citizenship and Immigration Service (USCIS), Refugee, Asylum, and Parole System (RAPS).

Table 19.
INDIVIDUALS GRANTED ASYLUM DEFENSIVELY BY REGION AND COUNTRY OF NATIONALITY: FISCAL YEARS 2004 TO 2013

Region and country of nationality	2004	2005	2006	2007	2008	2009	2010	2011	2012	2013
REGION										
Total	13,022	11,757	13,304	12,859	10,892	10,300	9,904	11,528	11,978	9,933
Africa	2,413	2,276	2,830	2,522	2,046	2,326	2,226	2,691	2,433	1,968
Asia	6,073	5,286	6,668	6,707	5,509	5,423	5,536	6,517	7,364	6,134
Europe	1,696	1,621	1,441	1,318	1,177	927	893	996	951	870
North America	937	1,016	1,007	1,071	1,083	856	645	663	747	682
Oceania	95	36	45	25	36	32	20	25	24	8
South America	1,748	1,448	1,226	1,132	975	646	487	509	337	216
Unknown	60	74	87	84	66	90	97	127	122	55
COUNTRY										
Total	13,022	11,757	13,304	12,859	10,892	10,300	9,904	11,528	11,978	9,933
Afghanistan	58	33	25	22	28	7	6	19	36	16
Albania	724	610	497	421	324	213	149	140	93	71
Algeria	13	23	13	6	5	6	D	5	7	D
Angola	9	6	16	7	8	6	D	5	D	D
Argentina	18	10	9	15	14	10	8	9	5	3
Armenia	305	268	289	179	149	202	206	143	100	54
Azerbaijan	31	30	27	23	12	14	9	11	17	5
Bangladesh	149	120	113	100	81	51	48	48	80	63
Belarus	56	89	106	76	80	73	67	72	87	62
Bosnia-Herzegovina	6	8	7	18	6	17	4	6	D	3
Brazil	33	24	33	33	31	22	17	20	19	14
Bulgaria	43	77	72	67	48	42	20	23	21	5
Burkina Faso	3	5	13	20	23	39	49	37	57	59
Burma	138	166	157	129	126	108	80	71	64	33
Burundi	12	11	13	13	12	15	7	8	10	13
Cambodia	31	29	20	13	12	12	13	10	12	7
Cameroon	273	263	357	205	161	211	196	198	184	137
Canada	5	4	9	9	3	11	5	10	7	D
Central African Republic	D	18	10	13	13	16	10	4	5	7
Chad	5	10	16	21	24	40	28	23	21	4
China, People's Republic	3,419	3,014	4,048	4,552	3,457	3,449	3,802	4,705	5,383	4,532
Colombia	1,473	1,151	782	683	548	368	234	213	131	72
Congo, Democratic Republic	24	38	29	28	27	18	17	16	13	19
Congo, Republic	129	76	89	73	70	49	56	57	57	46
Cote d'Ivoire	77	111	159	135	92	96	66	72	75	55
Cuba	33	21	26	26	23	15	9	14	5	6
Dominican Republic	3	D	D	5	D	3	11	8	8	4
Ecuador	4	11	11	10	13	6	7	20	16	25
Egypt	268	194	239	235	185	174	216	275	306	305
El Salvador	42	65	95	139	173	120	146	164	191	181
Eritrea	61	68	96	120	120	198	181	483	351	240
Estonia	8	6	3	13	3	8	D	D	-	D
Ethiopia	260	266	345	352	315	410	407	507	458	399
Fiji	95	35	45	24	24	29	18	19	14	3
Gambia	16	30	46	59	53	49	42	45	81	75
Georgia	66	64	59	27	26	24	32	26	22	10
Germany	4	5	9	4	5	D	11	4	4	-
Ghana	5	4	6	8	12	7	8	7	10	10
Greece	3	8	3	12	-	-	D	D	D	3
Guatemala	177	140	161	136	168	159	167	200	222	153
Guinea	258	257	356	325	242	194	186	179	157	101
Guyana	32	30	16	15	D	-	4	4	5	7
Haiti	535	653	569	586	530	410	168	56	49	53
Honduras	46	67	65	86	73	47	65	72	93	92
India	452	311	450	359	272	263	244	262	282	322
Indonesia	427	375	314	211	195	157	116	111	126	76
Iran	203	143	117	108	71	92	83	108	109	63
Iraq	115	94	192	277	410	364	151	117	111	54
Israel	9	17	25	18	16	17	10	13	6	3
Jamaica	3	D	3	D	3	D	6	7	15	6

See footnotes at end of table.

Table 19.
INDIVIDUALS GRANTED ASYLUM DEFENSIVELY BY REGION AND COUNTRY OF NATIONALITY:
FISCAL YEARS 2004 TO 2013 – *Continued*

Region and country of nationality	2004	2005	2006	2007	2008	2009	2010	2011	2012	2013
Jordan	28	21	27	16	19	20	19	7	17	13
Kazakhstan	28	13	25	31	14	20	17	15	14	24
Kenya	62	54	60	51	60	97	90	96	76	40
Kosovo	X	X	X	3	D	7	6	13	27	31
Kyrgyzstan	16	12	20	7	6	7	10	14	30	35
Laos	5	19	11	6	4	13	7	D	D	D
Latvia	17	4	12	6	3	D	-	6	3	6
Lebanon	42	23	26	29	20	9	26	24	19	16
Liberia	91	70	59	53	32	31	25	23	20	12
Lithuania	9	5	18	4	D	D	D	6	-	D
Macedonia	14	21	20	27	11	15	10	8	3	5
Mali	10	18	62	60	28	71	74	79	80	76
Mauritania	220	193	219	174	94	95	59	63	44	39
Mexico	68	34	49	49	73	65	49	107	126	155
Moldova	13	6	D	7	16	22	46	72	93	69
Mongolia	13	25	39	49	42	28	55	48	35	39
Morocco	D	4	8	4	23	4	3	D	10	4
Nepal	93	85	165	131	152	172	231	323	403	381
Nicaragua	7	16	15	23	23	19	15	19	14	17
Niger	6	3	10	10	8	14	4	6	8	5
Nigeria	50	33	30	39	28	29	35	28	35	31
Niue	-	-	-	D	11	3	D	5	7	4
Pakistan	164	140	178	140	142	104	115	149	191	127
Peru	111	59	88	54	52	39	25	24	23	8
Philippines	29	26	17	9	15	13	5	7	8	5
Romania	61	18	43	31	56	31	31	14	12	39
Russia	320	251	203	209	201	128	161	195	176	187
Rwanda	28	19	24	22	20	24	25	16	24	27
Saudi Arabia	5	6	13	5	5	3	3	D	12	7
Senegal	17	26	15	30	18	25	18	27	31	21
Serbia and Montenegro	207	228	179	152	152	148	108	89	67	53
Sierra Leone	122	82	79	48	47	29	27	24	33	11
Somalia	89	88	116	109	101	168	208	213	99	86
South Africa	5	5	20	8	D	3	D	16	3	D
Soviet Union, former	86	169	188	191	173	154	176	248	281	252
Sri Lanka	63	74	85	89	87	112	112	105	108	95
Sudan	68	55	45	19	30	40	35	35	50	34
Syria	10	11	20	23	11	18	13	14	37	48
Tajikistan	6	9	4	5	D	8	9	10	8	13
Tanzania	3	7	17	16	5	6	3	12	6	5
Togo	66	102	145	82	63	39	45	30	21	13
Turkey	27	12	34	23	11	18	12	13	24	4
Turkmenistan	16	13	23	12	15	14	7	8	7	D
Uganda	50	53	36	50	33	28	26	27	28	30
Ukraine	90	69	45	40	59	26	62	49	55	43
Uzbekistan	76	95	95	74	67	65	54	71	42	55
Venezuela	59	153	279	317	306	192	181	206	130	79
Vietnam	5	8	10	10	7	10	9	13	10	4
Yemen	9	10	10	8	8	7	7	29	16	9
Zimbabwe	71	58	56	97	68	69	52	44	42	24
All other countries	144	117	112	102	113	101	101	116	118	115
Unknown[1]	60	74	87	84	66	90	97	127	122	55

X Not applicable.

D Data withheld to limit disclosure.

- Represents zero.

[1] Includes admissions from Palestinian Territory.

Source: U.S. Department of Justice (DOJ), Executive Office for Immigration Review (EOIR).

Naturalizations

Table 20.
PETITIONS FOR NATURALIZATION FILED, PERSONS NATURALIZED, AND PETITIONS FOR NATURALIZATION DENIED: FISCAL YEARS 1907 TO 2013

Year	Petitions filed	Persons naturalized				Petitions denied
		Total	Civilian	Military[2]	Not reported	
1907[1]	21,113	7,941	7,941	NA	-	250
1908	44,032	25,975	25,975	NA	-	3,330
1909	43,141	38,374	38,374	NA	-	6,341
1910	55,750	39,448	39,448	NA	-	7,781
1911	74,740	56,683	56,683	NA	-	9,017
1912	95,661	70,310	70,310	NA	-	9,635
1913	95,380	83,561	83,561	NA	-	10,891
1914	124,475	104,145	104,145	NA	-	13,133
1915	106,399	91,848	91,848	NA	-	13,691
1916	108,767	87,831	87,831	NA	-	11,927
1917	130,865	88,104	88,104	NA	-	9,544
1918	169,507	151,449	87,456	63,993	-	12,182
1919	256,858	217,358	89,023	128,335	-	13,119
1920	218,732	177,683	125,711	51,972	-	15,586
1921	195,534	181,292	163,656	17,636	-	18,981
1922	162,638	170,447	160,979	9,468	-	29,076
1923	165,168	145,084	137,975	7,109	-	24,884
1924	177,117	150,510	140,340	10,170	-	18,324
1925	162,258	152,457	152,457	NA	-	15,613
1926	172,232	146,331	146,239	92	-	13,274
1927	240,339	199,804	195,493	4,311	-	11,946
1928	240,321	233,155	228,006	5,149	-	12,479
1929	255,519	224,728	224,197	531	-	11,848
1930	113,151	169,377	167,637	1,740	-	9,068
1931	145,474	143,495	140,271	3,224	-	7,514
1932	131,062	136,600	136,598	2	-	5,478
1933	112,629	113,363	112,368	995	-	4,703
1934	117,125	113,669	110,867	2,802	-	1,133
1935	131,378	118,945	118,945	NA	-	2,765
1936	167,127	141,265	140,784	481	-	3,124
1937	165,464	164,976	162,923	2,053	-	4,042
1938	175,413	162,078	158,142	3,936	-	4,854
1939	213,413	188,813	185,175	3,638	-	5,630
1940	278,028	235,260	232,500	2,760	-	6,549
1941	277,807	277,294	275,747	1,547	-	7,769
1942	343,487	270,364	268,762	1,602	-	8,348
1943	377,125	318,933	281,459	37,474	-	13,656
1944	325,717	441,979	392,766	49,213	-	7,297
1945	195,917	231,402	208,707	22,695	-	9,782
1946	123,864	150,062	134,849	15,213	-	6,575
1947	88,802	93,904	77,442	16,462	-	3,953
1948	68,265	70,150	69,080	1,070	-	2,887
1949	71,044	66,594	64,138	2,456	-	2,271
1950	66,038	66,346	64,279	2,067	-	2,276
1951	61,634	54,716	53,741	975	-	2,395
1952	94,086	88,655	87,070	1,585	-	2,163
1953	98,128	92,051	90,476	1,575	-	2,300
1954	130,722	117,831	104,086	13,745	-	2,084
1955	213,508	209,526	197,568	11,958	-	4,571
1956	137,701	145,885	138,681	7,204	-	3,935
1957	140,547	138,043	137,198	845	-	2,948
1958	117,344	119,866	118,950	916	-	2,688
1959	109,270	103,931	102,623	1,308	-	2,208
1960	127,543	119,442	117,848	1,594	-	2,277
1961	138,718	132,450	130,731	1,719	-	3,175
1962	129,682	127,307	124,972	2,335	-	3,557
1963	121,170	124,178	121,618	2,560	-	2,436
1964	113,218	112,234	109,629	2,605	-	2,309
1965	106,813	104,299	101,214	3,085	-	2,059

See footnotes at end of table.

Table 20.
PETITIONS FOR NATURALIZATION FILED, PERSONS NATURALIZED, AND PETITIONS FOR NATURALIZATION DENIED:
FISCAL YEARS 1907 TO 2013 - *Continued*

| Year | Petitions filed | Persons naturalized | | | | Petitions denied |
		Total	Civilian	Military[2]	Not reported	
1966.	104,853	103,059	100,498	2,561	-	2,029
1967.	108,369	104,902	102,211	2,691	-	2,008
1968.	103,085	102,726	100,288	2,438	-	1,962
1969.	102,317	98,709	93,251	5,458	-	2,043
1970.	114,760	110,399	99,783	10,616	-	1,979
1971.	109,897	108,407	98,858	9,549	-	2,028
1972.	121,883	116,215	107,740	8,475	-	1,837
1973.	126,929	120,404	112,628	7,776	-	1,708
1974.	136,175	131,153	124,342	6,811	-	2,210
1975.	149,399	140,749	134,586	6,163	-	2,300
1976[3]	199,152	189,988	182,887	7,101	-	2,799
1977.	186,354	159,873	154,568	5,305	-	2,845
1978.	168,854	171,971	166,911	5,060	-	3,894
1979.	165,434	163,107	157,305	5,802	-	3,987
1980.	192,230	156,627	152,073	4,554	-	4,370
1981.	171,073	164,389	160,342	4,047	-	4,316
1982.	201,507	141,004	138,188	2,816	-	3,994
1983.	187,719	178,415	175,159	3,182	74	3,160
1984.	286,440	195,862	190,984	2,944	1,934	3,373
1985.	305,981	242,451	236,202	3,237	3,012	3,610
1986.	290,732	279,497	274,263	2,886	2,348	5,980
1987.	232,988	223,249	220,393	2,362	494	6,771
1988.	237,752	240,775	238,275	2,278	222	4,304
1989.	227,692	232,655	230,088	1,947	620	5,200
1990.	233,843	267,586	245,410	1,618	20,558	6,516
1991.	206,668	307,394	298,741	1,802	6,851	6,268
1992.	342,238	239,664	221,997	5,699	11,968	19,293
1993.	521,866	313,590	302,383	7,062	4,145	39,931
1994.	543,353	429,123	398,364	5,890	24,869	40,561
1995.	959,963	485,720	472,518	3,855	9,347	46,067
1996.	1,277,403	1,040,991	924,368	1,214	115,409	229,842
1997.	1,412,712	596,010	532,871	531	62,608	130,676
1998.	932,957	461,169	437,689	961	22,519	137,395
1999.	765,346	837,418	740,718	711	95,989	379,993
2000.	460,916	886,026	812,579	836	72,611	399,670
2001.	501,643	606,259	575,030	758	30,471	218,326
2002.	700,649	572,646	550,835	1,053	20,758	139,779
2003.	523,370	462,435	449,123	3,865	9,447	91,599
2004.	662,796	537,151	520,771	4,668	11,712	103,339
2005.	602,972	604,280	589,269	4,614	10,397	108,247
2006.	730,642	702,589	684,484	6,259	11,846	120,722
2007.	1,382,993	660,477	648,005	3,808	8,664	89,683
2008.	525,786	1,046,539	1,032,281	4,342	9,916	121,283
2009.	570,442	743,715	726,043	7,100	10,572	109,813
2010.	710,544	619,913	604,410	9,122	6,381	56,994
2011.	756,008	694,193	677,385	8,373	8,435	57,065
2012.	899,162	757,434	745,932	7,257	4,245	65,874
2013.	772,623	779,929	769,073	6,652	4,204	83,112

NA Not available.

- Represents zero.

[1] Data on naturalizations were first compiled by a single federal agency with the establishment of the Naturalization Service in 1906. The year 1907 includes naturalizations from September 27, 1906 to June 30, 1907.

[2] Data on military naturalizations prior to 1918 not available. Special provisions for military naturalizations expired or suspended in 1925 and 1935.

[3] Includes the 15 months from July 1, 1975 to September 30, 1976 because the end date of fiscal years was changed from June 30 to September 30.

Source: U.S. Department of Homeland Security.

Table 21.
PERSONS NATURALIZED BY REGION AND COUNTRY OF BIRTH: FISCAL YEARS 2004 TO 2013

Region and country of birth	2004	2005	2006	2007	2008	2009	2010	2011	2012	2013
REGION										
Total....................	537,151	604,280	702,589	660,477	1,046,539	743,715	619,913	694,193	757,434	779,929
Africa	34,531	38,830	50,397	41,652	54,418	60,383	64,022	69,738	74,775	71,872
Asia	224,072	243,514	263,516	243,783	330,361	276,375	251,598	249,940	257,035	275,700
Europe	83,961	91,745	101,125	81,788	108,688	90,214	78,011	82,209	82,714	80,333
North America	151,008	180,525	223,034	241,136	462,312	250,209	163,836	217,750	261,673	271,807
Oceania................	3,551	3,898	3,657	3,342	4,781	3,928	3,646	3,734	3,886	3,849
South America	38,670	44,498	59,980	48,128	84,845	61,666	58,474	70,485	76,992	76,167
Unknown...............	1,358	1,270	880	648	1,134	940	326	337	359	201
COUNTRY										
Total....................	537,151	604,280	702,589	660,477	1,046,539	743,715	619,913	694,193	757,434	779,929
Afghanistan..............	1,323	1,464	2,018	2,013	2,650	2,588	2,230	1,998	1,758	2,074
Albania	3,324	3,830	3,964	2,786	2,972	3,483	5,088	4,267	3,615	3,538
Algeria..................	616	722	825	578	894	1,024	808	773	891	841
American Samoa	137	294	247	161	178	265	232	205	180	265
Angola..................	87	86	106	105	161	95	135	162	166	143
Anguilla	18	27	35	37	47	29	26	38	30	26
Antigua-Barbuda..........	357	371	520	416	661	456	341	386	390	366
Argentina................	1,965	1,976	2,695	2,348	4,170	3,153	3,140	3,870	3,909	4,177
Armenia.................	1,793	1,737	1,605	1,495	2,195	2,021	3,168	3,965	3,285	3,203
Aruba	30	39	44	36	55	37	27	40	27	42
Australia	1,295	1,155	1,240	1,067	1,636	1,392	1,202	1,291	1,312	1,296
Austria	277	307	359	292	357	303	277	271	241	248
Azerbaijan	793	904	997	606	834	1,005	1,233	1,153	958	786
Bahamas.................	378	343	574	397	838	569	475	609	647	681
Bahrain	54	57	81	56	85	91	102	80	93	76
Bangladesh	5,148	5,503	6,683	4,746	5,345	6,644	6,979	7,325	8,417	9,571
Barbados................	650	778	1,006	718	1,203	878	535	648	687	683
Belarus	1,464	1,549	1,769	1,401	1,767	1,583	1,523	1,814	1,896	1,797
Belgium.................	232	247	355	248	716	673	523	525	522	513
Belize	664	704	918	799	1,291	854	556	742	817	966
Benin	42	56	64	61	79	119	127	183	210	206
Bermuda.................	47	58	72	42	75	80	65	58	65	59
Bhutan	3	6	D	10	9	17	50	55	42	275
Bolivia..................	1,125	1,361	1,630	1,311	2,807	1,700	1,185	1,446	2,063	1,961
Bosnia-Herzegovina	8,013	8,921	9,686	8,175	8,176	4,544	4,012	4,259	4,904	3,662
Botswana	5	9	17	4	18	17	24	9	11	29
Brazil...................	4,074	4,583	7,028	5,745	8,808	7,960	8,867	10,251	9,884	9,565
British Virgin Islands..........	41	38	54	40	67	43	36	48	41	45
Brunei..................	10	13	13	20	25	14	15	11	17	11
Bulgaria.................	2,487	2,906	3,488	2,621	3,213	3,211	3,123	3,103	2,964	2,646
Burkina Faso	19	26	51	37	48	90	112	163	166	230
Burma..................	1,177	1,360	1,486	1,058	1,383	1,447	2,399	2,321	2,384	3,489
Burundi.................	59	56	71	95	76	90	145	168	209	379
Cambodia	3,975	4,806	4,778	4,197	5,869	4,673	3,756	4,589	6,189	4,161
Cameroon	575	661	771	611	967	1,098	1,519	2,172	2,459	2,541
Canada	7,682	7,815	9,607	8,473	12,387	9,753	8,539	9,318	9,077	8,690
Cape Verde	635	933	1,126	1,223	1,265	903	675	974	1,037	1,014
Cayman Islands	9	8	18	9	24	22	17	15	29	17
Central African Republic	5	10	14	17	19	22	27	34	56	54
Chad....................	27	19	18	22	22	27	39	50	69	64
Chile....................	1,142	1,183	1,549	1,346	2,851	1,585	1,249	1,527	1,586	1,649
China, People's Republic........	27,309	31,708	35,387	33,134	40,017	37,130	33,969	32,864	31,868	35,387
Colombia.................	9,819	11,396	15,698	12,089	22,926	16,593	18,417	22,693	23,972	22,196
Congo, Democratic Republic	88	122	229	164	211	349	744	908	1,173	1,250
Congo, Republic............	163	193	369	287	306	308	313	345	381	402
Costa Rica................	970	1,161	1,402	1,227	2,376	1,517	1,114	1,511	1,597	1,661
Cote d'Ivoire	317	324	491	382	479	589	549	694	868	958
Croatia	1,084	1,348	1,623	1,073	1,251	718	589	569	725	561
Cuba....................	11,236	11,227	21,481	15,394	39,871	24,891	14,050	21,071	31,244	30,482
Cyprus..................	104	134	140	109	160	160	118	115	92	112
Czech Republic	69	102	122	122	192	266	367	485	477	562

See footnotes at end of table.

Table 21.
PERSONS NATURALIZED BY REGION AND COUNTRY OF BIRTH: FISCAL YEARS 2004 TO 2013 – Continued

Region and country of birth	2004	2005	2006	2007	2008	2009	2010	2011	2012	2013
Czechoslovakia (former)	434	490	614	449	629	503	372	310	291	232
Denmark................	175	154	199	170	210	156	123	124	133	127
Djibouti................	12	17	18	14	25	19	17	22	26	39
Dominica...............	441	543	741	539	975	672	543	594	597	642
Dominican Republic	15,464	20,831	22,165	20,645	35,251	20,778	15,451	20,508	33,351	39,590
Ecuador................	5,616	7,091	8,321	7,229	11,908	7,609	5,931	6,929	8,783	9,470
Egypt.................	3,726	4,061	4,271	3,231	4,165	5,224	5,860	5,848	6,191	6,213
El Salvador	9,602	12,174	13,430	17,157	35,796	18,927	10,343	13,834	16,685	18,401
Equatorial Guinea............	3	4	D	6	9	D	12	9	19	14
Eritrea.................	829	692	653	553	694	760	991	985	1,059	1,145
Estonia	126	104	156	132	221	209	185	217	234	213
Ethiopia...............	4,255	4,621	5,397	5,165	7,160	8,698	8,903	8,519	8,803	8,323
Fiji..................	1,267	1,503	1,163	1,118	1,508	998	1,140	1,118	1,134	1,003
Finland	352	431	532	359	549	385	286	344	329	300
France................	1,847	2,016	2,506	2,011	2,835	2,529	2,263	2,527	2,358	2,534
French Polynesia	10	22	16	19	15	12	12	14	15	8
Gabon................	12	18	23	18	24	35	43	53	80	72
Gambia	136	189	286	246	330	419	444	505	556	573
Georgia	382	443	628	514	627	864	1,107	1,253	1,271	1,205
Germany	3,836	3,811	4,556	3,617	4,708	4,564	4,001	4,461	4,192	4,066
Ghana................	3,577	3,561	4,760	3,181	4,557	4,819	4,211	4,690	5,344	5,105
Greece	1,100	1,075	1,291	1,200	1,314	1,067	800	844	867	938
Grenada	530	649	781	511	850	683	446	528	683	717
Guatemala...............	5,080	6,250	6,551	8,181	17,087	8,619	5,375	7,285	8,797	9,530
Guinea	124	137	194	191	225	304	418	575	787	958
Guinea-Bissau	10	10	14	5	14	17	17	29	30	24
Guyana	4,877	5,543	7,434	5,631	8,290	6,840	4,932	5,413	6,201	6,295
Haiti	8,215	9,740	15,979	11,552	21,229	13,290	12,291	14,191	19,114	23,480
Honduras...............	3,455	3,953	4,949	4,669	8,794	4,858	3,056	3,980	5,294	5,462
Hong Kong..............	3,713	4,479	4,263	3,871	4,940	3,329	2,198	2,184	1,980	2,093
Hungary...............	738	720	955	788	1,089	1,142	916	953	1,014	984
Iceland	79	82	70	62	83	75	51	76	97	75
India	37,975	35,962	47,542	46,871	65,971	52,889	61,142	45,985	42,928	49,897
Indonesia	1,131	1,234	1,287	1,213	1,823	1,794	2,765	2,345	2,123	2,190
Iran..................	11,781	11,031	11,363	10,557	11,813	12,069	9,337	9,286	9,627	11,623
Iraq..................	3,646	3,273	3,614	2,967	5,057	4,197	3,489	3,360	3,523	7,771
Ireland................	2,421	1,995	1,754	1,335	2,179	1,296	1,178	1,171	1,239	1,295
Israel	2,373	2,436	2,905	2,363	2,933	3,410	3,205	3,153	2,859	3,466
Italy.................	2,295	2,511	2,769	2,217	2,991	2,552	2,064	2,231	2,234	2,355
Jamaica................	12,271	13,674	18,953	12,314	21,324	15,098	12,070	14,591	15,531	16,442
Japan	1,955	2,154	2,192	1,934	2,712	2,192	1,622	1,744	1,663	1,837
Jordan................	2,324	2,464	2,634	2,125	2,632	2,891	2,436	2,345	2,436	2,816
Kazakhstan	572	726	872	725	908	917	763	891	1,040	909
Kenya	997	1,158	1,636	1,396	2,218	2,546	3,043	3,621	4,170	4,257
Korea, North	NA	NA	NA	NA	NA	28	13	13	19	27
Korea, South[1]...............	17,184	19,223	17,668	17,628	22,759	17,576	11,170	12,664	13,790	15,786
Kosovo	X	X	X	X	89	397	590	465	510	487
Kuwait................	796	846	903	755	1,031	1,152	919	869	820	920
Kyrgyzstan..............	159	217	246	331	361	338	380	440	420	395
Laos	5,678	5,261	4,114	3,787	5,553	3,081	2,743	5,452	7,027	3,932
Latvia	335	348	347	327	455	404	342	401	392	364
Lebanon	3,314	3,288	3,393	2,779	3,399	3,787	3,266	3,127	2,914	3,002
Lesotho................	8	4	7	11	6	D	7	11	7	10
Liberia................	1,218	1,548	2,193	1,815	2,468	2,767	3,360	3,794	4,322	3,923
Libya.................	130	173	142	136	198	249	173	180	195	206
Lithuania	738	887	964	819	969	786	843	973	938	933
Luxembourg.............	9	7	9	9	17	22	18	18	23	16
Macau................	146	195	163	158	181	158	94	86	106	97
Macedonia..............	601	651	837	597	756	741	682	578	635	665
Madagascar..............	30	29	36	26	43	49	55	44	37	50
Malawi	52	60	67	46	64	58	80	86	85	83
Malaysia	1,019	1,221	1,264	1,217	1,705	1,178	1,211	1,137	1,150	1,169
Mali	66	85	118	93	124	149	200	274	288	332

See footnotes at end of table.

Table 21.
PERSONS NATURALIZED BY REGION AND COUNTRY OF BIRTH: FISCAL YEARS 2004 TO 2013 – *Continued*

Region and country of birth	2004	2005	2006	2007	2008	2009	2010	2011	2012	2013
Malta	80	67	86	66	71	72	46	54	44	59
Marshall Islands	9	4	14	12	12	29	21	32	21	17
Mauritania	53	56	106	72	122	175	281	405	495	520
Mauritius	43	46	65	55	70	89	79	64	57	67
Mexico	63,840	77,089	83,979	122,258	231,815	111,630	67,062	94,783	102,181	99,385
Micronesia, Federated States	14	22	41	41	62	125	84	74	73	96
Moldova	711	927	988	1,068	1,328	1,239	1,235	1,398	1,602	1,594
Mongolia	21	41	60	53	129	137	157	242	286	347
Montenegro	X	X	X	-	32	140	167	205	227	231
Montserrat	54	78	96	51	87	59	57	63	51	65
Morocco	1,841	2,628	3,643	2,684	3,383	4,556	3,710	3,656	3,872	3,768
Mozambique	40	50	62	45	73	47	41	49	48	51
Namibia	13	18	17	22	38	27	38	29	42	40
Nepal	408	417	575	638	953	1,632	2,185	2,235	2,448	2,711
Netherlands	722	860	1,008	819	1,219	889	691	778	919	786
Netherlands Antilles	23	25	33	28	43	40	56	60	76	82
New Zealand	420	444	440	447	649	562	495	480	563	482
Nicaragua	3,444	5,080	9,283	8,164	17,954	7,445	4,047	5,092	5,870	5,064
Niger	46	48	46	52	73	67	89	124	143	167
Nigeria	6,470	6,894	8,652	6,582	8,597	9,298	9,126	9,344	9,322	9,545
Norway	137	136	145	105	153	128	91	90	87	80
Oman	13	16	23	15	33	32	30	37	48	39
Pakistan	8,744	9,699	10,411	9,147	11,813	12,528	11,601	10,655	11,150	12,948
Palau	19	18	36	40	62	54	71	68	72	64
Panama	1,462	1,643	1,930	1,617	2,870	1,694	1,215	1,340	1,532	1,598
Papua New Guinea	3	10	12	5	14	18	16	17	16	20
Paraguay	178	202	285	234	386	310	212	289	338	331
Peru	6,980	7,904	10,063	7,965	15,016	10,349	8,551	10,266	11,814	11,782
Philippines	31,448	36,673	40,500	38,830	58,792	38,934	35,465	42,520	44,958	43,489
Poland	10,335	9,801	10,230	9,320	14,237	10,604	8,038	8,844	8,715	8,697
Portugal	2,173	2,403	2,638	2,506	3,988	2,143	1,266	1,426	1,607	1,585
Qatar	48	66	59	60	85	106	115	101	101	107
Romania	4,388	4,602	5,484	3,986	4,515	4,388	4,385	4,314	4,253	4,050
Russia	7,586	8,297	9,412	7,660	10,778	9,490	7,566	8,257	8,154	8,222
Rwanda	116	123	178	91	101	161	278	265	285	374
Saint Kitts-Nevis	282	331	483	334	529	389	305	306	319	315
Saint Lucia	359	515	623	506	779	583	554	600	724	856
Saint Vincent and the Grenadines	388	491	624	450	623	513	375	416	511	574
Samoa	157	165	201	163	204	185	154	172	178	206
Saudi Arabia	354	397	511	504	615	768	739	814	779	927
Senegal	371	401	503	386	566	640	633	752	790	869
Serbia	X	X	X	-	3	15	27	85	109	117
Serbia and Montenegro	3,159	5,857	5,555	3,382	3,582	2,597	2,653	2,185	2,012	1,830
Seychelles	13	8	22	5	26	19	12	19	8	15
Sierra Leone	945	1,043	1,683	1,485	2,018	1,868	1,878	1,831	1,861	1,613
Singapore	332	338	347	315	433	403	336	311	293	263
Slovakia	318	362	479	380	498	488	485	421	401	413
Slovenia	60	58	61	60	80	64	64	57	64	58
Somalia	2,714	3,238	4,242	3,594	3,816	3,818	5,728	7,971	9,286	6,875
South Africa	1,453	1,495	2,225	2,069	2,980	2,436	2,550	2,566	2,294	2,283
South Sudan	X	X	X	X	X	X	X	-	81	139
Soviet Union (former)	3,772	3,668	3,831	2,813	3,538	4,263	2,954	2,812	2,610	2,807
Spain	1,120	1,256	1,465	1,175	1,958	1,420	1,115	1,253	1,242	1,367
Sri Lanka	980	927	1,023	1,024	1,377	1,367	1,421	1,334	1,146	1,258
Sudan	1,104	1,551	2,587	2,785	2,893	2,855	2,885	2,444	2,291	1,924
Suriname	97	125	222	159	202	198	161	194	189	160
Swaziland	5	5	10	4	8	21	8	15	10	15
Sweden	1,016	980	984	786	1,207	940	774	872	798	783
Switzerland	487	541	539	501	658	529	484	427	427	452
Syria	2,385	2,252	2,395	1,799	2,105	2,484	2,029	1,981	1,814	2,196
Taiwan	7,889	8,295	8,819	7,486	8,711	7,606	5,621	5,065	4,573	5,255
Tajikistan	117	116	147	109	168	156	178	155	142	168
Tanzania	348	363	490	356	464	567	466	516	543	647

See footnotes at end of table.

Table 21.
PERSONS NATURALIZED BY REGION AND COUNTRY OF BIRTH: FISCAL YEARS 2004 TO 2013 – *Continued*

Region and country of birth	2004	2005	2006	2007	2008	2009	2010	2011	2012	2013
Thailand	3,779	4,314	4,583	4,438	6,930	4,962	4,112	5,299	6,585	5,544
Togo	204	291	536	473	673	1,132	1,253	1,523	1,448	1,380
Tonga	207	246	235	251	421	269	208	251	306	371
Trinidad and Tobago	3,958	4,832	6,612	4,514	7,305	5,726	4,740	5,014	5,596	5,784
Tunisia	192	226	315	299	390	479	407	377	345	362
Turkey	1,964	2,231	2,742	2,009	2,771	3,219	3,213	3,100	3,329	3,390
Turkmenistan	58	59	75	58	99	91	138	146	136	160
Turks and Caicos Islands	16	21	30	14	33	21	20	36	49	47
Uganda	327	340	477	344	541	489	637	838	820	763
Ukraine	8,069	9,343	10,184	8,594	10,992	9,123	7,345	8,489	9,459	8,624
United Arab Emirates	168	197	277	253	328	383	404	425	431	499
United Kingdom	7,785	8,087	9,104	7,752	12,095	10,060	8,401	9,246	9,145	9,459
United States	36	29	57	41	67	51	45	45	60	55
Uruguay	412	475	579	496	924	634	585	751	849	933
Uzbekistan	1,224	1,588	1,821	1,148	1,377	1,513	1,472	2,463	3,071	2,482
Venezuela	2,385	2,659	4,476	3,575	6,557	4,735	5,243	6,856	7,404	7,648
Vietnam	27,480	32,926	29,917	27,921	39,584	31,168	19,313	20,922	23,490	24,277
Yemen	822	814	989	734	1,080	1,243	1,186	1,320	1,452	1,355
Zambia	180	159	239	212	290	289	317	337	338	352
Zimbabwe	225	260	322	312	413	489	546	715	691	658
All other countries	32	37	27	35	59	48	37	45	40	41
Unknown	1,358	1,270	880	648	1,134	940	326	337	359	201

NA Not available.

X Not applicable.

D Data withheld to limit disclosure.

- Represents zero.

[1] Data for South Korea prior to Fiscal Year 2009 include a small number of cases from North Korea.

Note: Based on N-400 data for persons aged 18 and over.

Source: U.S. Department of Homeland Security.

Table 22.
PERSONS NATURALIZED BY STATE OR TERRITORY OF RESIDENCE: FISCAL YEARS 2004 TO 2013

State or territory of residence	2004	2005	2006	2007	2008	2009	2010	2011	2012	2013
Total...................	537,151	604,280	702,589	660,477	1,046,539	743,715	619,913	694,193	757,434	779,929
Alabama..................	734	795	1,946	1,343	1,982	1,775	2,027	2,439	2,084	1,811
Alaska..................	777	951	831	849	1,145	1,100	831	1,115	1,186	1,083
Arizona	6,500	6,785	9,707	12,091	24,055	12,377	10,340	12,784	13,090	13,165
Arkansas.................	823	990	1,133	1,214	2,330	1,648	1,275	1,559	1,605	1,567
California................	145,593	170,489	152,836	181,684	297,909	179,754	129,354	151,183	158,850	164,792
Colorado	6,007	5,681	5,526	7,829	11,972	6,813	7,165	7,805	7,726	6,263
Connecticut...............	5,957	8,169	7,231	4,552	9,589	10,421	7,452	8,370	8,332	9,253
Delaware.................	982	945	1,187	1,094	1,425	1,545	1,829	1,470	1,456	1,460
District of Columbia	882	939	1,089	1,334	1,492	2,188	1,319	1,016	1,958	1,854
Florida..................	43,795	42,999	90,846	54,563	128,328	82,788	67,484	87,309	100,890	101,773
Georgia..................	6,880	7,903	19,785	14,181	20,417	15,408	18,253	17,761	17,093	19,534
Guam...................	1,052	682	873	1,057	998	654	644	675	800	691
Hawaii..................	2,050	4,663	5,276	4,521	5,205	3,744	3,190	3,450	3,144	3,494
Idaho	864	1,097	980	1,261	2,240	1,674	1,102	1,473	1,384	1,305
Illinois..................	29,432	27,739	30,156	38,735	45,224	28,112	26,180	29,133	28,376	27,706
Indiana	2,455	2,650	3,885	3,652	5,104	4,261	3,866	4,085	4,146	4,369
Iowa	1,314	234	805	2,093	3,503	2,198	1,858	1,840	2,255	2,503
Kansas	2,093	1,814	2,509	2,406	4,072	3,129	2,492	2,687	2,905	2,761
Kentucky	1,307	1,820	2,049	2,256	3,093	2,390	2,398	2,778	2,686	3,341
Louisiana................	1,458	1,700	1,336	2,240	3,018	3,402	2,423	2,496	2,344	2,543
Maine	548	772	802	728	924	729	839	999	941	988
Maryland................	12,295	11,503	14,465	11,613	23,342	17,099	16,220	15,790	16,160	17,752
Massachusetts	16,263	22,685	22,932	20,952	28,728	21,748	21,095	22,812	22,753	21,404
Michigan	14,615	11,418	11,675	10,678	14,634	10,703	11,162	10,414	11,069	12,950
Minnesota	7,713	7,383	9,137	9,124	9,220	9,089	9,020	11,044	12,016	10,526
Mississippi	557	520	495	657	944	1,170	967	965	972	973
Missouri	3,999	2,733	3,711	4,237	5,849	4,526	4,388	4,175	4,794	4,817
Montana	285	209	225	251	358	267	259	297	325	294
Nebraska................	1,537	1,365	1,797	2,188	2,866	1,644	1,590	1,876	2,039	2,418
Nevada	4,622	5,901	8,202	8,363	13,150	8,470	6,791	8,519	7,667	8,507
New Hampshire	958	971	2,483	1,821	1,617	1,492	1,670	1,607	1,507	1,589
New Jersey	30,291	33,160	39,801	35,235	59,950	35,077	33,864	33,826	42,622	41,173
New Mexico...............	1,449	1,401	1,538	1,704	3,058	3,062	2,205	2,434	2,689	2,371
New York................	66,234	84,624	103,870	73,676	90,572	88,733	67,972	76,603	93,584	107,330
North Carolina	5,084	5,862	12,592	6,606	8,509	16,294	9,988	11,360	11,848	12,150
North Dakota..............	267	203	329	415	336	273	286	369	377	532
Ohio	8,590	9,415	8,796	9,250	11,142	8,072	8,617	9,326	10,194	10,664
Oklahoma	1,765	1,799	2,246	1,812	3,335	2,256	2,678	2,966	3,133	3,487
Oregon	3,612	4,777	4,332	5,572	9,257	5,051	4,910	5,657	5,872	5,784
Pennsylvania	10,205	13,307	15,846	11,371	19,673	16,905	16,143	16,162	16,470	17,813
Puerto Rico	512	1,641	1,413	1,518	2,622	1,253	1,318	1,692	2,212	2,447
Rhode Island	2,185	2,604	2,266	2,088	3,721	2,458	2,078	2,682	2,854	2,816
South Carolina.............	1,748	916	2,940	1,499	3,488	3,506	3,081	4,033	4,124	4,770
South Dakota..............	257	354	342	460	572	415	399	420	467	464
Tennessee...............	2,613	3,578	3,334	2,927	5,560	4,938	4,229	5,396	5,557	5,004
Texas	35,417	38,553	37,835	53,032	82,129	54,024	49,699	52,927	57,762	57,947
Utah	3,110	2,874	2,740	2,777	5,394	2,823	2,908	3,595	3,848	3,026
Vermont.................	419	488	569	468	518	426	407	431	546	496
Virginia	13,478	17,653	20,401	14,171	29,949	24,730	17,815	13,782	24,224	22,279
Washington	12,667	14,817	12,762	14,671	18,665	19,853	16,830	17,317	17,524	17,589
West Virginia	237	362	390	310	505	361	550	348	478	443
Wisconsin	3,570	4,040	3,247	4,485	5,200	3,845	3,864	4,434	4,379	4,532
Wyoming	146	134	169	190	245	186	229	228	220	242
Other[1].................	287	480	608	643	1,499	1,051	590	1,853	1,120	983
Unknown	8,661	6,733	8,313	6,030	5,907	5,805	3,770	6,426	2,777	2,101

[1] Includes U.S. territories and armed forces posts.

Note: Based on N-400 data for persons aged 18 and over.

Source: U.S. Department of Homeland Security.

Table 23.
PERSONS NATURALIZED BY CORE BASED STATISTICAL AREA (CBSA) OF RESIDENCE: FISCAL YEARS 2004 TO 2013
(Ranked by 2013 Naturalizations)

Geographic area	2004	2005	2006	2007	2008	2009	2010	2011	2012	2013
Total...............................	537,151	604,280	702,589	660,477	1,046,539	743,715	619,913	694,193	757,434	779,929
New York-Northern New Jersey-Long Island, NY-NJ-PA	89,923	108,437	132,321	99,006	134,570	112,797	91,256	99,153	123,891	136,513
Los Angeles-Long Beach-Santa Ana, CA	66,733	78,182	65,811	78,454	138,618	84,061	51,977	62,373	65,679	70,189
Miami-Fort Lauderdale-Pompano Beach, FL......	28,846	24,110	63,621	36,159	89,440	54,202	42,220	55,560	68,072	66,925
Washington-Arlington-Alexandria, DC-VA-MD-WV ...	19,711	22,473	26,463	19,367	40,731	32,690	24,861	20,591	31,601	30,030
Chicago-Joliet-Naperville, IL-IN-WI.............	28,264	27,054	29,047	37,736	43,548	26,676	25,053	27,607	26,942	26,173
San Francisco-Oakland-Fremont, CA	22,929	25,484	24,038	25,872	37,850	20,954	21,281	22,046	20,474	23,506
Houston-Sugar Land-Baytown, TX..............	12,816	13,401	13,893	18,398	28,275	18,379	18,343	18,467	22,056	22,581
Boston-Cambridge-Quincy, MA-NH	13,177	18,273	18,585	16,954	22,859	17,429	17,027	18,834	18,264	17,384
Atlanta-Sandy Springs-Marietta, GA	5,634	6,647	16,823	11,720	16,812	12,651	15,519	14,335	14,205	16,753
Dallas-Fort Worth-Arlington, TX................	11,248	12,748	12,110	18,068	25,172	17,423	16,568	16,048	16,892	16,267
San Diego-Carlsbad-San Marcos, CA	11,184	12,265	12,682	17,924	21,154	12,978	11,473	12,326	12,876	14,376
Philadelphia-Camden-Wilmington, PA-NJ-DE-MD ...	7,623	10,526	13,251	9,272	16,720	14,285	13,452	13,139	13,036	13,781
Seattle-Tacoma-Bellevue, WA.................	9,586	11,318	9,407	10,066	12,534	15,061	12,774	12,820	12,939	13,064
San Jose-Sunnyvale-Santa Clara, CA	15,408	15,494	14,129	12,347	24,142	14,201	13,455	11,303	11,473	12,974
Riverside-San Bernardino-Ontario, CA..........	8,368	13,417	11,311	12,253	23,627	19,422	8,724	12,339	11,530	11,749
Orlando-Kissimmee-Sanford, FL..............	2,382	5,326	9,247	3,622	11,914	7,181	6,744	8,578	8,661	10,294
Detroit-Warren-Livonia, MI	10,811	8,271	8,724	7,868	10,731	7,494	8,084	7,515	7,985	9,434
Phoenix-Mesa-Glendale, AZ..................	4,144	4,365	6,771	7,908	16,867	7,926	7,336	9,149	8,923	9,357
Minneapolis-St. Paul-Bloomington, MN-WI.......	6,776	6,388	7,932	7,839	7,834	7,969	7,917	9,534	10,258	8,916
Tampa-St. Petersburg-Clearwater, FL.........	4,650	4,754	5,394	4,721	9,623	7,587	5,786	7,502	8,081	8,248
Sacramento–Arden-Arcade–Roseville, CA	5,913	7,556	6,424	8,968	11,347	6,372	6,099	7,895	10,620	7,808
Las Vegas–Paradise, NV	3,905	4,833	6,986	6,829	11,058	7,357	5,724	7,291	6,532	7,347
Baltimore-Towson, MD	3,452	3,391	4,310	3,490	6,920	5,296	5,150	5,026	4,807	5,368
Portland-Vancouver-Hillsboro, OR-WA	3,585	4,425	4,044	5,037	7,779	4,821	4,611	5,184	5,369	5,283
Columbus, OH	2,529	3,624	3,090	3,141	4,014	2,742	3,075	3,456	3,895	4,263
Denver-Aurora-Broomfield, CO	4,221	3,987	3,688	5,414	8,047	4,497	4,751	5,198	5,101	4,184
Bridgeport-Stamford-Norwalk, CT	2,291	3,319	2,441	1,625	3,534	3,930	2,732	3,244	3,272	3,701
Providence-New Bedford-Fall River, RI-MA	3,024	3,746	3,390	3,202	5,536	3,470	2,819	3,538	3,771	3,613
Charlotte-Gastonia-Rock Hill, NC-SC..........	1,195	1,455	3,277	1,850	2,620	4,243	2,650	2,981	3,216	3,611
Austin-Round Rock-San Marcos, TX	1,935	2,043	2,120	3,004	4,707	2,829	2,953	3,528	3,472	3,534
San Antonio-New Braunfels, TX	1,714	2,069	1,757	2,568	5,387	2,594	2,457	3,334	3,253	3,413
Fresno, CA.............................	1,483	1,579	1,812	3,070	5,133	2,396	2,152	3,432	4,383	2,938
Hartford-West Hartford-East Hartford, CT	1,874	2,561	2,496	1,510	3,142	3,323	2,466	2,614	2,570	2,885
St. Louis, MO-IL.........................	2,471	1,656	2,119	2,711	3,532	2,549	2,531	2,499	2,607	2,718
El Centro, CA...........................	473	364	765	1,380	1,887	942	730	1,020	1,682	2,680
Honolulu, HI............................	1,854	4,326	4,207	3,585	4,082	2,950	2,551	2,684	2,418	2,673
Raleigh-Cary, NC........................	996	1,148	2,774	1,398	1,553	4,114	2,558	2,875	2,823	2,672
Jacksonville, FL.........................	1,860	2,491	2,278	2,626	3,208	2,305	2,859	2,930	2,865	2,658
El Paso, TX	1,975	2,056	1,239	2,314	4,436	3,512	1,980	2,559	2,739	2,652
Nashville-Davidson–Murfreesboro–Franklin, TN ...	932	1,835	1,661	1,422	2,619	2,290	2,112	2,482	2,570	2,612
Stockton, CA	1,848	2,218	2,102	3,157	4,196	2,044	1,845	3,043	3,712	2,605
Cleveland-Elyria-Mentor, OH.................	3,014	2,568	2,583	2,599	2,975	2,173	2,122	2,135	2,213	2,374
Bakersfield-Delano, CA	810	1,024	1,357	2,576	3,961	1,951	1,492	2,098	1,677	2,372
Oxnard-Thousand Oaks-Ventura, CA	2,087	3,387	2,743	3,221	5,235	3,371	1,823	2,134	1,949	2,372
Cape Coral-Fort Myers, FL..................	872	836	1,039	1,086	2,172	1,504	1,322	2,024	2,365	2,284
Kansas City, MO-KS	1,724	1,485	1,770	2,016	3,250	2,439	2,199	2,228	2,447	2,284
San Juan-Caguas-Guaynabo, PR.............	448	1,443	1,255	1,355	2,374	1,135	1,187	1,564	2,036	2,253
Richmond, VA...........................	969	1,237	1,386	1,276	2,376	1,633	1,689	1,784	2,047	2,208
Oklahoma City, OK	901	945	1,173	960	1,647	1,048	1,575	1,777	1,792	2,067
Indianapolis-Carmel, IN....................	883	873	1,617	1,421	2,058	1,766	1,834	1,865	1,708	1,999
Other CBSAs	82,145	89,390	108,501	107,281	166,550	127,014	110,282	126,263	133,157	132,579
Other metropolitan areas	72,210	78,908	94,452	93,711	145,676	110,136	96,611	109,798	115,991	115,050
Other micropolitan areas..................	9,935	10,482	14,049	13,570	20,874	16,878	13,671	16,465	17,166	17,529
Non-CBSA	4,894	4,742	6,158	6,807	10,284	7,939	5,964	7,865	7,748	7,305
Unknown..............................	8,661	6,735	8,467	6,024	5,899	5,800	3,769	6,424	2,780	2,100

Note: Based on N-400 data for persons aged 18 and over.
Source: U.S. Department of Homeland Security.

Table 24.
PERSONS NATURALIZED BY SEX, AGE, MARITAL STATUS, AND OCCUPATION: FISCAL YEAR 2013

Characteristic	Total	Sex		
		Male	Female	Unknown
AGE				
Total	779,929	348,486	431,427	16
18 to 19 years.	10,649	5,135	5,514	-
20 to 24 years.	61,065	28,545	32,520	-
25 to 29 years.	94,872	40,164	54,706	2
30 to 34 years.	100,600	41,778	58,821	1
35 to 39 years.	107,488	47,721	59,766	1
40 to 44 years.	100,520	47,269	53,248	3
45 to 49 years.	77,061	36,216	40,844	1
50 to 54 years.	65,184	29,958	35,225	1
55 to 59 years.	53,645	24,179	29,464	2
60 to 64 years.	39,408	17,783	21,622	3
65 to 74 years.	49,560	21,680	27,878	2
75 years and over	19,876	8,057	11,819	-
Unknown	1	1	-	-
BROAD AGE GROUPS				
Total	779,929	348,486	431,427	16
18 to 20 years.	20,016	9,815	10,201	-
21 years and over	759,912	338,670	421,226	16
Unknown	1	1	-	-
MARITAL STATUS				
Total	779,929	348,486	431,427	16
Single	175,367	88,369	86,998	-
Married	496,262	223,639	272,623	-
Widowed	25,173	3,708	21,465	-
Divorced/separated	81,079	31,886	49,193	-
Unknown	2,048	884	1,148	16
OCCUPATION				
Total	779,929	348,486	431,427	16
Management, professional, and related occupations.	54,678	21,813	32,865	-
Service occupations.	100,545	35,801	64,744	-
Sales and office occupations	59,702	22,494	37,208	-
Farming, fishing, and forestry occupations	2,426	1,777	649	-
Construction, extraction, maintenance and repair occupations.	15,065	14,522	543	-
Production, transportation, and material moving occupations.	93,869	62,735	31,134	-
Military	3,526	2,805	721	-
No occupation/not working outside home	216,617	68,036	148,581	-
Homemakers.	48,587	1,076	47,511	-
Students or children.	53,759	21,857	31,902	-
Retirees.	26,207	12,940	13,267	-
Unemployed.	88,064	32,163	55,901	-
Unknown	233,501	118,503	114,982	16

- Represents zero.

Note: Based on N-400 data for persons aged 18 and over.

Source: U.S. Department of Homeland Security.

Nonimmigrant Admissions

Table 25.
NONIMMIGRANT ADMISSIONS BY CLASS OF ADMISSION: FISCAL YEARS 2004 TO 2013

Class of admission	2004	2005	2006	2007	2008
Total all admissions[1]	180,200,000	175,300,000	175,100,000	171,300,000	175,400,000
Total I-94 admissions[2]	30,781,330	32,003,435	33,667,328	37,149,651	39,381,928
Temporary workers and families	1,507,769	1,572,863	1,709,268	1,932,075	1,949,695
Temporary workers and trainees	831,144	882,957	985,456	1,118,138	1,101,938
CNMI-only transitional workers (CW1)	X	X	X	X	X
Spouses and children of CW1 (CW2)	X	X	X	X	X
Temporary workers in specialty occupations (H1B)	386,821	407,418	431,853	461,730	409,619
Chile and Singapore Free Trade Agreement aliens (H1B1)	4	47	129	170	153
Registered nurses participating in the Nursing Relief for Disadvantaged Areas (H1C)	70	31	24	49	170
Agricultural workers (H2A)[3,4]	22,141	NA	46,432	87,316	173,103
Nonagricultural workers (H2B)[3]	86,958	NA	97,279	75,727	104,618
Returning H2B workers (H2R)[3,5]	X	NA	36,792	79,168	5,003
Trainees (H3)	2,226	2,938	4,134	5,540	6,156
Spouses and children of H1, H2, or H3 (H4)	130,847	130,145	133,437	144,136	122,423
Workers with extraordinary ability or achievement (O1)	27,127	29,715	31,969	36,184	41,238
Workers accompanying and assisting in performance of O1 workers (O2)	6,332	7,635	9,567	10,349	12,497
Spouses and children of O1 and O2 (O3)	3,719	4,154	4,674	5,377	6,386
Internationally recognized athletes or entertainers (P1)	40,466	43,766	46,205	53,050	57,030
Artists or entertainers in reciprocal exchange programs (P2)	3,810	4,423	4,604	4,835	4,358
Artists or entertainers in culturally unique programs (P3)	10,038	10,836	12,630	11,900	12,767
Spouses and children of P1, P2, or P3 (P4)	1,853	1,938	2,067	2,223	2,229
Workers in international cultural exchange programs (Q1)	2,113	2,575	2,423	2,412	3,231
Workers in religious occupations (R1)	21,571	22,362	22,706	25,162	25,106
Spouses and children of R1 (R2)	6,443	6,712	7,330	6,881	6,421
North American Free Trade Agreement (NAFTA) professional workers (TN)	65,970	64,713	73,880	85,142	88,382
Spouses and children of TN (TD)	12,635	14,222	17,321	20,787	21,048
Intracompany transferees	456,583	455,350	466,009	531,073	558,485
Intracompany transferees (L1)	314,484	312,144	320,829	363,536	382,776
Spouses and children of L1 (L2)	142,099	143,206	145,180	167,537	175,709
Treaty traders and investors	182,934	192,824	216,842	238,936	243,386
Treaty traders and their spouses and children (E1)	47,083	49,037	50,230	51,722	50,377
Treaty investors and their spouses and children (E2)	135,851	143,786	164,795	177,920	180,270
Treaty investors and their spouses and children CNMI only (E2C)	X	X	X	X	X
Australian Free Trade Agreement principals, spouses and children (E3)	X	D	1,817	9,294	12,739
Representatives of foreign information media	37,108	41,732	40,961	43,928	45,886
Representatives of foreign information media and spouses and children (I1)	37,108	41,732	40,961	43,928	45,886
Students	656,373	663,919	740,724	841,673	917,373
Academic students (F1)	613,221	621,178	693,805	787,756	859,169
Spouses and children of F1 (F2)	35,771	33,756	35,987	40,178	42,039
Vocational students (M1)	6,989	8,378	10,384	13,073	15,496
Spouses and children of M1 (M2)	392	607	548	666	669
Exchange visitors	360,777	382,463	427,067	489,286	506,138
Exchange visitors (J1)	321,975	342,742	385,286	443,482	459,126
Spouses and children of J1 (J2)	38,802	39,721	41,781	45,804	47,012
Diplomats and other representatives	276,817	287,484	292,846	303,290	314,920
Ambassadors, public ministers, career diplomatic or consular officers and their families (A1)	28,046	28,488	29,337	30,291	30,882
Other foreign government officials or employees and their families (A2)	122,809	126,827	127,296	131,583	136,699
Attendants, servants, or personal employees of A1 and A2 and their families (A3)	1,794	1,630	1,496	1,602	1,686
Principals of recognized foreign governments (G1)	13,189	13,606	14,523	15,099	15,348
Other representatives of recognized foreign governments (G2)	13,685	16,608	15,661	15,160	18,367
Representatives of nonrecognized or nonmember foreign governments (G3)	593	740	811	816	844
International organization officers or employees (G4)	80,515	82,826	85,119	88,374	89,711
Attendants, servants, or personal employees of representatives (G5)	1,373	1,336	1,411	1,477	1,399
North Atlantic Treaty Organization (NATO) officials, spouses, and children (N1 to N7)	14,813	15,423	17,192	18,888	19,984
Temporary visitors for pleasure	22,653,699	23,701,858	24,788,438	27,486,177	29,442,168
Temporary visitors for pleasure (B2)	9,185,492	9,758,617	11,269,933	13,087,974	13,371,671
Visa Waiver Program – temporary visitors for pleasure (WT)	13,380,069	13,462,507	12,827,677	13,469,851	15,099,059
Guam Visa Waiver Program – temporary visitors for pleasure to Guam (GT)	88,138	480,734	690,828	928,352	971,438
Guam – Commonwealth of Northern Mariana Islands (CNMI) Visa Waiver Program – temporary visitors for pleasure to Guam or Northern Mariana Islands (GMT)	X	X	X	X	X

See footnotes at end of table.

Table 25.
NONIMMIGRANT ADMISSIONS BY CLASS OF ADMISSION: FISCAL YEARS 2004 TO 2013 - *Continued*

Class of admission	2004	2005	2006	2007	2008
Temporary visitors for business	4,576,783	4,684,164	5,030,779	5,418,884	5,603,668
Temporary visitors for business (B1)	2,352,404	2,432,587	2,673,309	2,928,875	3,052,581
Visa Waiver Program – temporary visitors for business (WB)	2,223,331	2,249,816	2,355,332	2,486,015	2,546,322
Guam Visa Waiver Program – temporary visitors for business to Guam (GB)	1,048	1,761	2,138	3,994	4,765
Guam – Commonwealth of Northern Mariana Islands (CNMI) Visa Waiver Program – temporary visitors for business to Guam or Northern Mariana Islands (GMB)	X	X	X	X	X
Transit aliens	338,170	361,597	378,749	396,383	387,237
Aliens in continuous and immediate transit through the United States (C1)	322,187	343,609	357,682	376,451	365,958
Aliens in transit to the United Nations (C2)	2,283	2,379	2,854	2,914	2,646
Foreign government officials, their spouses, children, and attendants in transit (C3)	13,700	15,609	18,213	17,018	18,633
Commuter students	-	33	188	310	1,102
Canadian or Mexican national academic commuter students (F3)	-	33	188	307	1,102
Canadian or Mexican national vocational commuter students (M3)	-	-	-	3	-
Alien Fiancé(e)s of U.S. citizens and children	33,061	38,027	34,947	38,507	34,863
Fiancé(e)s of U.S. citizens (K1)	28,546	32,900	30,021	32,991	29,916
Children of K1 (K2)	4,515	5,127	4,926	5,516	4,947
Legal Immigration Family Equity (LIFE) Act	70,778	46,727	41,779	37,594	24,172
Spouses of U.S. citizens, visa pending (K3)	17,864	16,249	14,739	15,065	12,849
Children of U.S. citizens, visa pending (K4)	4,253	4,098	3,692	3,430	2,845
Spouses of permanent residents, visa pending (V1)	17,866	10,157	9,321	6,960	3,609
Children of permanent residents, visa pending (V2)	15,239	7,159	6,070	5,435	2,270
Dependents of V1 or V2, visa pending (V3)	15,556	9,064	7,957	6,704	2,599
Other	433	241	208	100	103
Unknown	306,670	264,059	222,335	205,372	200,489

See footnotes at end of table.

Table 25.
NONIMMIGRANT ADMISSIONS BY CLASS OF ADMISSION: FISCAL YEARS 2004 TO 2013 – *Continued*

Class of admission	2009	2010	2011	2012	2013
Total all admissions [1]	162,600,000	159,700,000	158,500,000	165,500,000	173,100,000
Total I-94 admissions [2]	36,231,554	46,471,569	53,082,286	53,887,286	61,052,260
Temporary workers and families	1,703,697	2,816,485	3,385,775	3,049,419	2,996,743
Temporary workers and trainees	936,272	1,682,111	2,092,028	1,900,582	1,853,915
CNMI-only transitional workers (CW1)	X	-	-	D	1,642
Spouses and children of CW1 (CW2)	X	-	-	-	404
Temporary workers in specialty occupations (H1B)	339,243	454,757	494,565	473,015	474,355
Chile and Singapore Free Trade Agreement aliens (H1B1)	213	163	30	D	8
Registered nurses participating in the Nursing Relief for Disadvantaged Areas (H1C)	231	295	124	29	7
Agricultural workers (H2A) [3,4]	149,763	139,403	188,411	183,860	204,577
Nonagricultural workers (H2B) [3]	56,381	69,395	79,794	82,906	104,984
Returning H2B workers (H2R) [3,5]	162	104	68	15	9
Trainees (H3)	4,168	3,078	3,279	4,081	4,117
Spouses and children of H1, H2, or H3 (H4)	105,429	141,571	155,936	156,668	163,786
Workers with extraordinary ability or achievement (O1)	45,600	49,995	51,775	53,941	66,604
Workers accompanying and assisting in performance of O1 workers (O2)	12,966	13,989	15,949	16,670	20,762
Spouses and children of O1 and O2 (O3)	6,533	6,764	6,985	6,853	8,238
Internationally recognized athletes or entertainers (P1)	54,432	72,915	84,545	84,209	85,583
Artists or entertainers in reciprocal exchange programs (P2)	4,028	11,213	13,359	12,826	12,306
Artists or entertainers in culturally unique programs (P3)	11,441	9,669	9,301	9,290	9,512
Spouses and children of P1, P2, or P3 (P4)	2,359	2,836	2,944	3,155	3,565
Workers in international cultural exchange programs (Q1)	2,555	2,430	2,331	2,494	2,685
Workers in religious occupations (R1)	17,362	21,043	19,683	15,906	14,191
Spouses and children of R1 (R2)	4,481	7,966	5,682	4,738	4,337
North American Free Trade Agreement (NAFTA) professional workers (TN)	99,018	634,116	899,455	733,692	612,535
Spouses and children of TN (TD)	19,907	40,409	57,812	56,223	59,708
Intracompany transferees	493,992	702,447	788,187	717,893	723,641
Intracompany transferees (L1)	333,386	502,723	562,776	498,899	503,206
Spouses and children of L1 (L2)	160,606	199,724	225,411	218,994	220,435
Treaty traders and investors	229,301	383,694	454,101	386,472	373,360
Treaty traders and their spouses and children (E1)	49,111	87,988	110,169	81,337	71,652
Treaty investors and their spouses and children (E2)	166,983	281,868	329,230	288,217	279,288
Treaty investors and their spouses and children CNMI only (E2C)	X	-	-	D	5
Australian Free Trade Agreement principals, spouses and children (E3)	13,207	13,838	14,702	16,916	22,415
Representatives of foreign information media	44,132	48,233	51,459	44,472	45,827
Representatives of foreign information media and spouses and children (I1)	44,132	48,233	51,459	44,472	45,827
Students	951,964	1,595,072	1,788,962	1,653,576	1,669,225
Academic students (F1)	895,392	1,514,777	1,702,730	1,566,815	1,577,509
Spouses and children of F1 (F2)	40,956	61,036	66,449	67,563	71,167
Vocational students (M1)	14,632	17,641	18,824	17,600	19,106
Spouses and children of M1 (M2)	984	1,618	959	1,598	1,443
Exchange visitors	459,408	543,335	526,931	475,232	492,937
Exchange visitors (J1)	413,150	484,740	469,993	421,425	433,534
Spouses and children of J1 (J2)	46,258	58,595	56,938	53,807	59,403
Diplomats and other representatives	323,183	380,241	377,830	365,779	373,330
Ambassadors, public ministers, career diplomatic or consular officers and their families (A1)	31,038	38,948	37,692	33,700	34,548
Other foreign government officials or employees and their families (A2)	142,315	173,293	175,651	172,096	164,896
Attendants, servants, or personal employees of A1 and A2 and their families (A3)	1,766	1,870	1,843	1,553	1,381
Principals of recognized foreign governments (G1)	14,876	16,452	15,649	15,669	15,254
Other representatives of recognized foreign governments (G2)	17,529	17,711	20,395	17,118	16,011
Representatives of nonrecognized or nonmember foreign governments (G3)	912	904	967	886	864
International organization officers or employees (G4)	92,878	105,040	100,858	100,760	108,478
Attendants, servants, or personal employees of representatives (G5)	1,389	1,385	1,509	1,190	1,137
North Atlantic Treaty Organization (NATO) officials, spouses, and children (N1 to N7)	20,480	24,638	23,266	22,807	30,761
Temporary visitors for pleasure	27,800,027	35,135,270	40,591,607	42,041,426	48,346,018
Temporary visitors for pleasure (B2)	12,680,504	19,144,019	23,806,138	24,476,086	29,915,467
Visa Waiver Program – temporary visitors for pleasure (WT)	14,272,553	14,825,553	15,718,710	16,380,307	17,168,958
Guam Visa Waiver Program – temporary visitors for pleasure to Guam (GT)	846,970	120,544	X	X	X
Guam – Commonwealth of Northern Mariana Islands (CNMI) Visa Waiver Program – temporary visitors for pleasure to Guam or Northern Mariana Islands (GMT)	X	1,045,154	1,066,759	1,185,033	1,261,593

See footnotes at end of table.

Table 25.
NONIMMIGRANT ADMISSIONS BY CLASS OF ADMISSION: FISCAL YEARS 2004 TO 2013 - *Continued*

Class of admission	2009	2010	2011	2012	2013
Temporary visitors for business	4,390,888	5,206,234	5,696,503	5,707,218	6,299,533
Temporary visitors for business (B1)	2,408,092	2,944,372	3,055,932	2,972,355	3,498,688
Visa Waiver Program – temporary visitors for business (WB)	1,977,361	2,256,890	2,637,166	2,731,887	2,798,130
Guam Visa Waiver Program – temporary visitors for business to Guam (GB)	5,435	904	X	X	X
Guam – Commonwealth of Northern Mariana Islands (CNMI) Visa Waiver Program – temporary visitors for business to Guam or Northern Mariana Islands (GMB)	X	4,068	3,405	2,976	2,715
Transit aliens	346,695	327,572	322,499	313,514	628,711
Aliens in continuous and immediate transit through the United States (C1)	326,704	304,012	296,636	289,105	608,396
Aliens in transit to the United Nations (C2)	2,613	2,986	4,397	4,158	2,269
Foreign government officials, their spouses, children, and attendants in transit (C3)	17,378	20,574	21,466	20,251	18,046
Commuter students	6,488	53,711	108,894	115,561	105,263
Canadian or Mexican national academic commuter students (F3)	6,488	53,711	108,892	115,561	105,263
Canadian or Mexican national vocational commuter students (M3)	-	-	D	-	-
Alien Fiancé(e)s of U.S. citizens and children	32,009	34,891	27,700	32,102	29,773
Fiancé(e)s of U.S. citizens (K1)	27,754	30,444	24,112	27,977	26,046
Children of K1 (K2)	4,255	4,447	3,588	4,125	3,727
Legal Immigration Family Equity (LIFE) Act	20,960	38,810	30,099	8,227	3,014
Spouses of U.S. citizens, visa pending (K3)	12,937	25,615	17,874	4,534	1,262
Children of U.S. citizens, visa pending (K4)	2,578	4,557	3,103	618	417
Spouses of permanent residents, visa pending (V1)	2,482	3,620	3,659	1,928	867
Children of permanent residents, visa pending (V2)	1,424	2,206	2,546	449	271
Dependents of V1 or V2, visa pending (V3)	1,539	2,812	2,917	698	197
Other	74	92	93	91	87
Unknown	196,161	339,856	225,393	125,141	107,626

NA Not available.

X Not applicable.

D Data withheld to limit disclosure.

- Represents zero.

[1] Estimated admission totals rounded to the nearest hundred thousand. Excludes sea and air crew admissions (D1 and D2 visas).

[2] Beginning in 2010, the number of I-94 admissions greatly exceeds totals reported in previous years due to a more complete count of land admissions.

[3] Data are not available separately for 2005; during 2005 there were 129,327 admissions for H2 classes (H2A, H2B, H2R).

[4] Beginning in 2006, annual increases in H2A admissions may be due to more complete recording of pedestrian admissions along the Southwest border.

[5] Issuances of H2R (returning H2B workers not subject to annual numerical limits) ceased at the end of 2007.

Notes: Admissions represent counts of events, i.e., arrivals, not unique individuals; multiple entries of an individual on the same day are counted as one admission. The majority of short-term admissions from Canada and Mexico are excluded.

Source: U.S. Department of Homeland Security.

Table 26.
NONIMMIGRANT ADMISSIONS (I-94 ONLY) BY REGION AND COUNTRY OF CITIZENSHIP: FISCAL YEARS 2004 TO 2013

Region and country of citizenship	2004	2005	2006	2007	2008	2009	2010[1]	2011	2012	2013
REGION										
Total............	30,781,330	32,003,435	33,667,328	37,149,651	39,381,928	36,231,554	46,471,569	53,082,286	53,887,286	61,052,260
Africa	384,442	395,734	394,163	426,922	474,160	452,693	485,110	508,489	573,184	645,919
Asia	7,856,176	8,157,755	8,371,244	8,781,480	8,795,236	7,820,986	9,404,375	10,027,386	11,062,760	12,230,911
Europe	12,524,817	12,950,441	12,792,122	13,993,051	15,931,641	14,559,083	14,692,093	15,481,558	15,710,015	16,167,460
North America	6,662,475	6,988,624	8,491,307	9,963,858	9,832,557	8,963,282	16,449,861	20,940,354	19,996,738	24,561,055
Oceania...........	934,439	997,175	1,039,872	1,067,258	1,127,444	1,065,909	1,290,993	1,513,963	1,618,337	1,770,569
South America.......	2,167,603	2,333,652	2,432,010	2,763,355	3,039,883	3,075,013	3,587,883	4,126,385	4,651,162	5,511,558
Unknown...........	251,378	180,054	146,610	153,727	181,007	294,588	561,254	484,151	275,090	164,788
COUNTRY										
Total............	30,781,330	32,003,435	33,667,328	37,149,651	39,381,928	36,231,554	46,471,569	53,082,286	53,887,286	61,052,260
Afghanistan.........	1,526	1,784	2,020	2,539	2,323	2,616	2,589	2,856	2,772	2,837
Albania	6,812	8,842	8,118	7,902	9,939	8,768	8,921	8,065	7,942	7,889
Algeria............	3,968	4,406	4,633	5,151	6,215	6,491	6,319	7,545	8,402	9,558
Andorra...........	720	825	858	912	1,295	977	1,152	1,217	1,176	1,271
Angola............	4,432	4,807	5,206	6,235	6,509	7,147	7,557	8,293	10,592	12,617
Antigua and Barbuda ..	21,205	22,401	23,416	23,037	22,649	18,743	18,563	17,076	16,958	15,151
Argentina..........	242,103	256,680	275,778	337,511	383,803	395,781	482,637	566,010	646,929	744,864
Armenia...........	5,238	5,245	5,137	4,641	5,694	5,412	5,282	4,910	6,135	7,431
Australia[2]	645,236	702,108	750,504	813,558	867,121	834,000	1,037,672	1,246,091	1,331,669	1,453,814
Austria	152,285	156,511	157,474	168,857	201,070	201,339	209,633	219,476	232,276	237,429
Azerbaijan	2,523	2,570	3,142	3,839	4,591	4,938	5,596	5,623	6,464	7,162
Bahamas...........	321,046	284,825	351,244	368,687	332,571	282,172	276,899	254,335	251,759	244,650
Bahrain	2,667	3,593	3,701	4,334	5,287	4,500	5,549	5,560	6181	7341
Bangladesh	14,712	14,909	14,224	13,100	13,758	15,368	18,034	19,348	22,629	30,314
Barbados..........	55,198	58,826	60,494	62,107	65,434	57,993	62,971	60,445	59,032	58,558
Belarus	9,691	9,252	9,938	10,378	10,719	10,214	12,287	12,141	13,715	14,211
Belgium............	208,754	220,043	219,727	248,107	306,492	281,736	293,762	306,730	310,111	315,611
Belize	25,855	24,730	26,195	27,131	26,747	25,867	25,081	23,273	24,184	25,327
Benin	1,569	1,932	2,375	2,326	2,910	2,585	2,804	2,887	3,056	2,821
Bhutan	425	451	432	514	801	578	660	613	662	633
Bolivia............	33,652	31,606	31,341	39,206	41,622	40,408	44,761	43,893	44,658	50,838
Bosnia and Herzegovina........	7,048	7,278	7,371	7,412	7,190	6,170	5,838	6,492	6,843	7,465
Botswana	1,980	2,102	1,906	2,228	2,564	2,349	2,386	2,587	2,580	2,381
Brazil.............	534,164	636,119	698,808	784,758	893,186	959,448	1,233,457	1,539,015	1,792,425	2,143,154
Brunei............	686	773	847	998	1,216	1,110	1,217	1,448	1,747	2,022
Bulgaria...........	33,688	36,407	39,495	42,205	41,793	35,871	35,456	38,974	39,100	40,029
Burkina Faso	1,760	2,169	2,507	2,674	2,767	2,862	3,004	3,051	3,682	3,928
Burma............	2,029	1,816	2,069	2,361	2,515	2,937	3,383	3,632	3,983	4,967
Burundi	678	861	1,098	1,059	1,052	960	1,182	1,230	1,424	1,740
Cambodia	4,904	4,829	4,132	3,851	3,953	3,652	3,660	3,352	3,628	4,898
Cameroon	7,972	7,982	8,558	9,094	9,517	9,329	9,832	9,423	9,495	9,639
Canada[3]	238,897	231,171	247,828	276,399	285,359	291,642	1,428,931	1,868,179	1,466,120	4,445,881
Cape Verde	1,509	2,000	2,362	2,871	2,966	2,918	2,727	1,943	1,520	3,140
Central African Republic	145	387	407	339	299	253	282	213	202	189
Chad.............	355	478	532	652	522	541	441	456	436	550
Chile.............	139,261	134,593	141,658	157,973	169,166	152,676	174,645	203,206	209,144	245,792
China[4]............	446,838	505,479	596,171	685,026	753,037	729,931	1,038,271	1,364,078	1,756,747	2,098,801
Colombia..........	394,156	412,271	443,781	492,957	527,451	511,071	592,362	613,354	669,392	830,891
Comoros	78	106	90	63	106	92	90	114	123	158
Congo (Brazzaville)[5] ...	2,838	3,223	3,017	2,764	2,950	2,724	2,806	3,509	4,198	2,859
Congo (Kinshasa)[6]....	117	192	477	996	1,269	1,401	1,506	1,276	1,430	3,861
Costa Rica.........	156,610	160,273	158,216	176,882	195,459	176,284	189,999	192,350	197,136	207,840
Cote d'Ivoire	2,444	2,381	3,290	3,001	3,837	4,216	3,671	2,183	2,661	5,219
Croatia	22,097	22,413	23,141	25,435	27,772	26,461	26,056	26,761	26,452	26,905
Cuba.............	12,520	13,443	10,606	11,237	15,130	17,047	23,745	18,593	21,197	34,615
Cyprus............	9,406	9,656	8,942	9,637	11,003	9,935	10,294	10,355	9,789	8,699
Czech Republic	43,455	45,671	47,169	52,411	59,805	77,395	76,951	90,654	95,229	100,056

See footnotes at end of table.

Table 26.

NONIMMIGRANT ADMISSIONS (I-94 ONLY) BY REGION AND COUNTRY OF CITIZENSHIP: FISCAL YEARS 2004 TO 2013 – *Continued*

Region and country of citizenship	2004	2005	2006	2007	2008	2009	2010[1]	2011	2012	2013
Denmark[7]	186,886	212,501	228,269	261,192	310,371	298,098	309,372	323,255	327,854	324,608
Djibouti	232	213	186	204	283	437	443	463	416	338
Dominica	8,809	6,401	5,897	5,322	5,821	5,855	6,718	5,496	5,528	6,783
Dominican Republic	205,905	254,113	267,324	301,306	276,511	250,368	272,896	266,330	276,562	280,563
East Timor	-	18	11	5	D	-	5	-	-	34
Ecuador	152,958	161,243	163,917	179,450	174,104	177,441	205,174	228,159	230,644	268,332
Egypt	32,164	34,659	38,115	43,139	47,706	49,838	57,442	61,716	84,287	89,578
El Salvador	205,047	189,340	176,552	179,678	164,984	141,428	132,336	119,465	114,001	119,572
Equatorial Guinea	158	179	290	272	379	562	523	598	641	1,197
Eritrea	1,605	1,518	1,299	1,009	841	854	901	873	854	1,528
Estonia	8,230	10,113	10,057	12,785	13,179	20,437	14,195	15,950	18,868	20,942
Ethiopia	8,189	7,656	9,096	10,964	12,468	12,116	12,321	13,183	15,336	16,884
Fiji	9,595	9,878	9,944	9,755	10,261	8,602	10,948	13,136	13,084	13,996
Finland	101,983	113,782	112,950	117,829	140,266	144,335	138,310	147,834	154,994	161,020
France[8]	1,244,651	1,309,842	1,192,209	1,414,627	1,711,342	1,683,372	1,696,767	1,845,227	1,913,551	1,959,424
Gabon	1,427	1,775	1,560	1,811	2,099	2,170	2,452	2,706	2,546	2,792
Gambia	2,854	2,749	1,969	2,022	2,014	2,394	2,966	2,999	2,468	2,551
Georgia	5,064	4,266	4,868	4,967	5,341	5,196	5,728	5,694	6,128	6,628
Germany	1,630,249	1,711,433	1,704,168	1,839,544	2,119,640	2,023,971	2,076,215	2,182,441	2,308,207	2,359,681
Ghana	29,028	22,988	20,677	20,903	27,125	23,943	24,926	25,760	27,405	27,822
Greece	60,810	66,727	65,840	71,048	82,518	75,426	79,719	84,380	79,010	81,400
Grenada	11,254	11,212	10,976	11,513	11,773	11,069	11,487	11,289	11,163	10,674
Guatemala	190,044	194,638	199,623	213,213	224,030	204,994	213,056	208,885	216,670	224,006
Guinea	5,919	5,190	4,495	4,619	4,324	3,382	2,870	2,740	2,780	2,777
Guinea-Bissau	102	103	100	107	241	316	165	102	64	126
Guyana	26,680	27,734	25,331	25,465	24,862	25,985	28,146	28,995	34,970	39,412
Haiti	82,101	85,458	72,518	101,276	115,591	103,601	106,066	99,161	98,865	108,382
Holy See	146	141	118	113	122	127	125	123	118	130
Honduras	107,860	111,009	109,478	127,745	139,103	137,923	131,782	141,685	152,168	157,751
Hungary	44,163	47,441	47,707	51,054	53,664	60,937	66,516	73,475	75,947	81,213
Iceland	31,787	41,878	49,535	52,319	57,247	35,330	41,990	57,872	56,114	55,202
India	611,337	665,260	761,257	1,019,766	1,100,401	974,306	1,140,913	1,222,302	1,296,276	1,491,712
Indonesia	72,859	78,127	81,705	86,905	87,917	80,049	89,262	101,894	111,496	123,583
Iran	7,808	9,576	10,433	11,181	11,479	15,084	18,375	21,027	24,290	26,144
Iraq	2,041	2,999	2,893	2,569	3,351	3,999	6,161	7,868	12,215	17,077
Ireland	428,215	469,878	496,662	585,915	669,638	561,051	486,354	471,174	452,312	487,428
Israel	337,516	339,459	339,109	375,482	388,787	363,209	363,907	356,956	366,779	381,206
Italy	759,895	810,141	758,899	890,366	1,086,722	1,036,940	1,111,972	1,201,510	1,192,251	1,205,816
Jamaica	223,898	222,945	269,980	293,421	281,353	252,663	240,304	219,140	223,785	233,430
Japan	4,335,979	4,400,400	4,306,800	4,122,044	3,906,231	3,368,590	3,831,173	3,777,643	4,141,299	4,298,081
Jordan	22,068	23,967	24,540	27,075	27,950	27,848	30,200	31,982	35,620	38,867
Kazakhstan	6,275	8,044	10,434	13,681	16,515	13,756	16,826	20,027	21,249	22,422
Kenya	19,636	19,244	19,607	21,843	23,186	21,443	21,183	19,516	20,331	22,105
Kiribati	1,152	820	722	737	798	1,164	995	989	694	654
Korea, North[9]	72	60	75	50	34	34	130	232	24	59
Korea, South[10]	828,967	876,563	942,350	1,028,253	1,007,466	906,006	1,332,352	1,460,972	1,527,085	1,656,795
Kuwait	12,404	15,112	16,518	20,276	22,305	25,246	29,500	35,568	40,912	48,784
Kyrgyzstan	1,532	1,462	1,788	2,467	2,898	2,783	3,383	3,992	3,740	4,584
Laos	1,856	2,336	2,696	2,988	2,619	1,861	1,514	1,115	1,315	2,556
Latvia	10,140	11,888	11,938	13,975	14,533	15,892	16,177	18,453	20,748	22,330
Lebanon	22,615	23,202	24,008	28,232	28,669	26,894	30,733	32,915	36,527	42,775
Lesotho	372	406	403	429	425	434	509	571	532	524
Liberia	1,684	1,409	1,299	2,228	1,948	1,681	2,075	2,583	3,290	4,152
Libya	402	757	949	1,680	4,313	3,711	4,956	2,462	2,933	4,016
Liechtenstein	1,457	1,203	1,376	1,478	1,701	1,786	1,913	2,297	2,255	2,234
Lithuania	12,928	12,831	12,781	14,569	15,991	20,188	21,595	23,809	27,337	27,854
Luxembourg	8,581	9,240	9,330	9,939	12,918	12,878	14,349	14,926	15,519	15,785
Macedonia	5,420	5,233	5,929	7,508	7,964	7,618	8,441	9,419	9,520	9,436
Madagascar	939	1,015	945	1,015	1,267	1,084	1,189	1,117	1,145	1,265
Malawi	1,472	1,744	1,584	1,673	2,054	1,850	2,001	2,070	2,280	2,359

See footnotes at end of table.

Region and country of citizenship	2004	2005	2006	2007	2008	2009	2010[1]	2011	2012	2013
Malaysia	68,712	73,537	78,050	82,457	85,631	66,410	80,549	91,502	97,410	102,605
Maldives	208	291	349	381	403	343	368	410	368	420
Mali	2,609	2,646	3,567	4,055	4,549	4,464	4,405	4,121	3,370	3,806
Malta	6,756	6,391	5,367	6,055	5,556	5,258	5,835	6,053	6,301	6,379
Marshall Islands	7,914	7,403	5,679	244	207	238	179	174	148	176
Mauritania	1,194	1,339	1,211	1,123	1,125	955	1,130	988	1,086	1,303
Mauritius	1,510	2,054	2,376	2,962	3,491	3,411	4,455	4,746	5,632	5,892
Mexico	4,454,061	4,774,169	6,146,126	7,405,191	7,273,511	6,601,059	12,917,745	17,052,559	16,462,118	17,980,784
Micronesia, Federated States of	23,922	24,470	18,458	275	201	196	189	181	258	209
Moldova	3,313	4,233	5,764	10,382	11,402	8,369	10,596	10,669	11,293	12,604
Monaco	721	748	857	898	1,225	1,303	1,274	1,099	1,270	1,194
Mongolia	5,801	5,956	7,004	6,832	6,739	7,901	9,885	10,648	10,399	11,819
Morocco[11]	18,623	18,721	18,296	18,856	21,029	21,991	24,686	25,999	27,765	30,618
Mozambique	980	1,048	1,074	1,011	1,260	1,288	1,343	1,497	1,764	2,278
Namibia	1,265	1,374	1,365	1,455	1,568	1,613	1,714	2,002	2,249	2,165
Nauru	59	64	83	57	100	76	102	128	120	85
Nepal	10,327	11,690	14,440	15,986	20,924	18,003	18,537	18,937	18,475	19,419
Netherlands[12]	624,587	642,261	646,025	709,357	836,900	760,738	764,482	784,441	785,029	781,198
New Zealand[13]	226,166	231,438	238,215	234,932	241,458	215,037	233,987	246,787	266,494	295,210
Nicaragua	52,152	50,371	51,032	53,641	57,497	53,426	52,925	53,023	56,380	59,296
Niger	3,955	4,487	2,781	1,426	1,243	1,380	1,244	1,209	1,312	1,583
Nigeria	61,550	64,697	61,107	69,985	88,732	88,473	97,402	104,483	121,177	157,509
Norway	162,018	163,298	173,365	199,296	244,827	228,229	251,321	282,734	300,258	320,842
Oman	1,996	2,500	2,281	2,495	2,806	2,978	3,257	3,457	5,729	7,794
Pakistan	58,572	55,976	53,462	55,739	57,922	56,672	63,182	61,957	69,222	78,246
Palau	13,689	14,140	9,271	234	202	210	311	205	282	136
Panama	95,497	93,344	95,314	104,641	111,354	112,596	124,113	125,162	132,615	143,365
Papua New Guinea	588	681	732	599	878	862	1,091	1,100	1,020	1,301
Paraguay	13,983	14,161	12,517	14,568	15,833	15,290	17,501	19,356	20,825	27,498
Peru	219,765	216,147	199,288	211,340	227,158	221,301	223,750	223,732	231,103	261,827
Philippines	266,843	271,541	284,065	316,241	334,894	311,907	326,216	319,609	327,757	358,961
Poland	170,533	182,712	182,419	183,491	186,888	157,116	152,951	154,423	149,046	168,854
Portugal	98,887	103,473	108,123	124,574	143,053	128,463	148,962	161,699	164,200	174,757
Qatar	1,845	2,351	2,789	3,272	4,900	5,451	7,592	9,966	12,210	15,894
Romania	55,483	65,123	70,463	74,213	76,799	64,118	69,401	74,763	76,255	82,238
Russia	121,776	139,519	152,463	176,983	206,629	197,173	229,725	269,566	299,911	364,116
Rwanda	1,461	1,639	1,959	2,391	2,840	2,772	3,132	3,489	4,168	4,074
Saint Kitts and Nevis . .	14,313	16,497	16,057	15,720	15,761	13,243	13,450	12,584	11,734	11,559
Saint Lucia	17,206	17,566	18,797	19,891	19,458	17,573	20,100	18,237	16,767	15,959
Saint Vincent and the Grenadines	13,521	13,952	14,276	14,640	14,545	14,076	14,271	13,469	12,745	12,204
Samoa	1,599	1,773	2,061	2,418	2,305	2,251	2,425	1,965	1,812	2,021
San Marino	408	538	583	557	774	677	797	924	765	745
Sao Tome and Principe .	67	80	56	63	D	78	63	66	45	77
Saudi Arabia	16,092	20,232	31,733	38,087	46,853	61,530	91,934	138,055	193,462	232,782
Senegal	9,350	8,235	7,360	7,696	9,437	9,582	10,005	10,137	9,824	10,518
Serbia and Montenegro	8,088	6,835	5,884	4,785	3,737	1,787	1,151	663	173	3,376
Seychelles	282	289	285	290	363	277	340	333	365	429
Sierra Leone	2,594	2,257	2,362	2,630	2,892	2,711	2,900	3,052	3,059	3,188
Singapore	98,849	105,463	112,581	120,930	132,889	103,762	126,095	149,258	161,576	162,922
Slovakia	24,365	25,220	27,403	28,049	28,702	36,341	39,776	45,930	46,597	49,173
Slovenia	13,769	15,365	15,443	18,922	24,812	24,437	23,539	24,108	24,803	22,977
Solomon Islands	684	382	319	304	333	292	378	440	344	411
Somalia	383	328	223	271	248	243	279	182	252	215
South Africa	111,563	120,522	119,165	124,564	123,725	107,238	111,173	120,383	127,973	135,400
Spain	542,733	507,547	543,757	655,788	830,812	763,335	823,199	891,635	882,313	934,322
Sri Lanka	13,618	14,668	16,331	18,846	19,156	16,865	18,431	20,411	21,072	23,015

See footnotes at end of table.

Table 26.
NONIMMIGRANT ADMISSIONS (I-94 ONLY) BY REGION AND COUNTRY OF CITIZENSHIP: FISCAL YEARS 2004 TO 2013 – *Continued*

Region and country of citizenship	2004	2005	2006	2007	2008	2009	2010[1]	2011	2012	2013
Sudan	1,562	1,534	1,877	2,250	2,319	2,584	2,840	3,585	3,663	3,196
Suriname	6,252	6,025	5,538	6,166	6,926	7,851	8,535	9,057	10,642	12,618
Swaziland	337	462	452	406	556	649	678	593	664	863
Sweden	307,827	345,712	347,803	392,293	470,303	414,126	426,253	509,356	520,762	551,820
Switzerland	276,435	271,021	284,197	303,408	339,106	340,943	377,973	456,226	484,359	472,914
Syria	6,357	6,379	6,582	7,116	7,441	7,575	8,904	9,484	10,934	15,004
Taiwan	322,641	340,759	331,490	342,971	332,764	272,105	327,297	336,533	313,837	444,046
Tajikistan	636	762	896	1,442	2,372	1,948	2,037	2,160	1,975	1,709
Tanzania	4,762	5,051	5,231	6,247	6,736	6,855	7,277	7,168	7,731	7,635
Thailand	82,205	84,699	89,431	100,105	101,622	87,664	95,687	96,924	98,172	109,761
Togo	2,201	1,779	1,563	1,689	1,855	1,765	1,800	1,964	2,003	2,186
Tonga	3,405	3,642	3,498	3,683	3,110	2,572	2,373	2,336	2,016	2,202
Trinidad and Tobago . . .	149,476	151,940	159,358	171,180	177,916	173,660	166,423	159,618	169,251	164,705
Tunisia	4,906	5,448	5,363	5,725	6,241	6,334	7,713	8,187	9,556	11,287
Turkey	106,341	116,470	121,157	132,942	147,837	134,839	148,096	167,767	175,933	192,113
Turkmenistan	488	600	659	750	706	893	1,077	1,059	1,171	1,345
Tuvalu	244	222	247	283	257	208	193	240	198	151
Uganda	5,588	5,493	6,073	6,976	8,300	7,765	7,773	7,919	8,926	9,398
Ukraine	35,640	41,802	51,996	63,331	75,308	66,069	71,400	76,886	82,565	87,913
United Arab Emirates . .	5,645	6,929	7,592	8,749	11,165	13,258	16,889	20,452	23,110	28,897
United Kingdom[14]	5,051,387	5,087,129	4,949,151	5,132,789	5,480,917	4,713,284	4,539,392	4,547,728	4,486,666	4,566,669
Uruguay	40,666	40,228	40,466	43,423	44,087	43,515	49,013	54,053	59,590	70,535
Uzbekistan	6,038	6,535	6,480	5,361	5,203	5,723	7,123	6,740	7,694	9,930
Vanuatu	186	154	139	179	213	201	150	191	198	203
Venezuela	363,963	396,845	393,587	470,538	531,685	524,246	527,902	597,555	700,840	815,797
Vietnam	22,245	26,815	31,458	42,169	55,251	47,468	54,299	57,839	63,383	73,913
Yemen	1,370	1,646	2,112	1,828	1,616	1,853	2,223	2,256	3,179	3,904
Zambia	3,646	3,788	3,786	3,649	3,449	2,944	3,847	3,865	4,585	4,887
Zimbabwe	8,026	7,832	7,599	7,831	7,968	7,238	7,382	8,352	8,906	8,738
Unknown	251,378	180,054	146,610	153,727	181,007	294,588	561,254	484,151	275,090	164,788

D Data withheld to limit disclosure.

- Represents zero.

[1] Beginning in 2010 the number of I-94 nonimmigrant admissions greatly exceeds totals reported in previous years due to a more complete count of land admissions.

[2] Australia includes Australia, Norfolk Island, Christmas Island, and Cocos (Keeling) Island.

[3] The number of I-94 nonimmigrant admissions in 2013 greatly exceeds totals reported in previous years due to a more complete count of Canadian air and sea admissions.

[4] China includes the People's Republic of China, Hong Kong, and Macau.

[5] Congo (Brazzaville) refers to the Republic of the Congo.

[6] Congo (Kinshasa) refers to the Democratic Republic of the Congo.

[7] Denmark includes Denmark, Faroe Islands, and Greenland.

[8] France includes France, French Guiana, French Polynesia, French Southern and Antarctic Lands, Guadeloupe, Martinique, New Caledonia, Reunion, Saint Pierre and Miquelon, and Wallis and Futuna.

[9] North Korea refers to the Democratic People's Republic of Korea.

[10] South Korea refers to the Republic of Korea.

[11] Morocco includes Morocco and Western Sahara.

[12] Netherlands includes the Netherlands, Aruba, and the Netherlands Antilles.

[13] New Zealand includes New Zealand, Cook Islands, Tokelau, and Niue.

[14] United Kingdom includes the United Kingdom, Anguilla, Bermuda, British Virgin Islands, Cayman Islands, Falkland Islands, Gibraltar, Guernsey, Isle of Man, Jersey, Montserrat, Pitcairn Island, Saint Helena, and Turks and Caicos Islands.

Notes: Admissions represent counts of events, i.e., arrivals, not unique individuals; multiple entries of an individual on the same day are counted as one admission.
The majority of short-term admissions from Canada and Mexico are excluded.

Source: U.S. Department of Homeland Security.

Table 27.
NONIMMIGRANT ADMISSIONS (I-94 ONLY) BY REGION AND COUNTRY OF RESIDENCE: FISCAL YEARS 2004 TO 2013

Region and country of residence	2004	2005	2006	2007	2008	2009	2010[1]	2011	2012	2013
REGION										
Total	30,781,330	32,003,435	33,667,328	37,149,651	39,381,928	36,231,554	46,471,569	53,082,286	53,887,286	61,052,260
Africa	324,374	333,454	333,474	361,357	410,020	391,415	419,545	435,460	493,648	574,756
Asia	7,282,206	7,609,943	7,766,144	8,117,887	8,164,330	7,228,615	8,759,488	9,351,790	10,317,367	11,601,237
Europe	11,461,349	11,840,254	11,617,585	12,694,971	14,520,845	13,242,341	13,587,632	14,638,186	14,765,445	15,191,408
North America	8,171,106	8,466,488	10,030,590	11,592,193	11,517,852	10,619,982	17,843,932	22,218,603	21,585,748	25,886,751
Oceania.	872,054	934,173	975,487	999,083	1,050,825	1,003,953	1,250,507	1,484,496	1,584,781	1,755,197
South America	2,037,651	2,207,087	2,301,755	2,644,877	2,972,682	3,050,774	3,617,278	4,127,874	4,636,363	5,585,093
Unknown	632,590	612,036	642,293	739,283	745,374	694,474	993,187	825,877	503,934	457,818
COUNTRY[2]										
Total.	30,781,330	32,003,435	33,667,328	37,149,651	39,381,928	36,231,554	46,471,569	53,082,286	53,887,286	61,052,260
Afghanistan	745	1,090	1,415	2,011	1,845	2,167	2,266	3,120	2,570	2,770
Albania	4,544	6,619	5,975	5,500	7,110	6,186	6,500	5,854	5,699	6,328
Algeria.	2,498	2,980	3,295	3,837	4,710	5,123	4,813	5,637	6,392	7,569
American Samoa	1,505	1,618	1,650	1,410	1,384	1,402	1,485	1,226	1,093	818
Andorra	1,316	1,351	1,390	1,524	2,045	1,724	1,810	1,601	1,508	1,554
Angola.	4,027	4,445	5,144	6,136	6,577	7,351	7,592	8,208	10,747	12,810
Anguilla	5,270	5,700	6,919	8,139	8,851	6,192	4,764	3,075	2,709	1,839
Antigua and Barbuda . .	23,499	24,785	26,027	25,351	24,953	20,420	20,197	18,437	18,268	16,502
Argentina.	217,306	235,475	254,371	318,743	374,359	396,635	496,355	580,415	659,320	777,054
Armenia.	4,886	4,905	4,850	4,108	5,013	4,624	4,472	4,091	5,096	6,517
Aruba	22,212	23,792	25,213	26,222	28,146	24,991	22,366	16,542	19,611	18,256
Australia	596,906	653,076	694,222	748,489	795,931	770,481	996,293	1,219,635	1,301,382	1,437,767
Austria	135,062	135,780	137,134	148,588	179,014	181,219	192,187	205,473	217,798	223,610
Azerbaijan	2,509	2,467	3,016	3,647	4,411	4,786	5,296	5,141	5,908	6,545
Bahamas.	332,428	294,744	366,271	387,210	353,205	305,115	303,101	275,604	269,335	260,573
Bahrain	4,682	5,899	6,218	7,281	8,351	7,480	8,780	8,469	9,115	9,343
Bangladesh	10,731	11,364	10,441	9,485	10,369	11,780	14,045	15,238	18,024	25,200
Barbados.	58,832	63,380	65,211	66,572	70,150	62,348	67,828	64,063	61,981	61,495
Belarus	8,747	8,165	8,856	9,018	9,189	8,806	10,759	10,280	11,474	11,877
Belgium.	213,604	224,056	221,164	250,012	309,247	284,285	296,493	311,024	313,615	318,855
Belize	27,692	26,400	27,888	28,739	27,967	27,348	26,770	24,532	24,268	25,536
Benin	1,095	1,336	1,642	1,666	2,209	1,932	2,116	2,225	2,310	2,148
Bermuda	23,837	24,146	28,075	41,254	46,325	44,152	37,508	26,560	26,855	52,935
Bhutan	368	391	345	463	728	447	518	482	493	568
Bolivia.	31,755	28,974	29,061	36,752	38,919	38,447	42,719	40,874	41,460	48,676
Bosnia and										
Herzegovina	5,494	5,668	5,829	5,916	5,743	5,034	5,003	6,266	5,726	6,221
Botswana	2,771	2,912	2,558	2,846	3,216	2,849	2,871	2,832	2,795	2,483
Brazil.	512,992	602,819	663,587	749,025	877,517	956,443	1,263,944	1,578,535	1,833,397	2,203,777
Brunei.	911	982	1,055	1,375	1,586	1,404	1,443	1,718	2,089	2,261
Bulgaria.	29,117	31,795	34,693	36,934	36,344	31,007	30,663	33,933	33,752	34,762
Burkina Faso	1,502	1,758	2,081	2,171	2,151	2,256	2,328	2,298	2,829	3,345
Burma.	1,436	1,178	1,376	1,556	1,608	2,089	2,542	2,631	2,978	4,274
Burundi	426	687	977	866	788	676	852	995	1,077	1,604
Cambodia	4,778	4,696	4,038	3,890	4,040	3,708	3,742	3,470	3,565	4,808
Cameroon	5,507	5,318	5,783	5,977	6,459	5,935	6,645	6,249	6,278	6,799
Canada[3]	584,554	527,264	565,825	634,436	684,480	689,600	1,666,498	2,121,739	1,837,473	4,697,606
Cape Verde	1,418	1,559	1,590	2,226	2,365	2,796	2,782	2,255	1,796	3,527
Cayman Islands	57,565	66,414	60,831	70,342	70,826	69,384	66,974	60,245	57,741	56,007
Central African										
Republic.	73	379	532	420	335	245	377	418	334	340
Chad.	352	456	487	598	466	561	468	404	351	514
Chile.	137,227	134,524	142,210	160,434	173,832	157,291	182,609	208,855	214,913	256,171
China	225,978	285,928	346,824	432,507	540,617	568,703	838,165	1,136,479	1,495,782	1,858,989
Christmas Island	16	7	D	5	D	D	D	10	7	17
Cocos (Keeling) Island .	5	11	7	10	24	10	6	10	9	19
Colombia.	347,509	368,464	399,385	448,429	484,296	473,213	557,943	574,544	624,480	794,972
Comoros	71	92	77	50	82	77	48	76	75	125

See footnotes at end of table.

Region and country of residence	2004	2005	2006	2007	2008	2009	2010[1]	2011	2012	2013
Congo (Brazzaville)[4]	1,796	2,087	2,024	1,773	2,248	2,284	2,583	3,063	3,404	2,428
Congo (Kinshasa)[5]	107	177	432	851	1,142	1,283	1,591	1,261	1,513	3,709
Cook Islands	617	523	409	537	523	418	221	78	70	76
Costa Rica	168,281	171,157	168,477	188,135	207,211	187,689	203,062	202,164	204,976	215,633
Cote d'Ivoire	1,985	1,668	2,432	2,095	2,886	3,193	3,065	1,783	2,355	4,780
Croatia	18,678	18,832	19,477	21,310	23,035	22,220	21,739	22,177	21,392	22,225
Cuba	13,039	14,139	10,964	11,137	15,200	17,113	26,773	21,163	24,957	41,406
Cyprus	10,862	10,976	10,327	11,094	12,725	11,379	11,506	10,821	10,197	8,672
Czech Republic	41,299	43,257	44,255	49,474	56,679	73,490	72,028	86,714	91,273	95,636
Denmark	166,511	191,121	205,880	237,139	284,832	275,140	290,173	307,458	310,295	308,960
Djibouti	224	187	211	210	282	420	463	497	447	339
Dominica	10,426	7,683	7,572	6,742	7,797	8,101	9,425	7,730	7,476	8,241
Dominican Republic	202,766	253,343	266,787	301,790	276,677	252,070	281,719	269,641	274,396	276,142
East Timor	-	43	17	5	D	-	3	6	8	14
Ecuador	151,937	161,010	162,829	179,944	175,195	180,542	211,325	230,599	230,402	270,299
Egypt	27,126	29,644	32,879	37,072	41,169	43,065	48,687	51,149	69,834	75,169
El Salvador	203,823	188,672	175,672	178,822	163,772	140,383	132,873	119,300	111,019	117,335
Equatorial Guinea	140	184	245	280	384	579	502	549	570	1,056
Eritrea	1,220	1,051	873	516	318	312	322	309	290	873
Estonia	7,996	9,721	9,590	12,181	12,444	19,372	12,978	14,714	17,587	19,350
Ethiopia	6,356	5,927	7,242	8,971	10,450	10,080	10,349	11,175	12,983	14,724
Falkland Islands	83	85	121	80	143	156	70	67	101	111
Fiji	7,105	7,481	7,983	7,963	8,342	7,038	8,914	10,747	10,799	11,848
Finland	88,369	99,786	98,990	103,765	124,750	129,870	125,796	137,856	145,272	152,127
France	1,072,387	1,125,352	1,002,087	1,196,097	1,463,998	1,443,230	1,507,886	1,724,854	1,787,211	1,832,703
French Guiana	180	280	278	359	371	537	641	731	1,270	1,132
French Polynesia	12,316	13,758	14,707	16,739	17,169	18,848	13,469	7,024	6,470	7,005
Gabon	1,469	1,812	1,631	1,780	2,118	2,098	2,168	2,554	2,520	2,697
Gambia	2,558	2,352	1,552	1,598	1,594	2,042	2,620	2,760	2,133	2,261
Georgia	4,787	3,941	4,505	4,522	4,736	4,660	5,408	5,617	5,838	6,475
Germany	1,518,492	1,590,648	1,568,461	1,687,963	1,950,233	1,866,557	1,940,164	2,078,934	2,203,996	2,256,662
Ghana	23,451	17,509	15,157	15,790	22,180	19,546	20,996	21,907	23,584	24,442
Gibraltar	1,342	1,732	1,652	1,786	2,033	1,979	1,683	1,099	1,236	1,429
Greece	53,086	58,821	58,282	63,145	74,199	67,984	70,885	74,418	68,362	70,176
Greenland	307	391	565	768	585	553	393	159	187	207
Grenada	9,821	9,667	9,337	9,785	10,166	9,660	10,208	9,446	9,176	9,623
Guadeloupe	8,021	9,247	7,716	9,007	10,596	10,677	11,210	8,968	7,564	7,461
Guam	11,557	11,081	9,844	5,061	4,991	5,654	5,736	5,147	4,664	3,972
Guatemala	197,095	200,723	205,563	220,041	230,837	212,475	223,093	216,637	219,795	226,114
Guinea	4,357	3,672	3,124	3,106	3,056	2,400	1,913	2,015	2,057	2,092
Guinea-Bissau	31	39	30	38	35	53	51	75	38	130
Guyana	18,255	19,636	17,207	17,134	16,466	17,873	19,958	20,759	26,568	33,407
Haiti	70,187	76,092	62,650	89,990	103,784	92,335	96,071	90,611	90,807	99,385
Holy See	60	59	40	55	62	70	71	105	122	163
Honduras	109,156	112,179	110,599	128,407	140,122	139,364	134,485	141,548	149,665	155,310
Hong Kong	140,685	146,132	149,580	154,211	156,364	123,392	146,652	142,487	142,934	139,517
Hungary	41,078	44,153	44,522	47,762	49,874	55,392	60,474	67,628	69,214	73,351
Iceland	28,791	38,578	45,861	48,571	53,319	32,207	38,883	55,687	53,819	53,174
India	442,328	496,376	571,608	791,842	863,222	742,180	886,979	958,271	1,013,899	1,248,218
Indonesia	62,517	68,218	71,345	75,497	76,828	70,841	79,174	90,499	99,311	113,197
Iran	5,125	6,442	7,111	7,377	7,423	10,394	12,862	15,198	16,658	19,391
Iraq	1,410	2,146	2,022	1,720	2,181	2,639	4,158	5,430	9,232	14,256
Ireland	369,802	411,657	435,154	519,960	600,872	499,026	431,345	419,817	396,596	434,252
Israel	316,886	320,020	320,050	357,106	373,942	353,145	352,363	340,733	351,586	371,861
Italy	623,770	659,849	617,945	725,447	884,439	839,317	944,224	1,060,659	1,031,326	1,022,589
Jamaica	210,945	209,813	255,243	276,989	265,136	239,096	230,147	206,825	209,930	221,675
Japan	4,208,240	4,280,788	4,179,874	3,988,552	3,760,606	3,231,509	3,676,433	3,645,898	4,011,372	4,195,305
Jordan	16,292	18,325	18,857	21,117	21,707	21,893	22,958	23,432	25,615	30,099
Kazakhstan	5,763	7,297	9,695	12,901	15,660	13,020	15,952	19,064	20,136	21,241
Kenya	17,716	17,047	17,101	19,102	20,444	18,848	18,749	17,340	17,938	20,159

See footnotes at end of table.

Table 27.
NONIMMIGRANT ADMISSIONS (I-94 ONLY) BY REGION AND COUNTRY OF RESIDENCE: FISCAL YEARS 2004 TO 2013 – Continued

Region and country of residence	2004	2005	2006	2007	2008	2009	2010[1]	2011	2012	2013
Kiribati	1,524	1,198	1,071	947	1,025	1,372	1,243	1,311	1,038	876
Korea, North[6]	17	18	38	33	20	28	94	190	177	331
Korea, South[7]	714,803	767,671	827,685	898,194	877,374	778,910	1,196,416	1,335,464	1,397,408	1,560,177
Kuwait	16,523	19,713	21,607	26,195	28,918	31,418	35,230	40,701	46,848	52,637
Kyrgyzstan	1,376	1,320	1,569	2,149	2,574	2,443	2,884	3,576	3,347	4,219
Laos	1,716	2,141	2,503	2,711	2,418	1,773	1,498	1,152	1,367	2,619
Latvia	9,652	11,291	11,168	13,104	13,456	14,308	14,443	16,258	18,358	20,032
Lebanon	17,061	17,357	17,975	20,869	20,879	19,822	22,411	23,524	26,223	33,558
Lesotho	360	409	374	397	401	390	473	508	524	498
Liberia	1,290	1,132	1,095	2,107	1,840	1,533	2,024	2,577	3,278	3,868
Libya	405	659	817	1,540	4,152	3,643	4,853	2,247	2,459	3,653
Liechtenstein	1,654	1,403	1,676	1,765	1,920	2,024	2,152	2,547	2,469	2,483
Lithuania	11,958	11,505	11,101	12,582	13,650	16,750	13,369	6,955	6,260	23,297
Luxembourg	12,637	13,919	13,952	15,825	20,357	19,993	20,734	19,389	20,193	20,810
Macau	2,609	3,176	3,169	3,368	3,974	3,380	3,877	3,870	3,899	3,524
Macedonia	4,571	4,314	4,978	6,428	6,800	6,603	7,393	8,331	8,422	8,285
Madagascar	897	992	936	1,061	1,276	1,110	1,019	914	972	1,096
Malawi	1,400	1,601	1,468	1,569	1,846	1,688	1,894	1,826	2,021	1,974
Malaysia	52,371	56,474	60,123	62,697	64,938	50,510	61,463	69,651	74,413	84,886
Maldives	194	278	332	366	398	326	329	370	356	383
Mali	2,038	2,002	2,847	3,227	3,643	3,634	3,649	3,449	2,624	3,173
Malta	6,591	6,381	5,287	5,917	5,585	5,434	5,948	5,880	6,072	6,228
Marshall Islands	6,077	5,383	4,665	790	930	944	777	694	654	476
Martinique	6,416	6,175	5,613	7,526	9,284	8,497	9,695	9,624	8,137	5,930
Mauritania	884	868	762	642	792	754	956	772	841	1,126
Mauritius	1,089	1,531	1,756	2,074	2,532	2,580	3,433	3,846	4,752	5,016
Mexico	4,429,284	4,766,919	6,121,709	7,332,929	7,215,118	6,585,742	12,605,032	16,716,265	16,395,988	17,882,766
Micronesia, Federated States of	14,710	15,179	12,065	1,437	1,532	1,481	1,724	1,722	1,781	1,800
Moldova	2,721	3,550	4,984	9,503	10,510	7,520	9,628	9,567	10,130	11,261
Monaco	5,059	5,345	5,682	6,126	7,185	7,057	6,301	4,441	4,701	4,483
Mongolia	5,221	5,290	6,049	5,870	5,776	6,843	8,734	9,629	9,241	10,962
Montserrat	1,012	888	965	907	978	724	560	255	228	292
Morocco	15,600	15,697	15,369	15,975	18,427	19,288	21,498	22,318	23,815	25,940
Mozambique	1,148	1,210	1,222	1,116	1,452	1,505	1,567	1,682	2,021	2,824
Namibia	1,438	1,464	1,444	1,573	1,766	1,719	1,899	2,354	2,589	2,448
Nauru	50	50	70	41	81	60	100	192	158	174
Nepal	8,612	9,843	12,409	13,646	18,082	15,112	15,335	15,500	14,863	15,563
Netherlands	508,958	523,929	519,849	576,474	694,062	629,394	646,501	710,691	707,525	709,959
Netherlands Antilles	47,629	44,791	48,999	48,364	51,964	47,342	42,717	15,690	11,068	6,995
New Caledonia	1,643	1,763	1,672	1,614	2,031	2,067	1,254	541	577	797
New Zealand	197,426	202,453	211,267	204,320	207,537	185,885	208,729	227,965	247,739	280,309
Nicaragua	53,787	51,471	52,317	54,847	59,044	54,968	54,570	52,655	55,135	58,197
Niger	3,367	4,014	2,803	1,413	1,130	1,365	1,218	1,227	1,345	1,508
Nigeria	50,577	52,546	48,567	55,693	73,197	73,609	83,695	89,778	105,488	141,857
Niue	13	21	11	17	14	11	12	20	12	14
Northern Mariana Islands	28	16	11	152	166	332	104	56	36	76
Norway	151,788	153,800	162,861	188,472	234,819	219,670	244,707	278,019	296,102	319,158
Oman	4,146	4,363	4,253	4,769	5,599	5,786	5,933	6,342	8,900	10,057
Pakistan	41,876	40,480	39,190	41,334	43,538	42,488	47,749	46,694	52,528	60,805
Palau	14,881	14,508	9,978	3,100	2,938	2,683	5,063	3,118	3,703	3,447
Panama	109,047	104,940	107,812	120,276	130,199	133,978	152,097	150,959	159,249	170,543
Papua New Guinea	862	901	904	788	974	985	1,105	1,071	1,015	1,317
Paraguay	14,891	14,932	12,902	15,114	16,855	16,492	19,542	20,819	22,046	29,326
Peru	196,072	192,201	173,953	186,752	206,606	206,431	211,619	208,949	216,406	254,183
Philippines	227,691	234,547	247,055	275,675	292,964	270,467	292,817	281,097	277,183	312,706
Pitcairn Islands	3	7	D	5	D	D	D	9	14	62
Poland	161,885	172,801	171,179	170,132	170,534	142,831	138,410	137,774	132,328	151,148

See footnotes at end of table.

Region and country of residence	2004	2005	2006	2007	2008	2009	2010[1]	2011	2012	2013
Portugal.	75,660	78,150	78,373	89,246	100,269	85,138	105,319	117,841	113,823	117,951
Puerto Rico	4,693	4,560	4,655	4,490	4,131	3,646	4,219	3,677	3,588	2,306
Qatar.	3,829	4,932	6,411	8,052	11,794	13,455	17,259	21,025	25,536	29,609
Reunion.	231	310	226	234	562	636	518	580	747	707
Romania	47,052	56,895	61,886	65,085	67,100	55,135	59,413	63,760	65,211	71,721
Russia.	109,863	127,987	140,338	164,228	193,745	185,386	208,627	249,412	276,956	346,800
Rwanda	1,235	1,380	1,660	1,923	2,286	2,309	2,551	2,806	3,430	3,488
Saint Helena	23	26	18	34	34	17	25	34	23	43
Saint Kitts and Nevis . .	12,545	14,726	14,367	13,914	14,041	11,994	12,456	11,417	10,706	11,045
Saint Lucia	16,155	16,479	17,446	18,153	18,011	15,932	18,741	16,399	14,880	14,662
Saint Pierre and Miquelon	26	49	38	61	43	84	122	75	88	122
Saint Vincent and the Grenadines	9,330	9,601	9,781	9,863	9,560	9,280	9,706	9,078	8,594	9,322
Samoa	1,394	1,473	1,558	1,982	1,937	1,686	1,730	1,376	1,258	1,610
San Marino	450	546	591	548	796	783	777	859	730	737
Sao Tome and Principe	77	79	77	72	68	70	129	269	215	79
Saudi Arabia	22,235	26,217	35,717	42,160	52,305	65,967	94,186	135,746	187,900	233,013
Senegal.	7,337	6,227	5,559	6,062	7,870	7,975	8,424	8,535	8,139	9,099
Serbia and Montenegro	4,392	3,842	3,202	2,339	1,972	965	869	579	177	4,157
Seychelles.	219	237	221	251	294	272	327	299	298	363
Sierra Leone	1,277	1,070	1,232	1,615	1,858	1,818	2,085	2,378	2,339	2,654
Singapore	118,345	126,714	135,328	146,288	160,356	123,309	152,902	175,908	187,781	182,455
Slovakia . . .	21,833	22,687	24,403	24,611	24,780	31,502	34,847	41,314	41,835	44,361
Slovenia	12,819	14,173	14,096	17,210	22,782	22,213	21,515	22,400	22,783	21,112
Solomon Islands	236	221	217	313	349	280	357	353	310	478
Somalia.	44	89	58	75	84	90	87	70	58	143
South Africa.	99,035	108,742	109,124	113,924	115,270	99,093	98,766	103,268	110,954	123,999
Spain	481,026	447,603	479,682	579,586	742,056	675,521	741,839	818,717	783,553	810,218
Sri Lanka.	9,513	10,785	12,362	14,308	14,440	12,298	13,428	15,430	15,918	18,211
Sudan	851	853	1,338	1,680	1,848	2,125	2,421	3,127	2,833	2,449
Suriname.	7,196	6,815	6,191	7,095	8,029	9,465	9,948	9,846	11,626	13,582
Swaziland	365	521	499	440	736	672	928	1,330	1,560	1,936
Sweden.	282,555	319,711	319,774	361,760	437,561	385,321	401,159	490,769	502,561	535,982
Switzerland	306,946	300,497	312,378	338,847	386,291	392,854	436,788	523,083	559,952	552,344
Syria	4,690	4,704	4,673	5,183	5,441	5,652	6,440	6,469	6,218	8,998
Taiwan.	333,528	348,405	338,605	347,638	336,190	273,211	335,734	345,767	325,883	430,906
Tajikistan.	613	727	834	1,323	2,167	1,808	1,930	2,018	1,837	1,590
Tanzania	4,313	4,606	4,980	5,962	6,490	6,585	6,900	6,814	7,613	7,375
Thailand	80,807	83,686	88,718	99,366	101,031	86,764	94,538	94,591	95,794	106,637
Togo	1,866	1,390	1,175	1,284	1,428	1,327	1,387	1,575	1,610	1,769
Tonga	2,394	2,705	2,546	2,693	2,153	1,752	1,678	1,658	1,430	1,661
Trinidad and Tobago . . .	144,512	148,013	155,305	167,780	175,352	170,702	164,803	156,232	164,773	161,669
Tunisia	3,979	4,634	4,474	4,708	5,196	5,412	6,426	6,733	8,053	9,724
Turkey	90,867	100,129	103,673	114,875	128,982	116,898	128,746	146,738	154,516	176,349
Turkmenistan.	459	572	577	671	626	804	997	916	991	1,231
Turks and Caicos Islands	14,583	15,770	20,289	25,259	26,314	19,942	16,367	13,750	13,680	11,851
Tuvalu	193	184	186	218	202	163	164	264	179	136
Uganda	4,765	4,630	5,176	5,880	7,248	6,700	6,578	6,795	7,879	8,586
Ukraine	30,719	37,124	46,913	58,226	69,768	60,875	65,855	70,932	75,982	80,485
United Arab Emirates . .	24,512	28,644	34,055	42,485	51,838	55,921	62,185	68,711	78,464	89,751
United Kingdom	4,781,015	4,815,801	4,655,995	4,814,810	5,165,386	4,430,949	4,339,294	4,412,117	4,322,049	4,382,392
United States[8].	948,221	934,668	977,185	1,033,607	1,011,283	956,051	1,137,530	1,126,684	1,083,403	954,222
Uruguay.	39,546	39,281	39,001	42,209	43,740	44,590	51,030	55,452	61,745	77,369
Uzbekistan.	5,688	6,019	5,953	4,777	4,547	5,028	6,293	5,968	6,757	9,094
Vanuatu.	305	313	263	336	408	311	270	248	337	317
Venezuela	362,702	402,591	400,659	482,807	556,354	552,659	549,575	597,429	692,629	825,034

See footnotes at end of table.

Table 27.
NONIMMIGRANT ADMISSIONS (I-94 ONLY) BY REGION AND COUNTRY OF RESIDENCE: FISCAL YEARS 2004 TO 2013 – *Continued*

Region and country of residence	2004	2005	2006	2007	2008	2009	2010[1]	2011	2012	2013
Vietnam.	19,854	24,666	28,920	39,120	51,860	44,561	52,786	54,958	58,877	69,129
Virgin Islands, British . .	33,328	36,957	40,061	43,725	45,031	41,359	39,241	30,407	27,632	27,244
Virgin Islands, U.S.	782	750	643	614	713	675	611	447	410	304
Wallis and Futuna.	288	243	173	116	180	81	67	21	46	125
Western Sahara	-	6	17	9	4	3	8	82	114	98
Yemen.	1,131	1,468	1,792	1,498	1,338	1,393	1,577	1,490	1,736	2,316
Zambia	3,665	3,576	3,627	3,508	3,299	2,756	3,728	3,620	4,359	4,558
Zimbabwe	6,323	5,675	5,454	5,334	5,327	4,733	5,128	5,613	6,045	6,582
Unknown	632,590	612,036	642,293	739,283	745,374	694,474	993,187	825,877	503,934	457,818

D Data withheld to limit disclosure.

- Represents zero.

[1] Beginning in 2010 the number of I-94 nonimmigrant admissions greatly exceeds totals reported in previous years due to a more complete count of land admissions.

[2] Includes countries and territories/dependencies.

[3] The number of I-94 nonimmigrant admissions in 2013 greatly exceeds totals reported in previous years due to a more complete count of Canadian air and sea admissions.

[4] Congo (Brazzaville) refers to the Republic of the Congo.

[5] Congo (Kinshasa) refers to the Democratic Republic of the Congo.

[6] North Korea refers to the Democratic People's Republic of Korea.

[7] South Korea refers to the Republic of Korea.

[8] United States includes nonimmigrants who self-report that they reside in the United States.

Notes: Admissions represent counts of events, i.e., arrivals, not unique individuals; multiple entries of an individual on the same day are counted as one admission.
The majority of short-term admissions from Canada and Mexico are excluded.

Source: U.S. Department of Homeland Security.

Table 28.

NONIMMIGRANT ADMISSIONS (I-94 ONLY) BY SELECTED CATEGORY OF ADMISSION AND REGION AND COUNTRY OF CITIZENSHIP: FISCAL YEAR 2013

Region and country of citizenship	Total	Tourists and business travelers		Students and exchange visitors[3]	Temporary workers and families[4]	Diplomats and other represen- tatives[5]	All other classes	Unknown
		Visa waiver[1]	Other[2]					
REGION								
Total..........................	61,052,260	21,231,396	33,414,155	2,162,162	2,996,743	373,330	766,848	107,626
Africa	645,919	X	529,629	47,185	23,580	33,880	9,737	1,908
Asia	12,230,911	5,622,402	4,543,031	1,041,784	733,843	101,707	163,172	24,972
Europe	16,167,460	13,987,858	1,083,929	360,112	520,299	118,059	89,828	7,375
North America	24,561,055	X	21,908,526	551,520	1,542,691	60,267	460,399	37,652
Oceania	1,770,569	1,621,136	52,919	19,840	55,664	13,451	6,256	1,303
South America..................	5,511,558	X	5,173,679	129,303	111,647	41,560	31,289	24,080
Unknown	164,788	X	122,442	12,418	9,019	4,406	6,167	10,336
COUNTRY								
Total..........................	61,052,260	21,231,396	33,414,155	2,162,162	2,996,743	373,330	766,848	107,626
Afghanistan	2,837	X	1,256	624	55	711	161	30
Albania	7,889	X	6,286	880	213	392	90	28
Algeria.........................	9,558	X	7,824	550	251	838	48	47
Andorra........................	1,271	1,073	25	61	75	34	D	D
Angola.........................	12,617	X	9,352	1,851	683	639	44	48
Antigua and Barbuda	15,151	X	14,274	357	133	296	48	43
Argentina.......................	744,864	X	707,863	8,082	17,308	5,974	1,921	3,716
Armenia........................	7,431	X	5,701	575	374	594	149	38
Australia[6]	1,453,814	1,351,238	25,477	14,811	48,980	9,469	2,865	974
Austria.........................	237,429	218,779	4,602	5,419	6,309	1,894	361	65
Azerbaijan	7,162	X	5,045	1,119	391	574	23	10
Bahamas........................	244,650	X	233,504	6,587	773	1,178	878	1,730
Bahrain	7,341	X	5,838	1,045	74	358	D	D
Bangladesh	30,314	X	21,912	4,889	1,142	1,753	423	195
Barbados.......................	58,558	X	56,123	707	500	761	237	230
Belarus	14,211	X	11,437	950	995	260	541	28
Belgium........................	315,611	293,217	4,564	4,917	9,464	2,982	401	66
Belize	25,327	X	23,009	612	261	512	868	65
Benin	2,821	X	2,015	310	50	420	20	6
Bhutan	633	X	268	158	14	163	13	17
Bolivia.........................	50,838	X	45,219	2,073	1,307	1,291	712	236
Bosnia and Herzegovina	7,465	X	5,462	771	240	414	546	32
Botswana	2,381	X	1,666	282	80	255	93	5
Brazil..........................	2,143,154	X	2,035,737	48,803	33,059	9,319	7,719	8,517
Brunei.........................	2,022	1,257	114	134	40	442	D	D
Bulgaria........................	40,029	X	24,668	8,907	2,191	936	3,223	104
Burkina Faso	3,928	X	2,575	669	87	479	109	9
Burma.........................	4,967	X	2,674	1,125	183	361	585	39
Burundi	1,740	X	1,084	250	28	349	20	9
Cambodia	4,898	X	3,362	595	246	239	445	11
Cameroon	9,639	X	7,128	891	353	1,113	125	29
Canada[7]	4,445,881	X	3,003,317	257,285	863,826	13,237	305,428	2,788
Cape Verde	3,140	X	2,826	90	32	119	42	31
Central African Republic	189	X	107	16	11	41	9	5
Chad...........................	550	X	313	50	12	165	6	4
Chile...........................	245,792	X	223,875	8,271	6,676	3,967	1,862	1,141
China[8,9].......................	2,098,801	2,837	1,620,453	391,068	53,736	7,462	10,013	13,232
Colombia.......................	830,891	X	773,375	22,075	17,442	9,736	5,190	3,073
Comoros	158	X	65	10	4	76	D	D
Congo (Brazzaville)[10]...........	2,859	X	1,873	348	76	504	17	41
Congo (Kinshasa)[11]	3,861	X	2,835	420	67	499	26	14
Costa Rica......................	207,840	X	197,828	2,951	3,422	1,370	1,544	725
Cote d'Ivoire	5,219	X	3,885	709	95	442	72	16
Croatia	26,905	X	19,012	1,737	1,207	544	4,315	90
Cuba...........................	34,615	X	31,695	71	549	492	503	1,305
Cyprus.........................	8,699	X	7,293	882	302	166	32	24
Czech Republic	100,056	72,733	18,697	4,548	2,540	1,141	332	65

See footnotes at end of table.

Region and country of citizenship	Total	Tourists and business travelers		Students and exchange visitors[3]	Temporary workers and families[4]	Diplomats and other represen-tatives[5]	All other classes	Unknown
		Visa waiver[1]	Other[2]					
Denmark[12]	324,608	299,941	5,283	6,289	9,378	3,016	621	80
Djibouti	338	X	194	12	D	120	D	7
Dominica	6,783	X	5,933	226	169	111	326	18
Dominican Republic	280,563	X	262,387	5,236	6,992	1,581	3,189	1,178
East Timor	34	X	6	D	D	16	6	-
Ecuador	268,332	X	253,225	7,001	2,969	2,210	1,658	1,269
Egypt	89,578	X	76,304	5,910	3,024	3,691	435	214
El Salvador	119,572	X	111,902	2,209	1,913	1,332	1,597	619
Equatorial Guinea	1,197	X	730	278	22	161	-	6
Eritrea	1,528	X	1,272	141	10	51	39	15
Estonia	20,942	15,563	2,821	1,204	562	588	183	21
Ethiopia	16,884	X	13,403	1,397	573	995	451	65
Fiji	13,996	X	12,085	136	142	373	1,243	17
Finland	161,020	148,524	1,938	3,322	4,930	1,956	318	32
France[13]	1,959,424	1,804,035	25,269	41,337	72,407	11,574	4,265	537
Gabon	2,792	X	1,812	391	43	516	17	13
Gambia	2,551	X	1,906	198	16	377	43	11
Georgia	6,628	X	3,700	1,151	271	849	620	37
Germany	2,359,681	2,173,849	38,586	50,957	74,328	16,442	5,052	467
Ghana	27,822	X	22,431	2,750	915	1,185	483	58
Greece	81,400	47,207	21,539	5,364	3,331	1,285	2,568	106
Grenada	10,674	X	9,447	242	123	196	479	187
Guatemala	224,006	X	210,641	3,281	6,000	1,584	1,457	1,043
Guinea	2,777	X	2,143	159	89	323	44	19
Guinea-Bissau	126	X	75	4	D	37	D	5
Guyana	39,412	X	36,411	335	140	516	1,910	100
Haiti	108,382	X	102,717	1,254	750	940	2,155	566
Holy See	130	X	20	D	-	103	D	D
Honduras	157,751	X	143,783	3,591	2,785	1,234	5,482	876
Hungary	81,213	61,027	11,039	3,806	3,313	956	1,020	52
Iceland	55,202	49,795	2,334	1,235	1,275	289	261	13
India	1,491,712	X	970,416	106,476	369,377	8,900	33,463	3,080
Indonesia	123,583	X	85,851	11,228	2,431	3,769	20,088	216
Iran	26,144	X	18,450	6,458	434	268	406	128
Iraq	17,077	X	13,290	2,671	115	820	53	128
Ireland	487,428	442,533	7,511	17,110	17,869	1,550	759	96
Israel	381,206	X	342,947	11,539	17,734	7,318	727	941
Italy	1,205,816	1,108,013	25,176	22,885	36,587	8,080	4,769	306
Jamaica	233,430	X	200,943	7,032	14,787	1,259	8,700	709
Japan	4,298,081	4,035,039	16,775	62,162	163,922	14,877	4,603	703
Jordan	38,867	X	28,838	4,166	895	4,478	375	115
Kazakhstan	22,422	X	14,338	6,400	724	815	113	32
Kenya	22,105	X	15,788	2,561	1,198	2,123	369	66
Kiribati	654	X	165	19	D	115	336	D
Korea, North[14]	59	X	24	7	D	10	D	15
Korea, South[15]	1,656,795	1,212,739	241,999	135,839	56,120	6,124	2,911	1,063
Kuwait	48,784	X	34,182	13,374	270	881	13	64
Kyrgyzstan	4,584	X	2,865	1,164	161	328	48	18
Laos	2,556	X	1,912	127	45	168	289	15
Latvia	22,330	15,166	3,520	891	688	407	1,640	18
Lebanon	42,775	X	36,281	3,183	1,856	1,142	209	104
Lesotho	524	X	317	50	21	122	14	-
Liberia	4,152	X	3,273	241	40	485	97	16
Libya	4,016	X	1,538	1,826	79	536	28	9
Liechtenstein	2,234	2,021	55	74	D	56	D	-
Lithuania	27,854	20,647	3,661	1,923	633	530	443	17
Luxembourg	15,785	14,565	244	317	242	392	D	D
Macedonia	9,436	X	5,459	2,323	299	378	939	38

See footnotes at end of table.

Table 28.
NONIMMIGRANT ADMISSIONS (I-94 ONLY) BY SELECTED CATEGORY OF ADMISSION AND REGION AND COUNTRY OF CITIZENSHIP: FISCAL YEAR 2013 - *Continued*

Region and country of citizenship	Total	Tourists and business travelers		Students and exchange visitors[3]	Temporary workers and families[4]	Diplomats and other represen-tatives[5]	All other classes	Unknown
		Visa waiver[1]	Other[2]					
Madagascar	1,265	X	836	109	45	219	41	15
Malawi	2,359	X	1,476	270	50	502	54	7
Malaysia	102,605	187	86,426	8,203	5,287	1,702	632	168
Maldives	420	X	155	103	D	101	52	D
Mali	3,806	X	2,935	376	134	341	16	4
Malta	6,379	5,018	952	67	201	111	D	D
Marshall Islands	176	X	57	6	3	47	38	25
Mauritania	1,303	X	848	101	21	277	50	6
Mauritius	5,892	X	4,516	255	128	265	701	27
Mexico	17,980,784	X	16,925,645	250,540	633,610	29,970	116,835	24,184
Micronesia, Federated States of	209	X	86	D	-	68	D	45
Moldova	12,604	X	8,088	3,531	412	371	174	28
Monaco	1,194	1,008	57	55	D	51	D	-
Mongolia	11,819	X	8,390	2,534	249	525	98	23
Morocco[16]	30,618	X	25,090	2,619	822	1,716	244	127
Mozambique	2,278	X	1,533	173	62	438	65	7
Namibia	2,165	X	1,492	133	54	367	107	12
Nauru	85	17	19	D	D	40	-	5
Nepal	19,419	X	12,664	3,629	1,625	718	663	120
Netherlands[17]	781,198	730,997	10,862	9,632	21,013	6,020	2,327	347
New Zealand[18]	295,210	269,654	10,514	4,517	6,388	2,642	1,323	172
Nicaragua	59,296	X	52,050	943	1,239	707	4,050	307
Niger	1,583	X	957	169	44	394	7	12
Nigeria	157,509	X	141,161	8,551	3,700	2,902	936	259
Norway	320,842	292,812	6,385	9,724	7,669	3,339	830	83
Oman	7,794	X	3,680	3,125	178	797	3	11
Pakistan	78,246	X	63,319	7,030	4,648	2,622	456	171
Palau	136	X	63	-	-	17	3	53
Panama	143,365	X	133,968	4,189	1,275	1,519	1,954	460
Papua New Guinea	1,301	227	652	158	D	183	67	D
Paraguay	27,498	X	24,618	1,182	373	960	206	159
Peru	261,827	X	233,948	8,342	6,009	3,804	8,503	1,221
Philippines	358,961	X	255,504	6,980	14,042	4,474	75,417	2,544
Poland	168,854	X	145,075	7,888	6,540	2,341	6,493	517
Portugal	174,757	160,183	3,566	3,281	4,777	1,121	1,770	59
Qatar	15,894	X	11,116	3,239	65	1,440	12	22
Romania	82,238	X	63,051	6,317	3,680	1,169	7,773	248
Russia	364,116	X	314,477	21,119	12,501	5,862	9,181	976
Rwanda	4,074	X	2,243	988	97	598	137	11
Saint Kitts and Nevis	11,559	X	10,701	398	83	294	56	27
Saint Lucia	15,959	X	13,934	454	107	338	1,065	61
Saint Vincent and the Grenadines	12,204	X	10,078	177	85	142	1,695	27
Samoa	2,021	X	1,685	53	53	112	115	3
San Marino	745	704	4	3	4	30	-	-
Sao Tome and Principe	77	X	33	6	-	38	-	-
Saudi Arabia	232,782	X	110,305	112,363	1,440	8,375	93	206
Senegal	10,518	X	8,153	908	269	1,081	76	31
Serbia and Montenegro	3,376	X	2,222	616	106	124	300	8
Seychelles	429	X	304	10	D	92	17	D
Sierra Leone	3,188	X	2,542	149	48	339	99	11
Singapore	162,922	141,828	1,566	9,712	5,451	3,628	617	120
Slovakia	49,173	35,865	6,565	4,342	1,571	538	264	28
Slovenia	22,977	20,485	632	738	676	331	110	5
Solomon Islands	411	X	209	19	-	100	83	-
Somalia	215	X	98	53	-	28	9	27
South Africa	135,400	X	116,369	4,640	8,198	2,294	3,481	418
Spain	934,322	838,935	19,467	27,389	39,170	6,892	1,654	815
Sri Lanka	23,015	X	16,989	2,526	1,571	735	1,113	81

See footnotes at end of table.

Table 28.
NONIMMIGRANT ADMISSIONS (I-94 ONLY) BY SELECTED CATEGORY OF ADMISSION AND REGION AND COUNTRY OF CITIZENSHIP: FISCAL YEAR 2013 – *Continued*

Region and country of citizenship	Total	Tourists and business travelers		Students and exchange visitors[3]	Temporary workers and families[4]	Diplomats and other represen- tatives[5]	All other classes	Unknown
		Visa waiver[1]	Other[2]					
Sudan	3,196	X	2,353	285	52	464	25	17
Suriname	12,618	X	11,717	226	65	385	169	56
Swaziland	863	X	523	151	34	121	16	18
Sweden	551,820	512,299	6,071	13,118	14,839	4,512	872	109
Switzerland	472,914	437,567	13,421	9,713	8,857	2,779	477	100
Syria	15,004	X	13,351	1,172	234	92	118	37
Taiwan	444,046	228,515	160,294	39,044	14,969	76	891	257
Tajikistan	1,709	X	921	464	25	277	16	6
Tanzania	7,635	X	5,192	958	259	1,052	153	21
Thailand	109,761	X	80,682	20,271	2,647	2,508	3,373	280
Togo	2,186	X	1,626	155	58	293	43	11
Tonga	2,202	X	1,770	94	58	157	117	6
Trinidad and Tobago	164,705	X	154,647	3,178	3,309	1,214	1,853	504
Tunisia	11,287	X	8,580	1,300	352	789	227	39
Turkey	192,113	X	146,944	29,163	8,338	5,003	2,259	406
Turkmenistan	1,345	X	704	415	57	143	26	-
Tuvalu	151	X	41	D	D	56	48	-
Uganda	9,398	X	6,593	891	579	1,218	95	22
Ukraine	87,913	X	63,605	7,866	4,093	1,142	10,938	269
United Arab Emirates	28,897	X	20,486	5,985	128	2,215	29	54
United Kingdom[19]	4,566,669	4,163,297	170,221	47,481	145,066	25,127	13,961	1,516
Uruguay	70,535	X	65,378	1,188	1,382	1,743	445	399
Uzbekistan	9,930	X	8,048	939	338	475	110	20
Vanuatu	203	X	96	10	D	72	17	D
Venezuela	815,797	X	762,313	21,725	24,917	1,655	994	4,193
Vietnam	73,913	X	53,453	15,716	1,593	1,626	1,373	152
Yemen	3,904	X	2,244	1,007	36	589	16	12
Zambia	4,887	X	3,400	518	119	773	67	10
Zimbabwe	8,738	X	6,042	1,053	591	618	413	21
Unknown	164,788	X	122,442	12,418	9,019	4,406	6,167	10,336

X Not applicable.

D Data withheld to limit disclosure.

- Represents zero.

[1] Includes GB, GMB, GT, GMT, WB, and WT admissions.

[2] Includes B1, B2 and a limited number of Border Crossing Card (BCC) admissions.

[3] Includes principals, spouses, and children (F1, F2, J1, J2, M1, and M2 admissions).

[4] Includes principals, spouses, and children (CW1, CW2, E1 to E3, H1B, H1B1, H1C, H2A, H2B, H2R, H3, H4, I1, L1, L2, O1 to O3, P1 to P4, Q1, R1, R2, TD and TN admissions).

[5] Includes principals, spouses, and children (A1 to A3, G1 to G5, and N1 to N7 admissions).

[6] Australia includes Australia, Norfolk Island, Christmas Island, and Cocos (Keeling) Island.

[7] The number of I-94 nonimmigrant admissions in 2013 greatly exceeds totals reported in previous years due to a more complete count of Canadian air and sea admissions.

[8] China includes the People's Republic of China, Hong Kong, and Macau.

[9] Admissions in the Visa Waiver category include only residents of Hong Kong admitted under the Guam and Commonwealth of Northern Mariana Islands Visa Waiver Program.

[10] Congo (Brazzaville) refers to the Republic of the Congo.

[11] Congo (Kinshasa) refers to the Democratic Republic of the Congo.

[12] Denmark includes Denmark, Faroe Islands, and Greenland.

[13] France includes France, French Guiana, French Polynesia, French Southern and Antarctic Lands, Guadeloupe, Martinique, New Caledonia, Reunion, Saint Pierre and Miquelon, and Wallis and Futuna.

[14] North Korea refers to the Democratic People's Republic of Korea.

[15] South Korea refers to the Republic of Korea.

[16] Morocco includes Morocco and Western Sahara.

[17] Netherlands includes the Netherlands, Aruba, and the Netherlands Antilles.

[18] New Zealand includes New Zealand, Cook Islands, Tokelau, and Niue.

[19] United Kingdom includes the United Kingdom, Anguilla, Bermuda, British Virgin Islands, Cayman Islands, Falkland Islands, Gibraltar, Guernsey, Isle of Man, Jersey, Montserrat, Pitcairn Island, Saint Helena, and Turks and Caicos Islands.

Notes: Admissions represent counts of events, i.e., arrivals, not unique individuals; multiple entries of an individual on the same day are counted as one admission. The majority of short-term admissions from Canada and Mexico are excluded.

Source: U.S. Department of Homeland Security.

Table 29.
NONIMMIGRANT ADMISSIONS (I-94 ONLY) BY SELECTED CATEGORY OF ADMISSION, AGE, AND SEX: FISCAL YEAR 2013

Characteristic	Total	Tourists and business travelers		Students and exchange visitors[3]	Temporary workers and families[4]	Diplomats and other represen-tatives[5]	All other classes	Unknown
		Visa waiver[1]	Other[2]					
AGE								
Total..................................	61,052,260	21,231,396	33,414,155	2,162,162	2,996,743	373,330	766,848	107,626
Under 5 years	1,128,661	373,506	660,256	20,878	58,174	5,674	7,826	2,347
5 to 9 years...........................	1,696,279	555,002	1,015,715	24,466	72,267	7,265	18,440	3,124
10 to 14 years.........................	2,280,920	759,049	1,377,702	39,191	58,709	7,001	35,511	3,757
15 to 19 years.........................	3,072,575	1,017,865	1,583,775	344,808	50,121	6,833	64,332	4,841
20 to 24 years.........................	4,417,064	1,488,604	1,833,245	876,147	119,850	12,963	79,942	6,313
25 to 29 years.........................	6,142,947	2,204,495	2,924,980	444,418	419,391	31,557	107,522	10,584
30 to 34 years.........................	6,786,102	2,313,428	3,549,722	208,172	553,619	50,658	96,719	13,784
35 to 39 years.........................	6,400,416	1,991,892	3,683,475	91,349	487,327	53,655	80,416	12,302
40 to 44 years.........................	6,465,742	2,116,009	3,736,996	49,885	428,067	52,945	70,037	11,803
45 to 49 years.........................	5,780,318	2,060,087	3,253,738	28,601	319,118	48,673	59,912	10,189
50 to 54 years.........................	5,105,456	1,851,972	2,919,592	15,475	216,158	42,024	51,999	8,236
55 to 59 years.........................	3,990,610	1,424,233	2,364,604	6,833	119,314	30,500	38,479	6,647
60 to 64 years.........................	3,141,633	1,233,450	1,803,947	3,517	56,374	14,645	24,500	5,200
65 years and over	4,580,183	1,836,715	2,657,943	4,982	35,045	7,706	29,909	7,883
Unknown age..........................	63,354	5,089	48,465	3,440	3,209	1,231	1,304	616
SEX AND AGE								
Total..................................	61,052,260	21,231,396	33,414,155	2,162,162	2,996,743	373,330	766,848	107,626
Male	31,420,318	11,206,030	16,296,348	1,118,591	2,033,740	243,536	470,448	51,625
Under 5 years	565,319	187,696	329,214	10,729	29,546	2,834	4,128	1,172
5 to 9 years...........................	846,990	279,934	504,638	11,955	36,465	3,589	8,835	1,574
10 to 14 years.........................	1,125,915	379,704	674,680	18,772	29,213	3,648	18,019	1,879
15 to 19 years.........................	1,435,847	466,374	723,374	178,108	28,829	3,480	33,473	2,209
20 to 24 years.........................	2,056,106	634,444	839,362	443,415	86,257	8,408	41,439	2,781
25 to 29 years.........................	2,988,456	1,025,328	1,382,017	232,753	260,613	19,290	63,787	4,668
30 to 34 years.........................	3,631,971	1,228,133	1,828,648	110,343	362,957	31,633	63,712	6,545
35 to 39 years.........................	3,629,783	1,160,883	1,979,637	50,790	340,769	34,972	56,522	6,210
40 to 44 years.........................	3,670,663	1,254,901	1,992,154	26,819	305,354	36,364	48,833	6,238
45 to 49 years.........................	3,201,174	1,215,132	1,657,205	15,690	233,667	33,444	40,619	5,417
50 to 54 years.........................	2,671,155	1,055,712	1,381,017	8,716	158,386	28,945	34,397	3,982
55 to 59 years.........................	1,964,735	770,158	1,052,956	3,959	89,543	20,491	24,723	2,905
60 to 64 years.........................	1,483,968	624,264	786,671	2,111	43,605	10,358	14,611	2,348
65 years and over	2,126,629	921,884	1,148,306	3,381	27,304	5,549	16,688	3,517
Unknown age..........................	21,607	1,483	16,469	1,050	1,232	531	662	180
Female	29,285,737	10,007,288	16,851,137	1,023,693	938,781	123,735	289,727	51,376
Under 5 years	557,532	184,993	327,019	9,943	28,040	2,760	3,650	1,127
5 to 9 years...........................	843,097	274,159	506,529	12,369	35,366	3,620	9,566	1,488
10 to 14 years.........................	1,148,594	378,656	697,874	20,265	29,244	3,302	17,459	1,794
15 to 19 years.........................	1,625,901	550,941	853,177	164,145	21,014	3,285	30,812	2,527
20 to 24 years.........................	2,338,145	852,757	981,689	425,369	32,691	4,368	37,962	3,309
25 to 29 years.........................	3,118,112	1,177,450	1,518,876	207,517	154,373	11,826	42,548	5,522
30 to 34 years.........................	3,113,733	1,083,660	1,691,617	95,921	185,589	18,324	31,900	6,722
35 to 39 years.........................	2,736,448	829,609	1,677,287	39,778	143,264	17,906	22,969	5,635
40 to 44 years.........................	2,763,924	859,880	1,720,023	22,661	120,155	15,785	20,421	4,999
45 to 49 years.........................	2,549,884	843,868	1,572,676	12,663	83,354	14,447	18,681	4,195
50 to 54 years.........................	2,406,273	795,206	1,514,781	6,624	56,356	12,377	17,190	3,739
55 to 59 years.........................	2,000,510	653,115	1,289,361	2,813	28,883	9,482	13,473	3,383
60 to 64 years.........................	1,637,277	608,250	998,888	1,361	12,348	4,050	9,765	2,615
65 years and over	2,422,849	913,073	1,481,586	1,471	7,445	1,995	13,159	4,120
Unknown age..........................	23,458	1,671	19,754	793	659	208	172	201
Unknown gender	346,205	18,078	266,670	19,878	24,222	6,059	6,673	4,625

[1] Includes GB, GMB, GT, GMT, WB, and WT admissions.

[2] Includes B1, B2 and a limited number of Border Crossing Card (BCC) admissions.

[3] Includes principals, spouses, and children (F1, F2, J1, J2, M1, and M2 admissions).

[4] Includes principals, spouses, and children (CW1, CW2, E1 to E3, H1B, H1B1, H1C, H2A, H2B, H2R, H3, H4, I1, L1, L2, O1 to O3, P1 to P4, Q1, R1, R2, TD and TN admissions).

[5] Includes principals, spouses, and children (A1 to A3, G1 to G5, and N1 to N7 admissions).

Notes: Admissions represent counts of events, i.e., arrivals, not unique individuals; multiple entries of an individual on the same day are counted as one admission. The majority of short-term admissions from Canada and Mexico are excluded.

Source: U.S. Department of Homeland Security.

Table 30.
NONIMMIGRANT ADMISSIONS (I-94 ONLY) BY SELECTED CATEGORY OF ADMISSION AND STATE OR TERRITORY OF DESTINATION: FISCAL YEAR 2013

State or territory of destination	Total	Tourists and business travelers		Students and exchange visitors[3]	Temporary workers and families[4]	Diplomats and other represen- tatives[5]	All other classes	Unknown
		Visa waiver[1]	Other[2]					
Total	61,052,260	21,231,396	33,414,155	2,162,162	2,996,743	373,330	766,848	107,626
Alabama	126,745	55,656	41,505	10,646	14,830	2,263	1,696	149
Alaska	131,918	73,177	50,244	2,390	3,552	525	1,827	203
Arizona	1,952,808	133,268	1,616,793	38,441	151,794	7,232	2,786	2,494
Arkansas	70,201	13,770	38,268	7,413	10,157	281	245	67
California	11,182,804	3,025,507	7,440,548	302,741	340,024	23,847	40,705	9,432
Colorado	559,247	172,192	336,402	23,335	23,409	2,273	920	716
Connecticut	218,108	77,465	84,875	25,163	28,297	1,290	663	355
Delaware	40,880	14,377	15,165	5,253	4,694	964	365	62
District of Columbia	434,495	174,944	152,239	26,336	14,277	64,751	1,292	656
Florida	8,089,139	2,871,429	4,823,058	93,064	158,389	17,039	100,612	25,548
Georgia	612,675	244,488	273,079	31,977	53,114	5,630	3,513	874
Guam	1,050,007	997,324	35,209	580	4,722	2,177	969	9,026
Hawaii	2,261,576	1,982,254	252,835	11,077	6,834	4,315	3,778	483
Idaho	41,208	15,293	15,186	5,401	4,592	547	130	59
Illinois	1,197,625	458,073	575,736	68,999	84,498	4,677	4,118	1,524
Indiana	192,018	55,340	81,235	35,128	19,094	447	510	264
Iowa	69,959	17,976	29,676	14,402	7,314	233	264	94
Kansas	103,292	15,700	67,173	11,940	6,909	1,142	308	120
Kentucky	93,191	28,336	35,383	10,435	18,493	157	256	131
Louisiana	252,353	93,384	120,153	10,648	18,478	994	8,333	363
Maine	106,407	37,230	29,514	18,041	20,618	212	665	127
Maryland	349,169	103,354	157,344	32,386	24,256	28,542	2,623	664
Massachusetts	1,056,505	510,996	346,945	125,379	63,810	4,285	3,857	1,233
Michigan	1,040,327	204,464	253,280	135,086	439,146	2,050	4,982	1,319
Minnesota	232,836	84,770	100,279	22,793	22,578	456	1,648	312
Mississippi	38,682	10,112	16,911	4,072	6,612	518	397	60
Missouri	149,231	38,201	73,022	23,475	13,012	910	440	171
Montana	51,189	28,276	14,925	4,930	2,692	64	134	168
Nebraska	312,883	188,243	105,796	9,599	7,300	1,408	413	124
Nevada	2,128,680	747,467	1,356,664	5,015	14,145	2,602	986	1,801
New Hampshire	60,918	28,268	17,054	8,772	6,376	218	151	79
New Jersey	1,010,849	377,873	476,195	43,593	100,683	4,941	5,660	1,904
New Mexico	587,505	18,074	552,203	7,057	5,885	2,949	438	899
New York	6,805,732	3,731,482	2,385,763	268,931	318,455	73,920	17,546	9,635
North Carolina	314,486	106,890	130,155	28,671	45,042	1,850	1,347	531
North Dakota	48,037	19,325	13,954	7,626	6,567	316	149	100
Ohio	317,313	95,715	123,996	46,675	47,973	1,549	1,033	372
Oklahoma	126,349	16,731	88,705	12,615	6,687	1,193	284	134
Oregon	205,807	82,962	82,977	22,250	16,052	319	956	291
Pennsylvania	505,507	192,962	187,122	69,883	49,707	2,045	3,122	666
Puerto Rico	148,816	52,668	84,802	1,575	5,951	528	2,951	341
Rhode Island	54,676	18,776	20,367	10,500	3,976	728	245	84
South Carolina	131,490	52,576	49,228	11,350	16,576	616	948	196
South Dakota	14,885	6,125	4,481	2,305	1,693	187	80	14
Tennessee	180,616	62,627	80,512	14,390	21,661	550	666	210
Texas	7,605,578	569,936	6,294,913	191,477	418,753	24,828	94,253	11,418
Utah	157,969	59,879	75,725	13,373	7,930	490	328	244
Vermont	65,965	34,034	16,046	6,263	9,185	72	166	199
Virginia	471,690	146,815	204,782	41,325	38,184	37,293	2,542	749
Washington	1,415,063	511,544	744,686	48,943	89,546	6,941	10,750	2,653
West Virginia	17,590	4,871	6,067	5,025	1,494	75	50	8
Wisconsin	157,128	52,046	67,843	22,240	14,090	276	462	171
Wyoming	22,856	11,025	7,892	2,477	1,343	37	51	31
Other	109,310	87,513	17,490	571	2,620	126	225	765
Unknown	6,369,967	2,417,613	3,141,755	158,130	172,674	29,452	433,010	17,333

See footnotes at end of table.

[1] Includes GB, GMB, GT, GMT, WB, and WT admissions.

[2] Includes B1, B2 and a limited number of Border Crossing Card (BCC) admissions.

[3] Includes principals, spouses, and children (F1, F2, J1, J2, M1, and M2 admissions).

[4] Includes principals, spouses, and children (CW1, CW2, E1 to E3, H1B, H1B1, H1C, H2A, H2B, H2R, H3, H4, I1, L1, L2, O1 to O3, P1 to P4, Q1, R1, R2, TD and TN admissions).

[5] Includes principals, spouses, and children (A1 to A3, G1 to G5, and N1 to N7 admissions).

Notes: Admissions represent counts of events, i.e., arrivals, not unique individuals; multiple entries of an individual on the same day are counted as one admission. The majority of short-term admissions from Canada and Mexico are excluded.

Source: U.S. Department of Homeland Security.

Table 31.
NONIMMIGRANT ADMISSIONS (I-94 ONLY) BY SELECTED CATEGORY OF ADMISSION AND MONTH OF ARRIVAL: FISCAL YEAR 2013

| Month of arrival | Total | Tourists and business travelers | | Students and exchange visitors[3] | Temporary workers and families[4] | Diplomats and other represen-tatives[5] | All other classes | Unknown |
		Visa waiver[1]	Other[2]					
Total	61,052,260	21,231,396	33,414,155	2,162,162	2,996,743	373,330	766,848	107,626
October 2012	4,525,678	1,835,435	2,303,209	91,618	214,260	29,446	40,955	10,755
November 2012	4,269,295	1,466,651	2,407,596	87,462	226,664	25,846	42,476	12,600
December 2012	5,307,873	1,677,125	3,202,027	116,249	237,147	24,312	34,955	16,058
January 2013	4,159,725	1,273,714	2,114,403	379,634	304,393	31,338	43,289	12,954
February 2013	3,671,074	1,397,660	1,890,837	86,452	222,530	23,545	38,640	11,410
March 2013	4,811,513	1,827,605	2,507,092	135,893	256,983	28,529	40,968	14,443
April 2013	4,329,370	1,705,516	2,215,371	90,110	238,131	31,215	39,171	9,856
May 2013	4,902,756	1,764,075	2,690,142	115,915	211,933	30,598	84,959	5,134
June 2013	5,568,390	1,831,094	3,174,116	185,482	253,482	35,324	84,996	3,896
July 2013	6,704,350	2,195,016	3,929,398	161,089	278,963	33,942	102,304	3,638
August 2013	6,914,843	2,243,852	3,709,158	515,643	286,023	39,006	117,535	3,626
September 2013	5,887,393	2,013,653	3,270,806	196,615	266,234	40,229	96,600	3,256

[1] Includes GB, GMB, GT, GMT, WB, and WT admissions.

[2] Includes B1, B2 and a limited number of Border Crossing Card (BCC) admissions.

[3] Includes principals, spouses, and children (F1, F2, J1, J2, M1, and M2 admissions).

[4] Includes principals, spouses, and children (CW1, CW2, E1 to E3, H1B, H1B1, H1C, H2A, H2B, H2R, H3, H4, I1, L1, L2, O1 to O3, P1 to P4, Q1, R1, R2, TD and TN admissions).

[5] Includes principals, spouses, and children (A1 to A3, G1 to G5, and N1 to N7 admissions).

Notes: Admissions represent counts of events, i.e., arrivals, not unique individuals; multiple entries of an individual on the same day are counted as one admission. The majority of short-term admissions from Canada and Mexico are excluded.

Source: U.S. Department of Homeland Security.

Table 32.
NONIMMIGRANT TEMPORARY WORKER ADMISSIONS (I-94 ONLY) BY REGION AND COUNTRY OF CITIZENSHIP: FISCAL YEAR 2013

Region and country of citizenship	Total temporary workers and families[1]	Workers in specialty occupations (H1B)	Agricultural workers (H2A)	Non-agricultural workers (H2B, H2R)[2]	Workers with extraordinary ability/ achievement (O1, O2)	Athletes, artists, and entertainers (P1 to P3)	Intra-company transferees (L1)	Treaty traders and investors (E1 to E3)[3]	Other
REGION									
Total..............	2,996,743	474,355	204,577	104,993	87,366	107,401	503,206	373,360	1,141,485
Africa	23,580	6,557	1,124	1,018	894	2,006	4,787	271	6,923
Asia	733,843	261,745	22	1,661	7,837	8,270	127,650	118,744	207,914
Europe	520,299	78,972	412	2,668	47,381	20,633	155,607	99,495	115,131
North America	1,542,691	92,258	201,325	98,744	20,145	67,004	171,561	122,641	769,013
Oceania............	55,664	3,586	148	78	4,945	2,713	10,645	24,881	8,668
South America	111,647	29,805	943	193	5,669	6,101	31,082	6,027	31,827
Unknown	9,019	1,432	603	631	495	674	1,874	1,301	2,009
COUNTRY									
Total..............	2,996,743	474,355	204,577	104,993	87,366	107,401	503,206	373,360	1,141,485
Afghanistan	55	10	-	-	D	D	3	3	36
Albania	213	85	-	D	16	40	18	D	51
Algeria..............	251	47	-	-	D	19	70	D	103
Andorra	75	11	-	-	D	-	22	-	D
Angola..............	683	24	-	-	20	D	327	D	303
Antigua and Barbuda	133	31	-	7	-	28	53	D	D
Argentina............	17,308	3,708	3	64	1,135	987	4,828	1,743	4,840
Armenia.............	374	95	-	-	45	104	17	23	90
Australia[4]	48,980	2,331	56	45	4,155	2,002	8,910	24,831	6,650
Austria	6,309	1,006	-	D	530	304	2,092	1,148	D
Azerbaijan	391	81	-	D	5	41	51	D	206
Bahamas.............	773	445	-	-	29	45	95	7	152
Bahrain	74	26	-	-	D	D	16	5	23
Bangladesh	1,142	442	-	D	6	61	147	9	D
Barbados............	500	197	-	D	97	91	55	D	57
Belarus	995	296	D	-	58	118	174	15	D
Belgium.............	9,464	1,130	-	5	916	187	3,263	1,564	2,399
Belize	261	91	4	86	3	15	5	-	57
Benin	50	32	-	-	3	D	D	D	12
Bhutan	14	6	-	-	-	-	-	D	D
Bolivia..............	1,307	522	-	-	24	97	291	52	321
Bosnia and Herzegovina ..	240	56	-	-	13	75	26	5	65
Botswana	80	35	-	-	3	D	5	-	D
Brazil..............	33,059	7,426	10	46	1,274	1,355	11,851	337	10,760
Brunei..............	40	10	-	-	-	-	12	-	18
Bulgaria.............	2,191	1,074	10	178	150	117	225	106	331
Burkina Faso	87	45	-	-	5	-	11	-	26
Burma..............	183	66	-	-	D	32	14	D	D
Burundi	28	19	-	-	-	4	D	-	D
Cambodia	246	16	-	-	D	181	6	D	D
Cameroon	353	142	-	-	14	14	55	7	121
Canada.............	863,826	59,451	5,350	337	11,632	28,718	124,567	42,199	591,572
Cape Verde	32	-	-	-	D	5	10	-	D
Central African Republic ..	11	3	-	-	-	D	4	-	D
Chad...............	12	D	-	-	-	-	6	-	D
Chile	6,676	2,216	21	20	314	201	1,416	427	2,061
China[5]............	53,736	24,957	D	13	728	2,135	11,810	510	D
Colombia............	17,442	5,261	-	15	1,072	1,363	3,708	2,042	3,981
Comoros	4	-	-	-	D	-	-	-	D
Congo (Brazzaville)[6]	76	8	-	-	D	16	18	3	D
Congo (Kinshasa)[7]	67	8	-	D	9	9	7	5	D
Costa Rica...........	3,422	929	98	284	67	77	1,093	132	742
Cote d'Ivoire	95	39	-	-	D	4	15	D	34
Croatia	1,207	332	-	4	123	111	305	71	261
Cuba	549	6	-	-	44	459	D	4	D
Cyprus..............	302	155	-	-	43	3	33	D	D
Czech Republic	2,540	422	-	13	210	265	783	190	657

See footnotes at end of table.

Region and country of citizenship	Total temporary workers and families[1]	Workers in specialty occupations (H1B)	Agricultural workers (H2A)	Non-agricultural workers (H2B, H2R)[2]	Workers with extraordinary ability/ achievement (O1, O2)	Athletes, artists, and entertainers (P1 to P3)	Intra-company transferees (L1)	Treaty traders and investors (E1 to E3)[3]	Other
Denmark[8]	9,378	1,008	-	6	1,058	294	3,420	796	2,796
Djibouti	D	-	-	-	D	D	-	-	-
Dominica	169	29	-	-	59	68	-	-	13
Dominican Republic	6,992	1,043	96	106	233	3,481	581	38	1,414
East Timor	D	-	-	-	-	-	-	-	D
Ecuador	2,969	1,181	3	14	138	130	657	48	798
Egypt	3,024	765	11	-	75	22	813	42	1,296
El Salvador	1,913	496	33	478	53	263	182	26	382
Equatorial Guinea	22	D	-	-	-	-	6	-	D
Eritrea	10	D	-	-	-	D	-	D	5
Estonia	562	110	-	D	97	48	124	27	D
Ethiopia	573	132	-	-	28	305	39	7	62
Fiji	142	14	-	-	10	16	20	-	82
Finland	4,930	674	D	D	340	401	1,784	290	D
France[9]	72,407	11,676	D	16	4,316	1,467	20,685	16,590	D
Gabon	43	6	-	D	D	D	20	D	11
Gambia	16	6	-	-	3	D	D	D	D
Georgia	271	81	-	-	22	60	18	3	87
Germany	74,328	7,894	D	17	3,454	1,133	17,648	33,007	D
Ghana	915	433	-	-	30	59	52	4	337
Greece	3,331	1,578	-	3	449	149	503	117	532
Grenada	123	69	-	-	3	20	3	7	21
Guatemala	6,000	677	972	2,734	84	225	515	57	736
Guinea	89	12	-	-	4	56	5	5	7
Guinea-Bissau	D	-	-	-	-	-	D	-	D
Guyana	140	55	-	-	8	9	17	4	47
Haiti	750	102	15	-	23	439	28	D	D
Honduras	2,785	643	109	409	19	302	507	330	466
Hungary	3,313	659	3	40	181	411	1,005	40	974
Iceland	1,275	237	-	D	395	126	194	7	D
India	369,377	188,776	-	132	740	2,112	50,120	363	127,134
Indonesia	2,431	952	-	4	60	41	503	34	837
Iran	434	164	-	-	17	21	24	33	175
Iraq	115	24	-	-	D	11	20	D	57
Ireland	17,869	3,581	39	178	1,425	1,148	6,418	1,613	3,467
Israel	17,734	3,462	-	18	1,248	480	4,646	1,952	5,928
Italy	36,587	6,777	-	13	2,986	913	9,615	10,098	6,185
Jamaica	14,787	1,019	4,381	5,828	1,762	934	229	71	563
Japan	163,922	7,651	D	302	2,348	791	37,401	88,317	D
Jordan	895	435	-	-	28	6	86	21	319
Kazakhstan	724	167	-	-	28	90	136	18	285
Kenya	1,198	599	-	D	16	270	92	9	D
Kiribati	18	-	-	D	-	-	-	-	D
Korea, North[10]	D	-	-	-	-	-	D	-	-
Korea, South[11]	56,120	9,692	-	214	1,086	770	11,377	19,887	13,094
Kuwait	270	37	-	D	9	6	39	43	D
Kyrgyzstan	161	39	-	-	19	45	D	-	D
Laos	45	3	-	-	-	15	D	-	D
Latvia	688	128	-	-	172	133	91	38	126
Lebanon	1,856	910	-	D	68	90	275	11	D
Lesotho	21	9	-	-	D	-	-	4	D
Liberia	40	4	-	-	12	14	-	-	10
Libya	79	18	-	-	4	D	8	D	D
Liechtenstein	26	12	-	-	8	-	D	D	-
Lithuania	633	190	D	57	159	15	73	18	D
Luxembourg	242	42	-	-	20	8	118	7	47
Macedonia	299	132	-	17	42	41	21	3	43
Madagascar	45	22	-	-	D	-	7	3	D
Malawi	50	11	-	-	3	5	7	D	D

See footnotes at end of table.

Table 32.
NONIMMIGRANT TEMPORARY WORKER ADMISSIONS (I-94 ONLY) BY REGION AND COUNTRY OF CITIZENSHIP: FISCAL YEAR 2013 – *Continued*

Region and country of citizenship	Total temporary workers and families[1]	Workers in specialty occupations (H1B)	Agricultural workers (H2A)	Non-agricultural workers (H2B, H2R)[2]	Workers with extraordinary ability/ achievement (O1, O2)	Athletes, artists, and entertainers (P1 to P3)	Intra-company transferees (L1)	Treaty traders and investors (E1 to E3)[3]	Other
Malaysia	5,287	1,636	-	D	62	19	2,142	31	D
Maldives	8	4	-	-	D	-	-	-	D
Mali	134	18	-	-	40	63	D	-	D
Malta	201	31	-	-	9	43	67	D	D
Marshall Islands	D	-	-	-	-	-	D	D	-
Mauritania	21	4	-	-	-	3	6	4	4
Mauritius	128	67	-	-	3	4	23	6	25
Mexico	633,610	25,191	189,956	88,329	5,682	30,922	42,591	79,455	171,484
Moldova	412	169	29	59	16	25	22	5	87
Monaco	22	8	-	-	7	-	-	D	D
Mongolia	249	75	-	-	3	43	8	29	91
Morocco[12]	822	339	-	-	17	47	103	52	264
Mozambique	62	4	-	-	5	6	-	-	47
Namibia	54	22	D	-	7	-	6	-	D
Nauru	D	D	-	-	-	-	-	-	-
Nepal	1,625	1,018	D	D	14	7	112	3	468
Netherlands[13]	21,013	2,297	8	21	2,329	837	7,499	2,929	5,093
New Zealand[14]	6,388	1,233	92	31	775	693	1,714	47	1,803
Nicaragua	1,239	307	310	97	15	187	121	3	199
Niger	44	10	-	-	-	13	3	D	D
Nigeria	3,700	1,416	-	D	35	254	640	15	D
Norway	7,669	637	D	D	655	296	1,478	2,794	1,805
Oman	178	27	-	D	-	D	50	5	D
Pakistan	4,648	1,977	-	D	132	111	517	149	D
Panama	1,275	372	D	47	55	160	208	86	D
Papua New Guinea	13	5	-	-	D	-	-	D	D
Paraguay	373	104	-	-	17	39	62	38	113
Peru	6,009	2,188	868	26	175	244	1,209	49	1,250
Philippines	14,042	4,353	D	922	392	229	2,327	614	D
Poland	6,540	1,396	D	42	375	676	1,895	170	D
Portugal	4,777	1,308	-	4	382	74	1,852	50	1,107
Qatar	65	5	-	-	4	-	27	5	24
Romania	3,680	1,290	175	306	209	116	743	133	708
Russia	12,501	2,848	10	88	1,150	1,938	2,455	136	3,876
Rwanda	97	35	-	-	5	20	14	-	23
Saint Kitts and Nevis	83	40	-	-	-	24	12	-	7
Saint Lucia	107	70	-	-	5	8	10	D	D
Saint Vincent and the Grenadines	85	33	-	-	13	9	6	6	18
Samoa	53	-	-	-	-	-	-	-	53
San Marino	4	-	-	-	-	-	-	-	4
Saudi Arabia	1,440	126	7	5	12	61	484	121	624
Senegal	269	136	-	-	10	39	28	5	51
Serbia and Montenegro	106	39	D	5	12	13	10	5	D
Seychelles	D	-	-	-	-	-	-	-	D
Sierra Leone	48	19	-	-	4	18	D	-	D
Singapore	5,451	2,280	-	8	91	16	1,531	176	1,349
Slovakia	1,571	316	-	57	156	101	457	109	375
Slovenia	676	112	-	5	106	78	127	153	95
South Africa	8,198	1,337	1,110	1,009	448	323	2,109	39	1,823
Spain	39,170	5,763	-	22	2,243	842	12,755	8,219	9,326
Sri Lanka	1,571	806	-	-	8	31	262	17	447
Sudan	52	16	-	-	D	-	5	D	D
Suriname	65	18	-	D	3	3	D	30	D
Swaziland	34	11	-	D	-	-	4	-	D
Sweden	14,839	1,846	-	D	2,130	1,147	4,263	1,939	D
Switzerland	8,857	1,450	D	5	707	221	2,975	1,543	D

See footnotes at end of table.

Table 32.
NONIMMIGRANT TEMPORARY WORKER ADMISSIONS (I-94 ONLY) BY REGION AND COUNTRY OF CITIZENSHIP: FISCAL YEAR 2013 – *Continued*

Region and country of citizenship	Total temporary workers and families[1]	Workers in specialty occupations (H1B)	Agricultural workers (H2A)	Non-agricultural workers (H2B, H2R)[2]	Workers with extraordinary ability/ achievement (O1, O2)	Athletes, artists, and entertainers (P1 to P3)	Intra-company transferees (L1)	Treaty traders and investors (E1 to E3)[3]	Other
Syria	234	61	-	-	3	24	28	3	115
Taiwan	14,969	5,642	-	D	298	284	1,755	4,326	D
Tajikistan	25	17	-	-	-	-	-	-	8
Tanzania	259	154	-	D	9	3	13	4	D
Thailand	2,647	848	9	D	78	52	489	459	D
Togo	58	31	-	-	9	-	-	-	18
Tonga	58	-	-	-	4	D	-	-	D
Trinidad and Tobago	3,309	1,017	-	D	267	529	699	214	D
Tunisia	352	95	-	-	19	12	89	20	117
Turkey	8,338	3,884	-	30	192	78	814	1,530	1,810
Turkmenistan	57	30	-	-	-	-	D	-	D
Tuvalu	D	-	-	-	-	-	-	-	D
Uganda	579	119	-	-	9	302	44	3	102
Ukraine	4,093	1,140	79	85	338	301	733	74	1,343
United Arab Emirates	128	11	-	-	D	5	34	8	D
United Kingdom[15]	145,066	19,212	48	1,414	19,437	6,421	49,665	15,479	33,390
Uruguay	1,382	414	38	D	80	69	368	103	D
Uzbekistan	338	89	-	-	17	49	33	3	147
Vanuatu	7	D	-	-	-	-	-	-	D
Venezuela	24,917	6,712	-	6	1,429	1,604	6,674	1,154	7,338
Vietnam	1,593	598	-	-	21	161	268	18	527
Yemen	36	D	-	-	D	-	10	D	22
Zambia	119	51	-	D	10	5	5	D	45
Zimbabwe	591	250	D	D	21	79	111	3	D
Unknown	9,019	1,432	603	631	495	674	1,874	1,301	2,009

D Data withheld to limit disclosure.

- Represents zero.

[1] Includes principals and dependents (CW1, CW2, E1 to E3, H1B, H1B1,H1C, H2A, H2B, H2R, H3, H4, I1, L1, L2, O1 to O3, P1 to P4, Q1, R1, R2, TD and TN admissions).

[2] Issuances of H2R (returning H2B workers not subject to annual numerical limits) ceased at the end of 2007.

[3] Includes principals and dependents.

[4] Australia includes Australia, Norfolk Island, Christmas Island, and Cocos (Keeling) Island.

[5] China includes the People's Republic of China, Hong Kong, and Macau.

[6] Congo (Brazzaville) refers to the Republic of the Congo.

[7] Congo (Kinshasa) refers to the Democratic Republic of the Congo.

[8] Denmark includes Denmark, Faroe Islands, and Greenland.

[9] France includes France, French Guiana, French Polynesia, French Southern and Antarctic Lands, Guadeloupe, Martinique, New Caledonia, Reunion, Saint Pierre and Miquelon, and Wallis and Futuna.

[10] North Korea refers to the Democratic People's Republic of Korea.

[11] South Korea refers to the Republic of Korea.

[12] Morocco includes Morocco and Western Sahara.

[13] Netherlands includes the Netherlands, Aruba, and the Netherlands Antilles.

[14] New Zealand includes New Zealand, Cook Islands, Tokelau, and Niue.

[15] United Kingdom includes the United Kingdom, Anguilla, Bermuda, British Virgin Islands, Cayman Islands, Falkland Islands, Gibraltar, Guernsey, Isle of Man, Jersey, Montserrat, Pitcairn Island, Saint Helena, and Turks and Caicos Islands.

Notes: Admissions represent counts of events, i.e., arrivals, not unique individuals; multiple entries of an individual on the same day are counted as one admission. The majority of short-term admissions from Canada and Mexico are excluded.

Source: U.S. Department of Homeland Security.

Enforcement Actions

Table 33.
ALIENS APPREHENDED: FISCAL YEARS 1925 TO 2013

Year	Number	Year	Number	Year	Number	Year	Number
1925.	22,199	1948.	192,779	1971.	420,126	1994.	1,094,719
1926.	12,735	1949.	288,253	1972.	505,949	1995.	1,394,554
1927.	16,393	1950.	468,339	1973.	655,968	1996.	1,649,986
1928.	23,566	1951.	509,040	1974.	788,145	1997.	1,536,520
1929.	32,711	1952.	543,535	1975.	766,600	1998.	1,679,439
1930.	20,880	1953.	885,587	1976[1]	1,097,739	1999.	1,714,035
1931.	22,276	1954.	1,089,583	1977.	1,042,215	2000.	1,814,729
1932.	22,735	1955.	254,096	1978.	1,057,977	2001.	1,387,486
1933.	20,949	1956.	87,696	1979.	1,076,418	2002.	1,062,270
1934.	10,319	1957.	59,918	1980.	910,361	2003.	1,046,422
1935.	11,016	1958.	53,474	1981.	975,780	2004.	1,264,232
1936.	11,728	1959.	45,336	1982.	970,246	2005.	1,291,065
1937.	13,054	1960.	70,684	1983.	1,251,357	2006.	1,206,412
1938.	12,851	1961.	88,823	1984.	1,246,981	2007.	960,772
1939.	12,037	1962.	92,758	1985.	1,348,749	2008[2]	1,043,799
1940.	10,492	1963.	88,712	1986.	1,767,400	2009[3]	889,203
1941.	11,294	1964.	86,597	1987.	1,190,488	2010.	796,587
1942.	11,784	1965.	110,371	1988.	1,008,145	2011.	678,606
1943.	11,175	1966.	138,520	1989.	954,243	2012.	671,327
1944.	31,174	1967.	161,608	1990.	1,169,939	2013.	662,483
1945.	69,164	1968.	212,057	1991.	1,197,875		
1946.	99,591	1969.	283,557	1992.	1,258,481		
1947.	193,657	1970.	345,353	1993.	1,327,261		

[1] Includes the 15 months from July 1, 1975 to September 30, 1976 because the end date of fiscal years was changed from June 30 to September 30.

[2] Beginning in 2008, includes all administrative arrests conducted by ICE ERO.

[3] Beginning in 2009, data include administrative arrests conducted by ICE ERO and administrative arrests conducted under the 287(g) program.

Note: Data refer to Border Patrol apprehensions and ICE administrative arrests. Prior to 1952, data refer to Border Patrol apprehensions.

Source: U.S. Department of Homeland Security, Customs and Border Protection (CBP) U.S. Border Patrol (USBP), Immigration and Customs Enforcement (ICE) Homeland Security Investigations (HSI), and the Office of Enforcement and Removal Operations (ERO).

Table 34.
ALIENS APPREHENDED BY REGION AND COUNTRY OF NATIONALITY: FISCAL YEARS 2004 TO 2013

Region and country of nationality	2004	2005	2006	2007	2008[1]	2009[2]	2010	2011	2012	2013
REGION										
Total.....................	1,264,232	1,291,065	1,206,412	960,772	1,043,799	889,203	796,587	678,606	671,327	662,483
Africa	2,092	2,804	3,544	3,085	5,218	5,652	5,762	5,209	4,755	3,772
Asia	7,229	9,273	10,342	7,348	13,201	13,351	14,877	15,875	12,424	10,771
Europe	2,826	2,926	3,025	2,466	5,150	5,100	5,571	5,520	5,548	4,447
North America............	1,214,322	1,237,532	1,179,600	938,932	1,003,176	848,794	754,307	637,356	634,713	629,886
Oceania.................	284	175	221	202	506	492	544	514	466	451
South America............	14,093	38,128	9,002	8,671	15,526	15,214	14,589	13,357	12,507	12,459
Unknown.................	23,386	227	678	68	1,022	600	937	775	914	697
COUNTRY										
Total.................	1,264,232	1,291,065	1,206,412	960,772	1,043,799	889,203	796,587	678,606	671,327	662,483
Afghanistan	57	55	53	28	74	76	92	111	98	70
Albania	163	253	350	259	362	331	321	258	277	423
Algeria..................	49	39	50	49	59	53	62	36	42	27
Angola..................	10	10	11	13	31	24	22	28	22	16
Antigua-Barbuda..........	14	30	29	23	69	59	57	47	56	40
Argentina................	325	296	293	227	440	507	431	421	324	235
Armenia.................	55	82	78	60	235	181	239	232	217	141
Australia	54	33	28	27	52	65	76	75	55	69
Austria	12	12	9	7	12	12	22	23	12	14
Azerbaijan	7	16	13	15	30	40	30	37	29	36
Bahamas................	68	122	101	62	269	288	279	311	275	288
Bahrain	11	6	5	D	4	4	5	3	D	D
Bangladesh	138	151	190	182	278	223	325	272	262	366
Barbados................	31	67	34	28	90	105	82	77	80	45
Belarus	25	28	22	17	52	72	66	58	51	42
Belgium.................	9	15	16	8	16	26	24	35	17	25
Belize	151	149	140	113	348	345	338	361	316	293
Benin	9	9	8	10	17	11	12	18	11	9
Bermuda................	4	4	8	3	14	20	18	23	21	18
Bolivia..................	221	329	310	189	328	351	307	387	290	226
Bosnia-Herzegovina	43	67	66	60	108	175	202	201	198	179
Brazil...................	10,082	32,103	2,957	2,902	3,889	3,392	3,532	3,228	2,433	1,702
British Virgin Islands......	D	D	4	-	8	8	10	12	12	8
Bulgaria.................	82	75	69	71	121	102	103	95	110	52
Burkina Faso	8	13	13	12	31	24	29	20	29	19
Burma..................	9	9	26	18	53	36	54	35	54	48
Burundi.................	D	D	8	3	12	13	17	17	27	21
Cambodia	102	104	124	79	344	330	384	347	268	204
Cameroon	34	45	79	79	153	149	152	164	130	102
Canada.................	1,806	1,486	1,200	767	1,378	1,306	1,486	1,131	1,172	822
Cape Verde	42	84	57	48	127	116	118	105	110	66
Cayman Islands	3	D	D	-	6	9	10	6	6	5
Central African Republic	D	3	5	6	9	12	12	10	9	14
Chad....................	D	-	4	6	14	9	5	8	7	12
Chile...................	116	156	190	135	255	284	285	248	193	128
China, People's Republic........	1,560	2,890	2,987	1,623	2,296	2,928	2,714	2,563	2,350	1,918
Colombia................	919	1,545	1,647	1,893	3,619	3,468	3,006	2,755	2,201	1,987
Congo, Democratic Republic	3	10	13	D	26	35	24	26	28	28
Congo, Republic..............	21	18	44	77	59	77	72	63	75	39
Costa Rica...............	571	1,321	804	377	629	582	548	503	518	409
Cote d'Ivoire	27	22	62	72	118	116	119	102	112	80
Croatia	12	13	15	13	23	25	34	31	31	29
Cuba...................	1,831	4,285	5,088	4,931	6,676	4,742	4,030	4,801	4,121	2,809
Czech Republic	150	50	44	42	96	66	107	71	68	56
Czechoslovakia, former..........	42	12	33	42	29	24	19	21	20	15
Denmark	6	8	6	12	17	21	14	9	8	7
Dominica................	20	44	35	34	72	57	64	65	41	41
Dominican Republic	3,635	4,586	3,713	2,118	5,470	5,106	5,274	4,433	4,506	3,893
Ecuador.................	1,173	2,048	1,931	1,771	3,676	3,483	3,890	3,298	4,374	5,680
Egypt...................	218	291	354	269	321	313	275	237	190	192
El Salvador	19,180	42,885	46,314	19,699	27,153	27,741	29,911	27,652	38,976	51,226
Equatorial Guinea..........	D	D	D	7	4	7	14	4	7	-
Eritrea..................	26	88	83	100	217	212	231	63	37	40
Estonia.................	18	23	13	13	34	32	22	35	30	18

See footnotes at end of table.

Table 34.
ALIENS APPREHENDED BY REGION AND COUNTRY OF NATIONALITY: FISCAL YEARS 2004 TO 2013 – *Continued*

Region and country of nationality	2004	2005	2006	2007	2008[1]	2009[2]	2010	2011	2012	2013
Ethiopia.	79	206	346	144	218	262	274	219	220	144
Fiji.	23	29	54	45	128	101	99	87	79	67
France.	109	115	75	69	124	136	151	145	131	106
Gabon.	D	D	4	10	7	17	28	13	13	10
Gambia.	64	79	71	87	126	131	130	148	119	100
Georgia.	42	45	50	59	105	157	121	101	58	65
Germany.	104	159	130	84	201	228	227	198	186	153
Ghana.	135	165	251	239	414	422	414	435	340	272
Greece.	28	29	36	16	61	58	53	48	34	29
Grenada.	21	23	28	15	56	63	76	61	35	44
Guam.	-	-	-	D	24	15	21	16	8	22
Guatemala.	14,288	25,909	25,144	23,907	33,690	34,992	39,050	41,708	57,486	73,208
Guinea.	36	67	64	86	163	185	154	147	142	112
Guinea-Bissau.	D	D	-	D	7	13	5	6	3	D
Guyana.	135	293	243	156	508	492	428	411	360	292
Haiti.	367	999	1,215	1,004	2,299	2,220	1,768	1,351	1,492	1,992
Honduras.	26,555	55,756	33,394	28,265	33,777	32,901	32,501	31,189	50,771	64,157
Hong Kong.	15	31	22	21	60	58	53	56	85	74
Hungary.	76	50	47	44	80	95	69	106	111	88
Iceland.	D	3	D	3	8	6	10	7	3	D
India.	895	770	769	795	1,218	1,155	2,175	3,859	1,566	1,791
Indonesia.	170	153	488	536	632	371	486	327	219	126
Iran.	138	166	215	128	239	291	297	305	301	257
Iraq.	135	164	170	138	222	291	280	285	244	169
Ireland.	41	53	52	27	94	94	72	88	89	70
Israel.	290	322	267	226	298	345	311	254	192	213
Italy.	81	104	90	60	201	205	174	149	153	138
Jamaica.	976	1,557	1,350	804	3,068	3,075	3,064	2,862	2,655	2,147
Japan.	101	41	33	19	68	68	72	63	59	47
Jordan.	258	309	338	318	437	359	368	305	281	198
Kazakhstan.	14	14	40	35	78	101	118	117	108	71
Kenya.	138	146	176	160	325	537	716	539	494	341
Korea, South.	503	604	519	307	545	580	594	714	627	470
Kosovo.	X	X	X	X	D	26	24	36	26	30
Kuwait.	24	16	80	57	27	29	27	23	22	26
Kyrgyzstan.	D	12	14	D	20	59	56	44	40	89
Laos.	148	237	199	117	712	657	703	758	754	561
Latvia.	25	14	22	16	29	30	44	38	35	36
Lebanon.	157	125	262	195	236	216	220	171	128	103
Liberia.	59	85	137	99	271	338	309	309	314	231
Libya.	7	5	10	8	21	14	16	24	23	16
Lithuania.	64	62	47	55	100	94	81	77	84	65
Macau.	-	D	D	21	D	D	5	D	-	-
Macedonia.	35	44	48	40	93	62	57	51	43	30
Malawi.	11	7	5	7	16	10	14	21	14	10
Malaysia.	67	51	104	58	91	60	73	53	49	31
Mali.	38	44	120	80	127	140	163	112	100	83
Malta.	10	3	D	-	D	D	-	D	D	8
Marshall Islands.	16	5	4	3	15	20	19	21	28	35
Mauritania.	20	33	46	62	128	141	81	70	55	57
Mexico.	1,142,807	1,093,340	1,057,222	854,275	884,043	731,218	632,034	517,472	468,766	424,978
Micronesia, Federated States.	55	22	23	13	83	88	110	106	106	113
Moldova.	10	20	28	46	82	98	129	144	93	93
Mongolia.	70	41	44	54	80	142	124	129	95	66
Montenegro.	X	X	X	-	D	4	D	11	18	6
Montserrat.	D	4	D	D	10	9	9	9	4	D
Morocco.	244	278	287	183	227	232	226	173	149	135
Nepal.	60	33	48	44	102	148	230	180	248	448
Netherlands.	55	53	29	25	59	92	76	72	64	57
Netherlands Antilles.	6	10	4	D	15	4	9	11	D	5
New Zealand.	42	25	33	55	45	38	55	63	35	30
Nicaragua.	1,664	4,272	3,228	2,119	2,801	2,739	2,587	2,278	2,532	2,712
Niger.	19	19	112	115	87	54	68	48	50	39
Nigeria.	279	375	363	351	680	624	599	633	543	492
Norway.	12	5	7	7	13	8	12	7	8	D
Pakistan.	641	792	721	654	654	578	612	538	470	334

See footnotes at end of table.

Table 34.
ALIENS APPREHENDED BY REGION AND COUNTRY OF NATIONALITY: FISCAL YEARS 2004 TO 2013 – *Continued*

Region and country of nationality	2004	2005	2006	2007	2008[1]	2009[2]	2010	2011	2012	2013
Palau.	8	5	8	3	20	19	20	20	26	21
Panama.	97	131	132	112	326	268	283	226	197	184
Paraguay	35	18	26	21	26	47	32	35	33	30
Peru	714	903	1,020	944	1,807	2,079	1,729	1,741	1,588	1,682
Philippines.	488	600	773	500	1,340	1,080	1,079	1,135	927	721
Poland.	440	348	337	309	602	571	635	519	494	328
Portugal.	86	145	106	70	234	220	205	194	215	131
Romania	153	232	309	196	287	255	630	869	1,220	865
Russia.	175	195	183	194	470	565	564	526	414	320
Rwanda.	6	5	4	8	19	23	12	19	13	21
Saint Kitts-Nevis.	11	20	24	9	41	45	30	46	49	32
Saint Lucia	22	44	45	37	79	71	82	58	57	45
Saint Vincent and the Grenadines . .	8	28	14	9	69	63	57	50	41	43
Samoa	30	20	21	25	33	57	26	36	32	37
Saudi Arabia	72	40	130	67	87	70	148	127	198	264
Senegal.	69	66	98	92	158	157	170	158	164	132
Serbia.	X	X	X	D	4	6	D	22	13	35
Serbia and Montenegro	150	122	176	222	302	219	174	142	86	64
Sierra Leone	31	63	75	98	158	192	147	171	162	145
Singapore	18	13	11	14	21	21	21	12	7	16
Slovakia	56	32	15	23	45	40	51	29	44	23
Slovenia	-	4	3	D	4	11	9	5	7	-
Somalia.	50	92	122	98	201	237	277	336	316	214
South Africa.	83	138	108	83	124	149	144	123	95	79
South Sudan	X	X	X	X	X	X	X	D	3	42
Soviet Union, former.	20	42	82	7	110	62	91	92	115	89
Spain	41	43	32	28	91	92	99	126	139	98
Sri Lanka.	26	46	67	47	107	135	284	316	223	134
Sudan.	50	81	74	38	164	202	252	226	253	168
Suriname.	10	8	20	10	28	28	18	19	20	15
Sweden.	18	23	10	19	30	44	37	42	33	27
Switzerland	11	10	8	12	22	19	22	19	14	11
Syria.	106	113	151	101	101	91	99	114	57	72
Taiwan.	37	51	44	34	52	61	55	58	46	55
Tajikistan.	8	8	13	15	43	90	80	82	51	33
Tanzania	44	37	49	45	64	81	82	64	73	72
Thailand	123	134	339	117	381	304	300	257	276	246
Togo	16	12	29	43	53	44	40	43	46	20
Tonga	52	33	43	27	99	76	100	82	86	49
Trinidad and Tobago	181	448	320	210	691	729	624	596	498	419
Tunisia	79	85	86	60	53	47	61	43	33	24
Turkey	232	392	250	221	310	317	326	224	265	216
Turkmenistan.	4	-	6	9	11	20	29	8	10	4
Turks and Caicos Islands	-	5	D	3	17	11	19	11	19	13
Uganda.	17	17	36	49	59	65	54	66	44	49
Ukraine.	137	154	193	177	403	374	392	393	394	290
United Arab Emirates	9	6	35	8	4	7	15	3	10	11
United Kingdom.	326	297	305	169	510	486	533	518	448	388
Uruguay.	114	128	110	109	200	221	190	239	144	116
Uzbekistan.	73	130	147	96	157	198	210	135	129	116
Venezuela	249	301	255	314	750	862	741	575	547	366
Vietnam.	271	421	442	212	1,342	1,374	1,313	1,413	1,313	875
Yemen.	88	67	64	106	90	82	130	86	69	68
Zambia	24	22	22	25	45	63	49	49	50	31
Zimbabwe	26	32	41	44	72	80	74	88	63	48
All other countries	24	36	45	35	83	80	95	68	73	55
Unknown.	23,386	227	678	68	1,022	600	937	775	914	697

X Not applicable.

- Represents zero.

D Data withheld to limit disclosure.

[1] Beginning in 2008 data include administrative arrests conducted by ICE ERO.

[2] Beginning in 2009 data include administrative arrests conducted by ICE ERO and administrative arrests conducted under the 287(g) program.

Note: CBP Border Patrol data are current as of April 2014. ICE Enforcement and Removal Operations (ERO) data are current as of October 2013. ICE Homeland Security Investigations (HSI) data current as of October 2013.

Source: U.S. Department of Homeland Security, Customs and Border Protection (CBP) U.S. Border Patrol (USBP), Immigration and Customs Enforcement (ICE) Homeland Security Investigations (HSI), and the Office of Enforcement and Removal Operations (ERO).

Table 35.
ALIENS APPREHENDED BY PROGRAM AND BORDER PATROL SECTOR, INVESTIGATIONS SPECIAL AGENT IN CHARGE (SAC) JURISDICTION, AND AREA OF RESPONSIBILITY: FISCAL YEARS 2004 TO 2013

Program and sector/jurisdiction/area	2004	2005	2006	2007	2008	2009	2010	2011	2012	2013
PROGRAM										
Total	1,264,232	1,291,065	1,206,412	960,772	1,043,799	889,203	796,587	678,606	671,327	662,483
CBP Border Patrol	1,160,395	1,189,031	1,089,096	876,803	723,865	556,032	463,382	340,252	364,768	420,789
ICE Homeland Security Investigations[1]	103,837	102,034	101,854	53,562	31,123	21,251	18,290	16,261	15,937	11,996
ICE Enforcement and Removal Operations[2]	X	X	15,462	30,407	288,811	311,920	314,915	322,093	290,622	229,698
BORDER PATROL SECTOR										
Total apprehensions	1,160,395	1,189,031	1,089,096	876,803	723,865	556,032	463,382	340,252	364,768	420,789
Southwest sectors	1,139,282	1,171,462	1,071,979	858,737	705,049	540,851	447,731	327,577	356,873	414,397
Big Bend, TX[3]	10,530	10,536	7,520	5,537	5,389	6,357	5,288	4,036	3,964	3,684
Del Rio, TX	53,794	68,504	42,630	22,919	20,763	17,082	14,694	16,144	21,720	23,510
EL Centro, CA	74,467	55,790	61,457	55,882	40,964	33,520	32,562	30,191	23,916	16,306
EL Paso, TX	104,399	122,691	122,264	75,464	30,311	14,998	12,251	10,345	9,678	11,154
Laredo, TX	74,706	75,330	74,845	56,716	43,663	40,571	35,287	36,053	44,872	50,749
Rio Grande Valley, TX	92,947	134,161	110,520	73,429	75,484	60,992	59,766	59,243	97,762	154,453
San Diego, CA	138,608	126,915	142,110	152,464	162,390	118,712	68,565	42,447	28,461	27,496
Tucson, AZ	491,771	439,105	392,101	378,332	317,724	241,667	212,202	123,285	120,000	120,939
Yuma, AZ	98,060	138,430	118,532	37,994	8,361	6,952	7,116	5,833	6,500	6,106
Other sectors	21,113	17,569	17,117	18,066	18,816	15,181	15,651	12,675	7,895	6,392
Blaine, WA	1,354	1,000	809	749	950	844	673	591	537	360
Buffalo, NY	671	406	1,518	2,190	3,338	2,672	2,422	2,114	1,143	796
Detroit, MI	1,912	1,793	1,282	902	960	1,157	1,669	1,531	950	650
Grand Forks, ND	1,225	754	517	500	542	472	543	468	418	469
Havre, MT	986	948	567	486	426	283	290	270	102	88
Houlton, ME	263	233	175	95	81	60	56	41	41	37
Livermore, CA[4]	1,850	X	X	X	X	X	X	X	X	X
Miami, FL	4,602	7,243	6,033	7,121	6,021	4,429	4,651	4,401	2,509	1,738
New Orleans, LA	2,889	1,358	3,053	4,018	4,303	3,527	3,171	1,509	474	500
Ramey, PR	1,813	1,619	1,435	548	572	418	398	642	702	924
Spokane, WA	847	279	184	338	341	277	356	293	317	299
Swanton, VT	2,701	1,936	1,544	1,119	1,282	1,042	1,422	815	702	531
HOMELAND SECURITY INVESTIGATIONS SAC JURISDICTION										
Total administrative arrests	103,837	102,034	101,854	53,562	31,123	21,251	18,290	16,261	15,937	11,996
Atlanta, GA	3,237	3,659	4,933	4,659	1,663	1,506	978	806	578	337
Baltimore, MD	990	980	974	1,156	511	403	394	316	135	75
Boston, MA	3,141	3,248	2,560	1,664	826	596	481	449	346	225
Buffalo, NY	1,031	892	795	485	438	257	200	138	183	153
Chicago, IL	8,113	7,056	7,722	4,770	2,929	1,946	1,709	1,451	1,658	1,239
Dallas, TX	5,160	4,902	4,336	3,011	973	641	628	557	508	256
Denver, CO	5,943	4,440	5,373	4,033	2,063	1,196	1,037	1,180	643	226
Detroit, MI	2,239	2,480	3,133	2,143	808	586	484	365	257	176
EL Paso, TX	2,017	1,624	1,786	1,511	1,103	499	508	513	446	367
Honolulu, HI	425	251	381	234	368	215	124	167	197	95
Houston, TX	4,251	4,449	4,760	2,516	1,612	1,139	967	743	1,044	1,071
Los Angeles, CA	13,253	11,514	11,328	2,034	1,641	1,164	1,012	640	536	507
Miami, FL	1,815	1,980	1,361	961	763	763	936	1,038	1,030	881
New Orleans, LA	2,357	2,220	3,333	3,094	3,229	1,630	949	923	686	508
New York, NY	4,019	4,953	3,632	1,732	725	572	681	600	461	219
Newark, NJ	1,892	1,594	1,584	512	273	365	239	372	194	118
Philadelphia, PA	2,506	2,696	2,935	2,602	2,295	1,057	884	578	373	178
Phoenix, AZ	12,385	10,621	10,526	1,029	1,189	1,044	654	401	403	457
Saint Paul, MN	2,596	2,925	3,149	2,585	1,145	591	607	582	381	174
San Antonio, TX	3,943	3,244	3,780	2,307	1,171	1,175	1,492	1,525	3,599	2,945
San Diego, CA	5,291	4,703	1,695	789	725	567	516	304	506	398
San Francisco, CA	9,088	11,089	9,893	1,565	896	715	691	749	355	252
San Juan, PR	1,185	1,691	1,862	1,227	503	293	271	158	178	242
Seattle, WA	3,254	4,302	5,088	3,517	1,103	835	661	659	424	376
Tampa, FL	1,571	2,226	2,794	1,739	1,001	661	615	488	421	168
Washington, DC	2,135	2,295	2,141	1,687	1,149	825	562	489	347	303
Other SAC jurisdictions abroad	-	-	-	-	21	10	10	70	48	50

See footnotes at end of table.

Table 35.
ALIENS APPREHENDED BY PROGRAM AND BORDER PATROL SECTOR, INVESTIGATIONS SPECIAL AGENT IN CHARGE (SAC) JURISDICTION, AND AREA OF RESPONSIBILITY: FISCAL YEARS 2004 TO 2013 – *Continued*

Program and sector/jurisdiction/area	2004	2005	2006	2007	2008	2009	2010	2011	2012	2013
ENFORCEMENT AND REMOVAL OPERATIONS AREA OF RESPONSIBILITY										
Total administrative arrests	X	X	15,462	30,407	288,811	311,920	314,915	322,093	290,622	229,698
Atlanta, GA	X	X	513	2,293	2,739	7,121	21,742	26,688	24,312	17,480
Baltimore, MD	X	X	591	925	1,018	2,773	2,973	3,178	2,953	2,562
Boston, MA	X	X	1,040	1,462	1,369	3,979	5,107	5,390	5,268	3,908
Buffalo, NY	X	X	369	503	390	659	1,169	1,635	1,666	1,668
Chicago, IL.	X	X	525	1,043	12,872	12,669	19,272	18,739	15,455	11,817
Dallas, TX	X	X	611	1,635	10,922	14,626	16,548	18,808	16,515	15,882
Denver, CO.	X	X	345	391	3,810	5,977	8,073	7,324	6,008	4,819
Detroit, MI	X	X	898	1,816	5,763	7,768	7,781	7,304	6,886	5,374
EL Paso, TX	X	X	318	604	1,261	3,345	6,432	5,046	4,407	3,244
Houston, TX.	X	X	842	1,236	277	2,688	19,052	19,579	17,126	13,866
Los Angeles, CA	X	X	1,496	2,667	1,562	6,767	27,748	33,728	31,078	24,582
Miami, FL.	X	X	1,470	2,579	7,599	15,441	13,656	15,940	16,011	11,147
New Orleans, LA.	X	X	271	448	3,245	5,743	12,179	14,258	12,584	8,972
New York City, NY	X	X	777	1,579	8,352	8,711	9,346	7,245	6,532	5,560
Newark, NJ	X	X	1,094	2,079	1,038	4,508	5,585	5,539	5,589	4,380
Philadelphia, PA	X	X	545	940	4,127	4,883	5,358	5,668	5,092	4,980
Phoenix, AZ	X	X	86	475	18,512	13,031	17,558	14,953	13,113	10,941
Saint Paul, MN.	X	X	661	914	3,132	4,747	7,371	7,770	6,960	5,505
Salt Lake City, UT	X	X	296	576	3,690	5,475	9,194	8,730	7,535	6,182
San Antonio, TX	X	X	180	1,327	3,948	17,199	24,337	28,292	28,947	25,658
San Diego, CA	X	X	691	817	12,382	12,031	10,608	13,016	11,196	6,521
San Francisco, CA	X	X	974	1,935	9,234	13,680	28,972	31,430	26,386	20,441
Seattle, WA	X	X	624	889	2,158	7,002	10,246	9,714	8,801	7,156
Washington, DC	X	X	245	1,274	1,906	4,851	5,069	8,322	7,383	5,557
Headquarters.	X	X	-	-	-	21	15	38	31	12
Unknown	X	X	-	-	167,505	126,225	19,524	3,759	2,788	1,484

X Not applicable.

- Represents zero.

[1] By 2008, no longer includes arrests under the 287(g) program.

[2] Data for 2006 and 2007 include only arrests of fugitive and nonfugitive aliens under the National Fugitive Operations Program of ICE ERO; 2008 data include administrative arrests conducted by ICE ERO; data from 2009 to 2013 include arrests conducted by ICE ERO and arrests conducted under the 287(g) program.

[3] Formerly known as Marfa, TX.

[4] Livermore sector closed September 30, 2004.

Source: U.S. Department of Homeland Security, Customs and Border Protection (CBP) U.S. Border Patrol (USBP), Immigration and Customs Enforcement (ICE) Homeland Security Investigations (HSI), and the Office of Enforcement and Removal Operations (ERO).

Table 36.
ALIENS DETERMINED INADMISSIBLE: FISCAL YEARS 2005 TO 2013

Year	Number
2005.	251,109
2006.	207,610
2007.	202,025
2008.	222,788
2009.	223,897
2010.	229,403
2011.	212,234
2012.	193,606
2013.	204,108

Note: Before April 2008, did not include all crew members detained on board vessels.

Source: U.S. Department of Homeland Security, Customs and Border Protection, Office of Field Operations, Enforcement Integrated Database (EID), October 2013.

Table 37.
ALIENS DETERMINED INADMISSIBLE BY REGION AND COUNTRY OF NATIONALITY: FISCAL YEARS 2005 TO 2013

Region and country of nationality	2005	2006	2007	2008	2009	2010	2011	2012	2013
REGION									
Total.................................	251,109	207,610	202,025	222,788	223,897	229,403	212,234	193,606	204,108
Africa	5,032	4,552	3,908	4,143	4,868	5,612	4,228	3,526	3,953
Asia	24,390	19,859	23,751	51,146	61,557	65,010	64,148	55,578	61,252
Europe	54,220	18,945	17,309	23,398	24,780	22,880	21,121	17,993	17,880
North America	155,402	154,105	147,768	134,940	124,543	129,214	117,255	111,729	115,513
Oceania..............................	2,194	1,469	1,237	1,227	1,432	1,054	835	851	917
South America	8,329	7,676	7,365	7,523	6,401	5,353	4,183	3,712	4,442
Unknown	1,542	1,004	687	411	316	280	464	217	151
COUNTRY									
Total.................................	251,109	207,610	202,025	222,788	223,897	229,403	212,234	193,606	204,108
Afghanistan	147	179	134	138	151	120	127	93	71
Albania	227	142	106	145	131	92	75	66	84
Algeria...............................	136	113	82	130	166	136	68	73	43
American Samoa	D	D	-	-	-	-	6	15	14
Angola...............................	73	24	23	39	24	13	24	27	54
Anguilla..............................	9	13	8	4	4	9	6	D	D
Antigua-Barbuda......................	59	56	53	39	41	47	39	41	25
Argentina.............................	571	411	297	342	263	210	148	129	178
Armenia..............................	126	67	91	72	97	64	57	66	56
Australia	851	719	607	542	605	553	444	444	567
Austria	348	200	136	136	131	112	86	77	71
Azerbaijan	26	10	21	21	49	32	63	31	37
Bahamas.............................	480	500	565	509	385	524	460	458	516
Bahrain	6	D	11	10	4	12	6	13	6
Bangladesh	374	319	263	299	375	332	310	316	292
Barbados.............................	144	104	97	78	82	82	72	63	48
Belarus	35	50	60	83	114	79	89	61	48
Belgium..............................	400	233	195	146	161	155	137	123	134
Belize	198	172	156	138	135	144	117	127	112
Benin	46	61	62	38	51	68	37	19	27
Bermuda	88	140	155	154	122	125	134	97	105
Bolivia...............................	266	272	355	268	225	178	84	78	67
Bosnia-Herzegovina	67	64	69	86	67	63	35	51	60
Botswana	8	7	5	16	11	8	4	13	5
Brazil................................	2,627	2,126	1,938	1,510	1,233	1,110	799	731	810
British Virgin Islands.................	18	14	36	70	62	9	10	19	26
Bulgaria..............................	218	230	216	348	336	334	272	278	228
Burkina Faso	46	57	30	28	24	22	12	22	23
Burma...............................	96	103	546	3,045	3,867	4,043	2,642	2,410	1,984
Burundi..............................	23	36	64	19	14	29	24	23	31
Cambodia	94	39	52	67	38	52	34	30	25
Cameroon	178	176	170	130	89	102	136	152	334
Canada	41,861	41,757	36,595	32,381	30,425	33,148	32,141	30,731	29,387
Cape Verde	32	29	15	37	52	74	61	48	22
Cayman Islands	37	35	22	32	21	19	16	20	12
Chad.................................	48	22	22	29	13	11	3	4	5
Chile.................................	337	296	292	309	252	209	162	111	184
China, People's Republic..............	4,886	3,227	5,257	13,494	15,975	17,173	16,931	12,888	13,552
Colombia.............................	1,303	1,618	1,692	1,951	1,916	1,567	1,241	1,113	1,260
Congo, Democratic Republic	15	8	11	10	22	27	25	64	58
Congo, Republic......................	117	99	94	99	99	76	65	18	27
Costa Rica............................	611	575	547	501	440	284	218	229	215
Cote d'Ivoire	137	111	109	101	89	154	63	27	33
Croatia	70	66	88	232	170	261	244	194	177
Cuba.................................	9,043	10,401	12,993	11,265	7,037	7,442	7,759	12,253	17,679
Cyprus...............................	32	28	17	32	21	15	8	11	9
Czech Republic	165	106	78	97	135	144	124	211	184
Czechoslovakia, former................	96	69	46	67	136	80	30	-	-
Denmark..............................	1,473	156	117	141	137	128	92	100	82
Djibouti	9	15	12	6	9	10	3	7	D
Dominica.............................	49	50	91	97	78	54	58	46	50
Dominican Republic	1,556	1,538	1,612	1,818	2,299	2,137	1,591	1,605	1,471
Ecuador..............................	581	542	508	577	495	431	308	369	408

See footnotes at end of table.

Table 37.
ALIENS DETERMINED INADMISSIBLE BY REGION AND COUNTRY OF NATIONALITY: FISCAL YEARS 2005 TO 2013 – Continued

Region and country of nationality	2005	2006	2007	2008	2009	2010	2011	2012	2013
Egypt.	401	333	276	382	534	599	438	418	329
El Salvador	1,427	1,683	1,133	1,064	1,195	1,099	853	1,028	2,194
Eritrea	48	30	26	17	45	393	336	188	139
Estonia	24	17	37	37	90	70	59	38	48
Ethiopia.	148	149	170	212	201	270	167	134	253
Fiji.	168	153	140	151	352	137	97	64	71
Finland	354	60	58	80	107	69	71	56	48
France.	10,397	3,532	2,584	1,644	1,514	1,417	1,144	872	858
French Polynesia	12	7	-	D	D	5	D	D	D
Gabon.	32	28	29	20	13	9	16	5	8
Gambia	41	60	32	38	37	27	40	30	33
Georgia.	35	20	75	288	440	329	134	116	96
Germany	3,761	1,369	1,314	1,079	1,073	941	835	770	735
Ghana.	330	296	218	266	363	278	239	267	349
Greece	267	211	233	386	395	450	415	367	477
Grenada	83	76	53	79	58	72	46	47	47
Guatemala.	1,500	1,470	1,391	1,715	1,859	1,767	1,612	1,757	1,919
Guinea	103	123	112	87	72	40	53	40	40
Guyana	536	412	432	432	362	317	280	183	164
Haiti	1,057	1,267	970	1,054	936	2,956	1,734	1,425	1,552
Honduras.	853	850	870	1,101	1,310	1,300	1,075	1,445	2,187
Hong Kong.	392	299	284	229	196	161	140	104	94
Hungary.	239	162	189	193	328	220	224	265	247
Iceland	629	28	33	25	28	20	24	28	16
India	3,152	2,907	3,083	5,023	5,846	6,577	5,983	6,907	11,815
Indonesia	446	797	1,268	3,974	3,003	2,236	1,941	1,401	1,020
Iran.	655	681	577	581	654	764	504	474	533
Iraq.	206	253	374	360	232	217	214	198	296
Ireland.	2,189	762	683	536	456	320	244	255	282
Israel	975	883	816	807	873	694	496	460	397
Italy.	6,866	1,681	1,326	1,153	1,204	1,089	1,024	1,043	1,030
Jamaica.	1,798	1,490	1,315	1,584	1,367	1,229	945	834	769
Japan.	3,184	1,106	850	881	671	645	723	538	620
Jordan.	307	333	293	275	281	230	206	198	204
Kazakhstan	33	45	25	34	34	44	29	43	30
Kenya	201	175	142	133	129	161	113	92	86
Kiribati	16	12	36	99	68	41	58	41	33
Korea, South	2,459	1,726	1,588	1,738	2,106	1,861	1,945	1,512	1,707
Kosovo	X	X	X	-	17	-	D	18	17
Kuwait.	37	36	35	31	47	36	42	29	53
Kyrgyzstan	12	5	10	4	11	12	19	6	9
Laos.	55	50	45	53	23	18	38	34	15
Latvia	44	64	60	179	354	310	218	139	145
Lebanon	380	413	432	346	296	247	209	141	185
Liberia.	51	55	72	53	71	69	67	58	29
Libya.	24	39	35	71	65	53	50	33	18
Lithuania.	89	84	114	622	760	685	519	397	179
Luxembourg.	25	7	11	D	D	D	6	4	D
Macau.	15	3	6	3	3	3	3	D	5
Macedonia.	47	77	48	98	66	56	64	53	56
Madagascar.	24	31	20	18	8	11	41	9	5
Malawi	7	13	10	6	12	7	6	7	D
Malaysia	203	178	288	285	341	310	257	402	316
Maldives	D	D	23	74	125	61	58	92	12
Mali	54	70	51	48	38	38	42	32	26
Malta	36	56	30	26	10	9	16	9	7
Marshall Islands	7	9	8	14	32	9	3	15	7
Mauritania.	40	22	19	31	20	24	14	22	14
Mauritius.	74	50	44	103	170	277	252	65	40
Mexico	92,760	90,209	87,632	79,686	75,151	75,464	67,410	58,658	56,267
Micronesia, Federated States	24	36	33	28	27	16	14	26	12
Moldova	51	46	35	52	72	73	75	64	51
Mongolia.	48	95	86	91	57	54	59	53	44
Montenegro.	X	X	-	-	-	-	25	36	32

See footnotes at end of table.

Table 37.
ALIENS DETERMINED INADMISSIBLE BY REGION AND COUNTRY OF NATIONALITY: FISCAL YEARS 2005 TO 2013 – Continued

Region and country of nationality	2005	2006	2007	2008	2009	2010	2011	2012	2013
Morocco	543	368	356	235	206	254	167	121	133
Nepal	90	70	65	122	66	63	104	67	77
Netherlands	1,266	681	599	625	583	541	399	372	384
Netherlands Antilles	26	23	12	14	14	14	7	-	-
New Zealand	948	381	274	225	169	171	138	126	152
Nicaragua	452	448	472	428	464	393	326	323	379
Niger	46	44	41	24	31	31	18	9	4
Nigeria	632	572	435	578	659	784	628	668	828
Norway	4,201	219	171	179	207	167	110	122	122
Oman	11	6	4	4	3	D	4	5	5
Pakistan	1,460	1,341	985	944	957	840	726	595	460
Palau	18	23	14	19	25	26	9	12	7
Panama	260	299	221	236	213	182	154	130	146
Paraguay	59	54	67	54	46	42	20	24	27
Peru	1,203	1,200	1,065	1,401	1,085	805	746	565	882
Philippines	1,636	2,162	3,506	14,032	20,188	22,917	25,197	22,486	23,389
Poland	851	946	910	1,258	1,295	1,108	1,148	763	762
Portugal	1,768	693	493	440	361	311	293	475	369
Qatar	7	27	D	5	6	16	7	7	18
Romania	487	521	611	1,015	1,044	1,150	973	719	580
Russia	549	430	822	2,753	3,774	3,676	3,905	2,946	2,618
Rwanda	40	47	28	37	41	18	59	56	81
Saint Kitts-Nevis	56	35	37	26	41	51	56	23	41
Saint Lucia	116	85	76	88	69	65	78	63	94
Saint Vincent and the Grenadines	104	96	109	97	97	103	77	64	64
Samoa	74	63	51	71	61	36	24	25	21
Saudi Arabia	115	118	148	148	170	232	310	311	369
Senegal	138	309	142	118	170	167	85	61	111
Serbia	X	X	-	-	-	-	86	-	-
Serbia and Montenegro	170	159	154	259	190	165	60	4	D
Sierra Leone	53	44	58	46	41	43	60	32	26
Singapore	246	128	135	147	146	109	92	141	130
Slovakia	88	94	72	66	145	118	135	103	119
Slovenia	53	32	20	21	27	33	22	32	28
Solomon Islands	-	D	D	3	12	D	5	D	7
Somalia	82	85	109	185	335	412	164	180	267
South Africa	369	278	258	289	277	248	188	240	209
Soviet Union, former	28	31	38	159	102	163	83	-	-
Spain	1,742	567	534	605	603	689	988	1,717	2,423
Sri Lanka	483	389	328	434	462	315	253	190	182
Sudan	72	79	73	92	69	56	78	60	46
Suriname	6	13	14	16	8	10	7	D	3
Swaziland	19	10	D	4	7	5	D	D	D
Sweden	1,161	283	247	233	253	215	202	168	220
Switzerland	1,566	285	190	197	153	155	114	143	122
Syria	133	82	112	135	94	106	108	168	416
Taiwan	500	431	494	386	459	399	367	466	656
Tajikistan	4	-	3	8	10	5	5	15	3
Tanzania	88	53	47	67	359	326	162	40	47
Thailand	249	244	327	558	485	527	638	318	282
Togo	58	46	49	34	45	84	32	16	22
Tonga	65	60	64	52	61	53	25	33	14
Trinidad and Tobago	711	674	512	635	609	466	236	221	186
Tunisia	224	192	166	57	49	67	56	36	43
Turkey	328	391	458	1,082	1,698	1,934	1,935	1,335	1,137
Turkmenistan	7	6	D	4	3	5	6	6	30
Turks and Caicos Islands	28	36	26	35	24	22	23	19	18
Tuvalu	-	-	D	3	5	-	7	24	-
Uganda	48	42	59	53	43	41	54	42	33
Ukraine	359	409	1,063	4,806	4,917	4,657	4,359	2,928	2,882
United Arab Emirates	24	21	23	32	13	21	13	18	22
United Kingdom	11,804	4,119	3,517	3,183	3,129	2,549	2,093	1,925	1,948
Uruguay	137	99	101	79	58	52	47	43	54
Uzbekistan	59	38	29	56	48	50	49	22	30

See footnotes at end of table.

Table 37.
ALIENS DETERMINED INADMISSIBLE BY REGION AND COUNTRY OF NATIONALITY: FISCAL YEARS 2005 TO 2013 – *Continued*

Region and country of nationality	2005	2006	2007	2008	2009	2010	2011	2012	2013
Vanuatu.	-	D	-	13	4	-	-	-	D
Venezuela	702	633	604	584	458	422	341	363	405
Vietnam.	598	504	498	733	865	1,061	1,094	796	503
Yemen.	51	92	69	58	65	61	47	54	48
Zambia	51	33	26	31	16	15	15	12	12
Zimbabwe	90	83	82	94	60	52	39	39	37
All other countries	77	54	55	58	40	44	45	52	43
Unknown.	1,542	1,004	687	411	316	280	464	217	151

X Not applicable.

D Data withheld to limit disclosure.

- Represents zero.

Note: Before April 2008, did not include all crew members detained on board vessels.

Source: U.S. Department of Homeland Security, Customs and Border Protection, Office of Field Operations, Enforcement Integrated Database (EID), October 2013.

Table 38.
ALIENS DETERMINED INADMISSIBLE BY FIELD OFFICE: FISCAL YEARS 2005 TO 2013

Field office	2005	2006	2007	2008	2009	2010	2011	2012	2013
Total..........................	251,109	207,610	202,025	222,788	223,897	229,403	212,234	193,606	204,108
Atlanta, GA	6,175	4,254	3,905	7,529	8,002	9,163	8,726	7,984	8,376
Baltimore, MD	4,054	2,039	2,006	2,231	2,428	2,775	3,108	3,613	3,120
Boston, MA	4,091	3,045	3,347	4,087	4,650	4,716	5,203	4,819	4,984
Buffalo, NY	49,655	37,488	28,945	21,369	18,683	17,763	15,712	14,050	13,425
Chicago, IL..........................	6,201	3,675	2,874	3,599	3,536	3,219	2,553	2,449	2,173
Detroit, MI..........................	11,844	10,403	8,546	7,748	7,428	7,398	7,250	6,743	6,564
El Paso, TX	9,689	8,713	8,370	7,912	7,712	7,898	6,909	6,954	7,900
Houston, TX.........................	4,426	3,512	3,641	12,061	16,428	18,963	19,528	12,706	10,909
Laredo, TX..........................	32,576	30,686	30,765	26,635	21,877	24,441	25,790	28,005	31,781
Los Angeles, CA.....................	8,526	4,372	6,962	12,148	11,724	8,556	6,692	3,928	3,905
Miami, FL...........................	13,069	8,085	6,842	7,765	7,032	9,161	6,896	7,593	8,684
New Orleans, LA.....................	162	182	331	12,293	18,153	19,162	20,855	20,204	21,011
New York, NY	14,990	6,113	5,723	6,834	11,268	9,918	6,892	4,912	4,650
Portland, OR	620	576	1,117	1,401	988	899	1,892	1,166	1,402
Pre-Clearance[1]	8,338	10,922	10,613	8,388	7,865	9,539	8,586	8,559	9,695
San Diego, CA	45,552	47,932	49,456	47,125	42,017	40,014	33,719	26,889	25,632
San Francisco, CA	4,910	2,914	3,418	7,305	6,880	6,279	6,954	9,832	14,939
San Juan, PR........................	2,008	1,501	2,674	4,247	4,754	5,458	2,927	1,984	2,071
Seattle, WA	11,383	10,338	10,605	10,867	9,080	10,738	10,650	10,529	9,343
Tampa, FL	2,008	1,260	3,396	3,778	4,501	4,099	3,142	2,941	3,173
Tucson, AZ..........................	10,531	9,450	8,268	7,110	8,377	8,735	7,951	7,612	9,991
Unknown office	301	150	221	356	514	509	299	134	380

[1] Refers to field offices abroad.

Note: Before April 2008, did not include all crew members detained on board vessels.

Source: U.S. Department of Homeland Security, Customs and Border Protection (CBP), Office of Field Operations (OFO), Enforcement Integrated Database (EID), October 2013.

Table 39.
ALIENS REMOVED OR RETURNED: FISCAL YEARS 1892 TO 2013

Year	Removals[1]	Returns[2]	Year	Removals[1]	Returns[2]	Year	Removals[1]	Returns[2]
1892.........	2,801	NA	1933.........	25,392	10,347	1974.........	19,413	718,740
1893.........	1,630	NA	1934.........	14,263	8,010	1975.........	24,432	655,814
1894.........	1,806	NA	1935.........	13,877	7,978	1976[3].........	38,471	955,374
1895.........	2,596	NA	1936.........	16,195	8,251	1977.........	31,263	867,015
1896.........	3,037	NA	1937.........	16,905	8,788	1978.........	29,277	975,515
1897.........	1,880	NA	1938.........	17,341	9,278	1979.........	26,825	966,137
1898.........	3,229	NA	1939.........	14,700	9,590	1980.........	18,013	719,211
1899.........	4,052	NA	1940.........	12,254	8,594	1981.........	17,379	823,875
1900.........	4,602	NA	1941.........	7,336	6,531	1982.........	15,216	812,572
1901.........	3,879	NA	1942.........	5,542	6,904	1983.........	19,211	931,600
1902.........	5,439	NA	1943.........	5,702	11,947	1984.........	18,696	909,833
1903.........	9,316	NA	1944.........	8,821	32,270	1985.........	23,105	1,041,296
1904.........	8,773	NA	1945.........	13,611	69,490	1986.........	24,592	1,586,320
1905.........	12,724	NA	1946.........	17,317	101,945	1987.........	24,336	1,091,203
1906.........	13,108	NA	1947.........	23,434	195,880	1988.........	25,829	911,790
1907.........	14,059	NA	1948.........	25,276	197,184	1989.........	34,427	830,890
1908.........	12,971	NA	1949.........	23,874	276,297	1990.........	30,039	1,022,533
1909.........	12,535	NA	1950.........	10,199	572,477	1991.........	33,189	1,061,105
1910.........	26,965	NA	1951.........	17,328	673,169	1992.........	43,671	1,105,829
1911.........	25,137	NA	1952.........	23,125	703,778	1993.........	42,542	1,243,410
1912.........	18,513	NA	1953.........	23,482	885,391	1994.........	45,674	1,029,107
1913.........	23,399	NA	1954.........	30,264	1,074,277	1995.........	50,924	1,313,764
1914.........	37,651	NA	1955.........	17,695	232,769	1996.........	69,680	1,573,428
1915.........	26,675	NA	1956.........	9,006	80,891	1997.........	114,432	1,440,684
1916.........	21,648	NA	1957.........	5,989	63,379	1998.........	174,813	1,570,127
1917.........	17,881	NA	1958.........	7,875	60,600	1999.........	183,114	1,574,863
1918.........	8,866	NA	1959.........	8,468	56,610	2000.........	188,467	1,675,876
1919.........	11,694	NA	1960.........	7,240	52,796	2001.........	189,026	1,349,371
1920.........	14,557	NA	1961.........	8,181	52,383	2002.........	165,168	1,012,116
1921.........	18,296	NA	1962.........	8,025	54,164	2003.........	211,098	945,294
1922.........	18,076	NA	1963.........	7,763	69,392	2004.........	240,665	1,166,576
1923.........	24,280	NA	1964.........	9,167	73,042	2005.........	246,431	1,096,920
1924.........	36,693	NA	1965.........	10,572	95,263	2006.........	280,974	1,043,381
1925.........	34,885	NA	1966.........	9,680	123,683	2007.........	319,382	891,390
1926.........	31,454	NA	1967.........	9,728	142,343	2008.........	359,795	811,263
1927.........	31,417	15,012	1968.........	9,590	179,952	2009.........	391,597	582,624
1928.........	30,464	19,946	1969.........	11,030	240,958	2010.........	382,265	474,233
1929.........	31,035	25,888	1970.........	17,469	303,348	2011.........	387,134	322,124
1930.........	24,864	11,387	1971.........	18,294	370,074	2012.........	418,397	230,386
1931.........	27,886	11,719	1972.........	16,883	450,927	2013.........	438,421	178,371
1932.........	26,490	10,775	1973.........	17,346	568,005			

NA Not available.

[1] Removals are the compulsory and confirmed movement of an inadmissible or deportable alien out of the United States based on an order of removal. An alien who is removed has administrative or criminal consequences placed on subsequent reentry owing to the fact of the removal.

[2] Returns are the confirmed movement of an inadmissible or deportable alien out of the United States not based on an order of removal.

[3] Includes the 15 months from July 1, 1975 to September 30, 1976 because the end date of fiscal years was changed from June 30 to September 30.

Source: U.S. Department of Homeland Security, ENFORCE Alien Removal Module (EARM), January 2014, Enforcement Integrated Database (EID), November 2013.

Table 40.
ALIENS RETURNED BY REGION AND COUNTRY OF NATIONALITY: FISCAL YEARS 2009 TO 2013

Region and country of nationality	2009	2010	2011	2012	2013
REGION					
Total	582,624	474,233	322,124	230,386	178,371
Africa	3,073	3,441	2,389	1,728	1,496
Asia	53,826	57,789	56,694	46,364	44,520
Europe	19,255	18,201	17,186	13,287	12,387
North America	501,573	390,739	241,976	166,088	117,077
Oceania	1,075	792	628	608	609
South America	3,640	3,139	2,961	2,174	2,201
Unknown	182	132	290	137	81
COUNTRY					
Total	582,624	474,233	322,124	230,386	178,371
Afghanistan	98	85	93	56	42
Albania	87	47	36	47	22
Algeria	141	131	56	57	39
American Samoa	-	-	4	11	8
Angola	13	7	11	20	21
Antigua-Barbuda	11	18	9	14	8
Argentina	120	98	89	62	70
Armenia	18	15	6	12	5
Australia	423	431	351	335	396
Austria	82	76	57	53	46
Azerbaijan	40	33	52	14	27
Bahamas	314	474	433	416	485
Bahrain	D	11	4	8	4
Bangladesh	310	281	248	238	167
Barbados	47	44	43	37	24
Belarus	91	52	71	44	24
Belgium	124	115	111	105	98
Belize	65	51	39	38	36
Benin	43	59	21	11	19
Bermuda	78	88	115	79	93
Bolivia	90	59	99	85	43
Bosnia-Herzegovina	32	26	24	22	10
Brazil	773	766	721	542	481
British Virgin Islands	42	5	5	11	19
Bulgaria	296	271	199	186	117
Burkina Faso	15	16	8	18	12
Burma	3,783	3,951	2,582	2,337	1,920
Burundi	9	19	11	12	12
Cambodia	21	28	15	16	13
Cameroon	54	55	66	49	47
Canada	25,373	29,144	28,274	27,039	23,963
Cape Verde	35	41	26	30	8
Cayman Islands	15	11	6	10	3
Chile	140	133	125	81	119
China, People's Republic	15,155	16,449	16,234	11,780	11,684
Colombia	893	777	645	435	448
Congo, Democratic Republic	D	7	10	29	17
Congo, Republic	50	47	33	14	19
Costa Rica	163	122	132	94	55
Cote d'Ivoire	45	120	43	18	18
Croatia	121	192	158	87	79
Cuba	85	108	105	90	77
Cyprus	16	10	5	10	5
Czech Republic	100	101	105	144	133
Czechoslovakia, former	82	54	23	4	5
Denmark	97	88	72	74	59
Dominica	59	30	37	24	27
Dominican Republic	786	741	763	764	531
Ecuador	411	328	336	303	209
Egypt	454	520	326	299	186
El Salvador	1,072	949	1,021	921	619
Eritrea	10	9	11	9	10
Estonia	70	55	42	28	35

See footnotes at end of table.

Table 40.
ALIENS RETURNED BY REGION AND COUNTRY OF NATIONALITY: FISCAL YEARS 2009 TO 2013 - *Continued*

Region and country of nationality	2009	2010	2011	2012	2013
Ethiopia	73	73	54	33	47
Fiji	333	109	72	51	57
Finland	79	39	50	39	34
France	917	970	842	661	609
Gabon	11	4	10	6	5
Gambia	14	9	14	11	8
Georgia	378	309	107	82	80
Germany	690	670	627	552	501
Ghana	231	159	150	128	83
Greece	311	365	291	294	375
Grenada	36	37	16	22	22
Guatemala	1,860	2,314	3,026	2,332	1,347
Guinea	29	17	25	16	5
Guyana	192	183	167	88	80
Haiti	272	297	210	163	156
Honduras	1,354	1,382	1,553	1,282	912
Hong Kong	137	102	92	75	54
Hungary	176	126	152	209	173
Iceland	17	13	9	19	8
India	4,233	4,695	4,136	3,273	2,462
Indonesia	2,685	1,907	1,587	1,171	719
Iran	304	433	315	306	353
Iraq	71	93	107	120	130
Ireland	300	202	182	180	200
Israel	495	429	341	275	232
Italy	790	771	739	692	631
Jamaica	555	508	458	344	332
Japan	461	482	461	354	381
Jordan	197	165	138	123	120
Kazakhstan	31	38	37	42	28
Kenya	96	127	124	92	91
Kiribati	63	37	46	40	24
Korea, South	1,634	1,561	1,619	1,191	1,259
Kosovo	8	D	D	9	11
Kuwait	36	26	40	22	40
Kyrgyzstan	13	18	15	5	8
Laos	21	12	6	12	3
Latvia	322	222	167	112	95
Lebanon	204	194	126	89	92
Liberia	39	16	25	24	14
Libya	59	49	41	34	17
Lithuania	703	638	470	371	153
Macedonia	39	28	37	15	12
Madagascar	7	10	40	9	4
Malaysia	267	231	156	124	53
Maldives	125	61	58	92	12
Mali	25	29	21	18	8
Malta	9	6	14	5	4
Marshall Islands	27	5	D	D	3
Mauritius	158	270	246	33	18
Mexico	468,699	353,850	205,158	131,983	88,042
Micronesia, Federated States	13	10	6	9	3
Moldova	53	56	64	41	42
Mongolia	39	36	54	35	39
Montenegro	-	-	13	22	13
Morocco	156	214	142	101	106
Nepal	52	43	63	36	25
Netherlands	392	393	295	287	280
Netherlands Antilles	6	11	7	-	-
New Zealand	128	136	104	97	94
Nicaragua	175	170	217	172	122
Niger	21	28	10	10	6
Nigeria	298	461	292	265	293
Norway	124	117	79	88	71

See footnotes at end of table.

Region and country of nationality	2009	2010	2011	2012	2013
Pakistan	658	647	586	477	296
Palau	19	23	7	10	5
Panama	119	73	98	53	53
Paraguay	20	21	9	14	16
Peru	659	460	521	356	510
Philippines	18,823	21,413	23,150	20,903	21,523
Poland	920	846	888	516	559
Portugal	211	169	205	294	266
Qatar	5	7	3	6	13
Romania	893	1,012	808	478	318
Russia	3,522	3,189	3,512	2,464	1,991
Rwanda	27	15	18	13	14
Saint Kitts-Nevis	12	13	22	6	18
Saint Lucia	41	31	39	21	27
Saint Vincent and the Grenadines	52	53	44	39	31
Samoa	24	20	10	9	D
Saudi Arabia	153	220	291	296	354
Senegal	106	127	56	38	87
Serbia	-	-	33	D	112
Serbia and Montenegro	135	119	48	9	4
Sierra Leone	16	19	28	18	10
Singapore	91	65	68	74	64
Slovakia	98	80	83	76	67
Slovenia	21	26	15	16	21
Solomon Islands	12	D	5	-	5
Somalia	23	25	10	5	10
South Africa	223	160	101	119	107
Soviet Union, former	94	150	61	-	D
Spain	348	461	649	874	1,139
Sri Lanka	342	254	182	151	125
Sudan	23	21	33	29	14
Sweden	157	152	145	119	142
Switzerland	94	108	87	104	85
Syria	56	89	71	72	79
Taiwan	325	293	286	374	473
Tajikistan	27	14	22	17	4
Tanzania	351	320	149	38	34
Thailand	394	463	530	231	202
Togo	40	75	19	11	13
Tonga	16	9	12	7	5
Trinidad and Tobago	267	199	130	117	67
Tunisia	37	57	35	21	22
Turkey	1,534	1,802	1,879	1,226	1,029
Turks and Caicos Islands	9	11	14	16	8
Tuvalu	5	-	5	20	-
Uganda	24	20	42	22	19
Ukraine	4,664	4,415	4,111	2,589	2,604
United Arab Emirates	10	18	8	13	13
United Kingdom	1,984	1,774	1,604	1,353	1,237
Uruguay	39	32	30	18	22
Uzbekistan	34	46	39	22	20
Venezuela	297	274	216	188	201
Vietnam	513	722	839	565	332
Yemen	19	23	23	26	12
Zambia	22	16	15	10	8
Zimbabwe	46	42	33	19	22
All other countries	87	89	70	73	57
Unknown	182	132	290	137	81

D Data withheld to limit disclosure.

- Represents zero.

Source: U.S. Department of Homeland Security. ENFORCE Alien Removal Module (EARM), January 2014, Enforcement Integrated Database (EID), November 2013.

Table 41.
ALIENS REMOVED BY CRIMINAL STATUS AND REGION AND COUNTRY OF NATIONALITY: FISCAL YEARS 2004 TO 2013

Region and country of nationality	2004 Total	2004 Criminal[1]	2004 Non-Criminal	2005 Total	2005 Criminal[1]	2005 Non-Criminal	2006 Total	2006 Criminal[1]	2006 Non-Criminal	2007 Total	2007 Criminal[1]	2007 Non-Criminal
REGION												
Total............	240,665	92,380	148,285	246,431	92,221	154,210	280,974	98,490	182,484	319,382	102,394	216,988
Africa	2,662	838	1,824	2,372	761	1,611	2,103	704	1,399	2,112	805	1,307
Asia	6,827	1,518	5,309	6,414	1,445	4,969	6,366	1,206	5,160	5,745	1,217	4,528
Europe	3,574	1,198	2,376	3,345	1,107	2,238	3,156	1,054	2,102	3,164	953	2,211
North America	213,592	85,267	128,325	219,432	84,632	134,800	256,952	92,206	164,746	96,082	96,498	199,584
Oceania..........	300	152	148	247	123	124	219	113	106	248	143	105
South America	13,618	3,400	10,218	14,535	4,152	10,383	12,102	3,199	8,903	11,988	2,774	9,214
Unknown	92	7	85	86	1	85	76	8	68	43	4	39
COUNTRY												
Total............	240,665	92,380	148,285	246,431	92,221	154,210	280,974	98,490	182,484	319,382	102,394	216,988
Afghanistan	38	14	24	37	21	16	20	12	8	27	11	16
Albania	209	26	183	236	32	204	252	32	220	246	23	223
Algeria...........	54	12	42	39	9	30	41	18	23	27	6	21
Angola...........	13	3	10	13	-	13	16	D	D	17	3	14
Antigua-Barbuda.....	36	25	11	34	26	8	40	33	7	45	37	8
Argentina..........	648	71	577	574	95	479	457	88	369	395	76	319
Armenia...........	144	38	106	120	32	88	97	27	70	74	34	40
Australia	62	12	50	39	11	28	54	20	34	52	21	31
Austria	16	8	8	11	D	D	10	D	D	13	8	5
Azerbaijan	9	D	D	10	D	D	6	D	D	8	D	D
Bahamas..........	132	95	37	153	120	33	91	68	23	97	72	25
Bangladesh	131	21	110	145	21	124	151	22	129	138	25	113
Barbados..........	75	68	7	65	55	10	46	41	5	40	33	7
Belarus	20	11	9	25	6	19	24	7	17	21	4	17
Belgium...........	38	10	28	19	7	12	14	4	10	17	4	13
Belize	202	119	83	219	118	101	211	112	99	233	116	117
Benin	3	-	3	D	D	D	11	4	7	7	3	4
Bermuda	3	-	3	-	-	-	D	-	D	D	-	D
Bolivia............	336	51	285	303	62	241	352	61	291	382	37	345
Bosnia-Herzegovina ..	26	21	5	23	14	9	42	28	14	42	29	13
Brazil.............	6,390	761	5,629	7,097	1,431	5,666	4,217	563	3,654	4,210	352	3,858
Bulgaria...........	84	12	72	82	15	67	64	10	54	80	23	57
Burkina Faso	10	D	D	11	3	8	17	3	14	13	4	9
Burma............	15	3	12	12	5	7	14	-	14	22	D	D
Cambodia	70	42	28	51	28	23	27	11	16	29	17	12
Cameroon	80	17	63	61	8	53	60	11	49	63	10	53
Canada	1,497	520	977	1,561	462	1,099	1,413	423	990	1,263	411	852
Cape Verde	42	31	11	47	38	9	37	30	7	61	50	11
Chad.............	7	-	7	9	D	D	D	D	-	3	D	D
Chile.............	227	73	154	225	61	164	245	60	185	237	73	164
China, People's Republic	1,225	144	1,081	1,252	147	1,105	1,362	132	1,230	864	97	767
Colombia..........	2,725	1,456	1,269	2,594	1,367	1,227	2,788	1,307	1,481	2,993	1,191	1,802
Congo, Democratic Republic	22	D	D	18	D	D	23	7	16	17	4	13
Congo, Republic.....	24	7	17	30	3	27	26	3	23	17	5	12
Costa Rica.........	599	74	525	676	82	594	795	100	695	655	88	567
Cote d'Ivoire	35	8	27	34	6	28	41	8	33	30	4	26
Croatia	19	7	12	11	4	7	15	5	10	13	6	7
Cuba.............	465	67	398	730	44	686	124	39	85	76	26	50
Czech Republic	34	5	29	30	D	D	34	D	D	41	8	33
Czechoslovakia, former	185	19	166	107	10	97	68	16	52	52	12	40
Denmark	14	3	11	14	6	8	8	D	D	14	3	11
Dominica..........	47	16	31	28	17	11	28	14	14	49	29	20
Dominican Republic ..	3,760	2,479	1,281	3,210	2,308	902	3,107	2,206	901	2,990	2,044	946
Ecuador...........	1,116	307	809	1,490	393	1,097	1,750	470	1,280	1,564	392	1,172
Egypt.............	256	59	197	233	47	186	172	30	142	145	29	116
El Salvador	7,269	2,805	4,464	8,305	2,827	5,478	11,050	3,850	7,200	20,045	4,949	15,096
Eritrea............	13	D	D	12	D	D	10	3	7	11	6	5

See footnotes at end of table.

Region and country of nationality	2004			2005			2006			2007		
	Total	Criminal[1]	Non-Criminal	Total	Criminal[1]	Non-Criminal	Total	Criminal[1]	Non-Criminal	Total	Criminal[1]	Non-Criminal
Estonia	14	4	10	22	4	18	23	4	19	21	8	13
Ethiopia	78	15	63	94	19	75	105	48	57	150	78	72
Fiji	65	27	38	74	18	56	47	19	28	45	21	24
Finland	4	D	D	8	-	8	6	D	D	D	-	D
France	121	36	85	136	45	91	124	35	89	100	22	78
Gabon	4	-	4	D	D	D	D	D	-	4	D	D
Gambia	72	16	56	61	16	45	43	7	36	35	10	25
Georgia	65	18	47	35	18	17	42	7	35	53	17	36
Germany	171	100	71	169	79	90	158	61	97	165	60	105
Ghana	299	53	246	218	76	142	187	69	118	231	88	143
Greece	36	22	14	50	24	26	35	19	16	30	13	17
Grenada	28	19	9	38	27	11	27	20	7	28	19	9
Guatemala	9,729	2,176	7,553	14,522	2,143	12,379	20,527	3,850	16,677	25,898	3,917	21,981
Guinea	92	22	70	92	24	68	78	18	60	66	20	46
Guyana	388	230	158	396	255	141	289	174	115	293	191	102
Haiti	878	222	656	1,204	591	613	907	290	617	1,492	519	973
Honduras	8,752	2,544	6,208	15,572	2,704	12,868	27,060	5,752	21,308	29,737	5,236	24,501
Hong Kong	22	5	17	20	7	13	15	8	7	28	4	24
Hungary	99	9	90	110	12	98	75	14	61	85	10	75
India	928	131	797	867	139	728	1,048	150	898	832	125	707
Indonesia	361	21	340	375	17	358	388	22	366	434	39	395
Iran	64	23	41	52	17	35	59	16	43	48	9	39
Iraq	26	3	23	24	8	16	21	4	17	27	3	24
Ireland	77	25	52	72	13	59	54	11	43	57	20	37
Israel	240	63	177	284	84	200	197	53	144	246	53	193
Italy	161	100	61	144	73	71	144	78	66	158	69	89
Jamaica	2,541	1,614	927	2,023	1,475	548	1,662	1,234	428	1,490	1,139	351
Japan	93	38	55	46	12	34	53	10	43	38	11	27
Jordan	207	74	133	223	81	142	190	75	115	212	65	147
Kazakhstan	17	-	17	18	3	15	15	3	12	19	D	D
Kenya	129	47	82	117	36	81	97	36	61	126	43	83
Korea, South	434	156	278	401	113	288	451	115	336	417	123	294
Kosovo	X	X	X	X	X	X	X	X	X	X	X	X
Kuwait	13	4	9	13	5	8	6	D	D	7	-	7
Kyrgyzstan	4	-	4	3	D	D	D	D	D	4	D	D
Laos	14	D	D	12	4	8	12	D	D	19	D	D
Latvia	23	5	18	28	7	21	19	4	15	19	3	16
Lebanon	172	32	140	149	38	111	154	36	118	128	33	95
Liberia	67	40	27	98	70	28	64	39	25	69	43	26
Lithuania	74	9	65	66	16	50	63	15	48	77	14	63
Macedonia	30	8	22	33	D	D	38	7	31	34	8	26
Malawi	7	3	4	10	4	6	D	-	D	7	D	D
Malaysia	108	15	93	89	13	76	66	8	58	65	21	44
Mali	47	6	41	34	4	30	24	3	21	35	4	31
Marshall Islands	10	D	D	7	D	D	D	D	-	10	10	-
Mauritania	44	6	38	32	-	32	46	3	43	21	4	17
Mexico	175,865	71,570	104,295	169,031	70,779	98,252	186,726	73,171	113,555	208,996	76,967	132,029
Micronesia, Federated States . . .	37	D	D	24	21	3	30	23	7	43	35	8
Moldova	12	4	8	12	4	8	12	6	6	16	6	10
Mongolia	42	4	38	27	D	D	48	4	44	46	6	40
Montenegro	X	X	X	X	X	X	X	X	X	-	-	-
Morocco	128	42	86	108	35	73	90	26	64	88	27	61
Nepal	49	4	45	38	8	30	30	8	22	43	5	38
Netherlands	88	53	35	103	65	38	89	47	42	75	36	39
New Zealand	38	9	29	35	13	22	32	11	21	35	13	22
Nicaragua	947	401	546	1,292	356	936	2,446	592	1,854	2,307	508	1,799
Niger	48	12	36	34	8	26	30	8	22	40	20	20
Nigeria	557	279	278	480	232	248	418	202	216	435	241	194
Norway	19	6	13	8	3	5	15	5	10	9	4	5

See footnotes at end of table.

Table 41.
ALIENS REMOVED BY CRIMINAL STATUS AND REGION AND COUNTRY OF NATIONALITY: FISCAL YEARS 2004 TO 2013 – *Continued*

Region and country of nationality	2004 Total	2004 Criminal[1]	2004 Non-Criminal	2005 Total	2005 Criminal[1]	2005 Non-Criminal	2006 Total	2006 Criminal[1]	2006 Non-Criminal	2007 Total	2007 Criminal[1]	2007 Non-Criminal
Pakistan	650	119	531	655	104	551	567	94	473	545	112	433
Palau	7	7	-	6	6	-	11	11	-	6	6	-
Panama	188	122	66	187	122	65	209	114	95	185	99	86
Paraguay	62	D	D	57	11	46	59	6	53	49	6	43
Peru	1,121	306	815	1,220	304	916	1,338	314	1,024	1,208	295	913
Philippines	936	364	572	755	357	398	658	260	398	697	278	419
Poland	426	107	319	449	135	314	450	116	334	410	112	298
Portugal	120	77	43	123	78	45	146	93	53	124	80	44
Romania	144	34	110	133	27	106	188	53	135	200	39	161
Russia	223	67	156	189	54	135	169	44	125	188	49	139
Rwanda	7	-	7	15	D	D	3	D	D	6	D	D
Saint Kitts-Nevis	26	15	11	24	21	3	25	22	3	14	D	D
Saint Lucia	50	18	32	50	18	32	35	13	22	46	27	19
Saint Vincent and the Grenadines	44	32	12	44	30	14	21	14	7	26	15	11
Samoa	27	14	13	21	15	6	7	3	4	23	12	11
Saudi Arabia	23	3	20	20	5	15	23	4	19	31	5	26
Senegal	121	23	98	91	22	69	124	23	101	79	15	64
Serbia	X	X	X	X	X	X	X	X	X	-	-	-
Serbia and Montenegro	117	22	95	145	35	110	105	29	76	137	32	105
Sierra Leone	62	22	40	60	16	44	35	15	20	51	16	35
Singapore	30	10	20	30	12	18	16	3	13	16	5	11
Slovakia	47	7	40	37	5	32	35	5	30	44	6	38
Slovenia	14	-	14	8	3	5	3	D	D	9	D	D
Somalia	30	D	D	40	5	35	39	5	34	19	3	16
South Africa	72	30	42	73	23	50	69	24	45	45	13	32
South Sudan	X	X	X	X	X	X	X	X	X	X	X	X
Soviet Union, former	17	9	8	22	14	8	8	5	3	5	D	D
Spain	109	56	53	66	29	37	59	25	34	65	25	40
Sri Lanka	94	8	86	85	4	81	82	6	76	60	6	54
Sudan	28	11	17	17	4	13	22	5	17	13	5	8
Suriname	24	7	17	24	6	18	21	7	14	12	6	6
Sweden	29	9	20	34	13	21	25	8	17	35	10	25
Switzerland	13	3	10	17	5	12	15	10	5	16	4	12
Syria	72	25	47	59	15	44	70	21	49	40	7	33
Taiwan	101	31	70	68	18	50	86	9	77	126	15	111
Tajikistan	6	-	6	4	D	D	D	-	D	D	-	D
Tanzania	27	9	18	18	5	13	20	5	15	23	8	15
Thailand	96	30	66	75	31	44	73	16	57	91	13	78
Togo	41	10	31	27	4	23	23	7	16	23	7	16
Tonga	50	38	12	41	34	7	32	23	9	32	23	9
Trinidad and Tobago	457	266	191	455	307	148	398	248	150	363	234	129
Tunisia	39	12	27	39	12	27	33	8	25	23	5	18
Turkey	149	24	125	184	26	158	158	25	133	155	35	120
Turks and Caicos Islands	D	-	D	3	-	3	-	-	-	3	-	3
Uganda	30	8	22	24	5	19	26	7	19	31	7	24
Ukraine	245	47	198	168	47	121	174	48	126	162	36	126
United Arab Emirates	D	D	D	D	-	D	10	-	10	5	-	5
United Kingdom	490	254	236	431	218	213	385	195	190	378	162	216
Uruguay	146	17	129	157	23	134	142	19	123	163	31	132
Uzbekistan	73	10	63	56	8	48	48	5	43	46	7	39
Venezuela	435	119	316	398	144	254	444	130	314	482	124	358
Vietnam	33	18	15	27	11	16	41	19	22	27	9	18
Yemen	52	12	40	76	23	53	47	16	31	64	17	47
Zambia	22	8	14	16	6	10	14	7	7	25	13	12
Zimbabwe	23	11	12	34	5	29	26	12	14	29	D	D
All other countries	57	16	41	53	11	42	56	10	46	49	10	39
Unknown	92	7	85	86	D	D	76	8	68	43	4	39

See footnotes at end of table.

Table 41.
ALIENS REMOVED BY CRIMINAL STATUS AND REGION AND COUNTRY OF NATIONALITY: FISCAL YEARS 2004 TO 2013 – *Continued*

Region and country of nationality	2008 Total	2008 Criminal[1]	2008 Non-Criminal	2009 Total	2009 Criminal[1]	2009 Non-Criminal	2010 Total	2010 Criminal[1]	2010 Non-Criminal	2011 Total	2011 Criminal[1]	2011 Non-Criminal
REGION												
Total............	359,795	105,266	254,529	391,597	131,837	259,760	382,265	169,656	212,609	387,134	188,964	198,170
Africa............	2,064	647	1,417	2,022	718	1,304	1,887	666	1,221	1,663	647	1,016
Asia	5,799	1,339	4,460	6,240	1,334	4,906	6,224	1,559	4,665	5,304	1,567	3,737
Europe	3,929	1,076	2,853	4,615	1,078	3,537	4,007	1,266	2,741	3,235	1,236	1,999
North America	335,707	99,139	236,568	366,261	125,416	240,845	358,762	162,443	196,319	367,251	181,887	185,364
Oceania...........	305	165	140	317	160	157	314	203	111	315	218	97
South America	11,831	2,890	8,941	12,069	3,118	8,951	11,012	3,500	7,512	9,288	3,396	5,892
Unknown..........	160	10	150	73	13	60	59	19	40	78	13	65
COUNTRY												
Total............	359,795	105,266	254,529	391,597	131,837	259,760	382,265	169,656	212,609	387,134	188,964	198,170
Afghanistan	31	11	20	18	6	12	17	5	12	17	9	8
Albania	331	34	297	296	42	254	238	51	187	171	37	134
Algeria............	21	4	17	27	3	24	16	D	D	13	4	9
Angola............	17	D	D	20	D	D	10	D	D	13	4	9
Antigua-Barbuda.....	28	23	5	43	28	15	24	18	6	19	12	7
Argentina..........	390	84	306	448	106	342	351	121	230	286	114	172
Armenia...........	86	43	43	95	29	66	83	31	52	58	31	27
Australia	47	14	33	83	19	64	69	30	39	52	21	31
Austria	18	3	15	20	D	D	19	7	12	25	5	20
Azerbaijan	9	D	D	7	D	D	5	D	D	9	D	D
Bahamas...........	105	82	23	143	99	44	106	89	17	134	110	24
Bangladesh	115	17	98	104	17	87	96	24	72	88	28	60
Barbados..........	44	39	5	48	36	12	44	34	10	41	32	9
Belarus	25	9	16	36	11	25	26	10	16	22	11	11
Belgium...........	21	D	D	27	3	24	31	7	24	17	7	10
Belize	213	109	104	242	126	116	253	157	96	215	155	60
Benin	14	3	11	9	4	5	8	4	4	5	D	D
Bermuda	9	3	6	15	9	6	13	8	5	15	12	3
Bolivia............	276	54	222	278	54	224	215	67	148	195	93	102
Bosnia-Herzegovina ..	45	31	14	57	49	8	61	50	11	63	53	10
Brazil.............	3,836	368	3,468	3,724	388	3,336	3,533	487	3,046	3,350	550	2,800
Bulgaria...........	77	11	66	82	14	68	73	17	56	68	17	51
Burkina Faso	18	6	12	11	5	6	8	3	5	4	-	4
Burma............	10	D	D	5	D	D	13	D	D	11	D	D
Cambodia	40	22	18	46	28	18	43	25	18	89	74	15
Cameroon	66	12	54	55	10	45	71	19	52	75	15	60
Canada	1,302	347	955	1,326	418	908	1,341	457	884	1,291	417	874
Cape Verde	35	26	9	49	42	7	47	36	11	27	10	17
Chad.............	7	-	7	6	-	6	10	D	D	4	D	D
Chile	211	68	143	205	70	135	185	95	90	155	87	68
China, People's Republic	877	188	689	966	135	831	1,060	166	894	1,025	217	808
Colombia..........	2,590	1,081	1,509	2,714	1,124	1,590	2,403	1,241	1,162	1,899	1,048	851
Congo, Democratic Republic	32	5	27	17	6	11	11	4	7	15	D	D
Congo, Republic.....	22	5	17	21	4	17	23	D	D	21	6	15
Costa Rica.........	692	132	560	695	123	572	553	157	396	378	157	221
Cote d'Ivoire	43	10	33	24	4	20	30	4	26	26	11	15
Croatia	24	9	15	23	7	16	23	7	16	18	8	10
Cuba.............	65	32	33	130	86	44	106	73	33	79	56	23
Czech Republic	52	13	39	66	17	49	78	19	59	46	18	28
Czechoslovakia, former	55	12	43	48	5	43	29	6	23	15	D	D
Denmark	17	D	D	31	5	26	27	4	23	9	5	4
Dominica..........	35	22	13	35	18	17	38	23	15	34	21	13
Dominican Republic ..	3,232	2,046	1,186	3,576	2,207	1,369	3,371	2,241	1,130	2,893	2,142	751
Ecuador...........	2,330	532	1,798	2,383	602	1,781	2,385	692	1,693	1,716	704	1,012
Egypt.............	166	37	129	157	36	121	123	40	83	109	29	80
El Salvador	20,050	5,558	14,492	20,844	6,344	14,500	20,347	8,368	11,979	17,381	8,507	8,874
Eritrea............	10	4	6	D	D	D	7	-	7	9	3	6

See footnotes at end of table.

Table 41.
ALIENS REMOVED BY CRIMINAL STATUS AND REGION AND COUNTRY OF NATIONALITY:
FISCAL YEARS 2004 TO 2013 – Continued

Region and country of nationality	2008 Total	2008 Criminal[1]	2008 Non-Criminal	2009 Total	2009 Criminal[1]	2009 Non-Criminal	2010 Total	2010 Criminal[1]	2010 Non-Criminal	2011 Total	2011 Criminal[1]	2011 Non-Criminal
Estonia	25	5	20	26	8	18	24	3	21	28	12	16
Ethiopia	87	32	55	76	18	58	79	30	49	53	28	25
Fiji	71	26	45	54	24	30	63	29	34	61	34	27
Finland	11	4	7	10	-	10	17	D	D	7	3	4
France	153	29	124	236	24	212	194	41	153	127	44	83
Gabon	3	D	D	7	D	D	4	D	D	14	3	11
Gambia	26	7	19	27	7	20	27	8	19	26	5	21
Georgia	55	15	40	71	23	48	59	21	38	45	24	21
Germany	178	63	115	204	53	151	201	84	117	154	65	89
Ghana	202	61	141	229	60	169	199	65	134	188	76	112
Greece	50	23	27	48	18	30	41	22	19	46	23	23
Grenada	28	17	11	29	21	8	47	29	18	46	26	20
Guatemala	27,527	5,138	22,389	29,641	6,547	23,094	29,709	9,432	20,277	30,343	11,718	18,625
Guinea	74	16	58	61	14	47	26	6	20	35	11	24
Guyana	284	188	96	302	216	86	221	167	54	187	139	48
Haiti	1,584	416	1,168	730	473	257	477	126	351	729	251	478
Honduras	28,885	5,476	23,409	27,283	6,998	20,285	25,121	10,420	14,701	22,027	10,825	11,202
Hong Kong	23	6	17	25	9	16	33	12	21	21	12	9
Hungary	95	19	76	131	19	112	89	10	79	84	19	65
India	932	164	768	1,046	186	860	959	177	782	723	161	562
Indonesia	489	68	421	431	42	389	361	43	318	324	31	293
Iran	40	11	29	55	15	40	74	15	59	57	14	43
Iraq	37	7	30	33	16	17	59	35	24	26	18	8
Ireland	79	19	60	129	19	110	107	21	86	59	28	31
Israel	258	41	217	413	50	363	327	55	272	205	38	167
Italy	215	74	141	244	61	183	201	62	139	124	44	80
Jamaica	1,628	1,214	414	1,662	1,246	416	1,483	1,169	314	1,474	1,225	249
Japan	88	17	71	87	12	75	46	16	30	37	14	23
Jordan	161	45	116	214	66	148	137	58	79	112	52	60
Kazakhstan	25	7	18	34	9	25	41	6	35	31	8	23
Kenya	140	44	96	175	70	105	171	56	115	139	56	83
Korea, South	419	116	303	394	129	265	356	156	200	424	156	268
Kosovo	-	-	-	14	4	10	22	8	14	28	14	14
Kuwait	10	-	10	14	D	D	8	D	D	7	4	3
Kyrgyzstan	10	3	7	10	D	D	13	4	9	10	D	D
Laos	20	5	15	21	D	D	14	D	D	17	4	13
Latvia	23	7	16	30	4	26	33	5	28	41	14	27
Lebanon	108	24	84	144	35	109	167	60	107	93	37	56
Liberia	26	10	16	51	22	29	47	26	21	40	28	12
Lithuania	69	13	56	72	14	58	66	17	49	47	20	27
Macedonia	60	8	52	49	11	38	45	13	32	33	11	22
Malawi	9	D	D	4	D	D	5	-	5	7	D	D
Malaysia	52	11	41	59	15	44	53	18	35	38	9	29
Mali	33	7	26	23	3	20	35	4	31	23	4	19
Marshall Islands	15	11	4	11	D	D	16	16	-	20	D	D
Mauritania	24	D	D	18	D	D	19	-	19	21	D	D
Mexico	247,263	77,531	169,732	276,850	99,616	177,234	273,150	128,396	144,754	288,078	145,133	142,945
Micronesia, Federated States	64	56	8	66	52	14	64	60	4	69	D	D
Moldova	45	9	36	44	14	30	44	9	35	61	19	42
Mongolia	50	10	40	48	9	39	53	17	36	77	26	51
Montenegro	-	-	-	-	-	-	-	-	-	10	5	5
Morocco	61	31	30	95	48	47	77	41	36	63	37	26
Nepal	46	8	38	55	11	44	57	8	49	50	9	41
Netherlands	93	29	64	129	29	100	95	27	68	65	24	41
New Zealand	39	13	26	35	6	29	35	17	18	44	20	24
Nicaragua	2,257	533	1,724	2,172	620	1,552	1,903	804	1,099	1,502	696	806
Niger	39	7	32	31	9	22	24	6	18	11	3	8
Nigeria	435	209	226	424	222	202	370	184	186	361	167	194
Norway	20	4	16	30	D	D	15	4	11	7	D	D

See footnotes at end of table.

Table 41.
ALIENS REMOVED BY CRIMINAL STATUS AND REGION AND COUNTRY OF NATIONALITY: FISCAL YEARS 2004 TO 2013 – *Continued*

Region and country of nationality	2008 Total	2008 Criminal[1]	2008 Non-Criminal	2009 Total	2009 Criminal[1]	2009 Non-Criminal	2010 Total	2010 Criminal[1]	2010 Non-Criminal	2011 Total	2011 Criminal[1]	2011 Non-Criminal
Pakistan	383	74	309	358	73	285	331	78	253	229	75	154
Palau.	10	6	4	14	10	4	11	11	-	13	13	-
Panama.	190	99	91	199	81	118	188	123	65	149	99	50
Paraguay	40	5	35	47	4	43	40	8	32	25	8	17
Peru	1,275	337	938	1,282	365	917	1,108	419	689	982	459	523
Philippines.	689	280	409	747	269	478	747	326	421	695	340	355
Poland.	498	115	383	595	135	460	550	169	381	426	140	286
Portugal.	158	87	71	206	92	114	184	84	100	148	76	72
Romania	216	50	166	153	34	119	168	56	112	204	78	126
Russia.	238	68	170	263	61	202	237	89	148	242	100	142
Rwanda	7	3	4	10	D	D	5	D	D	8	3	5
Saint Kitts-Nevis.	14	8	6	12	8	4	15	7	8	20	11	9
Saint Lucia	30	16	14	37	20	17	35	13	22	23	10	13
Saint Vincent and the Grenadines	23	12	11	32	16	16	26	18	8	20	17	3
Samoa	20	12	8	19	13	6	14	D	D	9	5	4
Saudi Arabia	32	11	21	18	6	12	38	11	27	16	4	12
Senegal.	87	20	67	88	24	64	65	13	52	51	21	30
Serbia	-	-	-	-	-	-	-	-	-	11	3	8
Serbia and Montenegro	165	30	135	101	24	77	109	27	82	79	18	61
Sierra Leone	27	7	20	17	4	13	36	11	25	44	25	19
Singapore	21	3	18	23	8	15	17	8	9	14	6	8
Slovakia	35	6	29	42	7	35	67	19	48	37	10	27
Slovenia	4	-	4	7	D	D	10	3	7	7	3	4
Somalia.	23	D	D	26	6	20	39	9	30	31	5	26
South Africa.	59	18	41	51	15	36	61	12	49	52	23	29
South Sudan	X	X	X	X	X	X	X	X	X	-	-	-
Soviet Union, former. .	14	6	8	5	D	D	4	D	D	4	D	D
Spain	94	27	67	156	21	135	137	30	107	122	38	84
Sri Lanka.	113	9	104	100	4	96	355	19	336	236	15	221
Sudan	15	4	11	19	10	9	27	16	11	17	9	8
Suriname.	14	4	10	17	7	10	11	5	6	13	7	6
Sweden.	38	7	31	64	8	56	48	8	40	29	7	22
Switzerland	20	5	15	22	D	D	13	D	D	12	6	6
Syria	46	9	37	34	12	22	54	17	37	36	12	24
Taiwan.	81	24	57	85	14	71	62	18	44	69	14	55
Tajikistan.	10	3	7	13	D	D	16	D	D	33	10	23
Tanzania	41	12	29	42	15	27	31	14	17	27	9	18
Thailand	102	20	82	105	25	80	115	26	89	87	15	72
Togo	30	4	26	28	14	14	18	6	12	16	5	11
Tonga	38	27	11	31	23	8	34	22	12	45	37	8
Trinidad and Tobago . .	478	273	205	484	258	226	380	264	116	326	236	90
Tunisia	38	9	29	15	3	12	30	10	20	14	6	8
Turkey	183	33	150	149	18	131	178	51	127	126	41	85
Turks and Caicos Islands	10	5	5	11	4	7	11	6	5	12	3	9
Uganda	28	10	18	31	13	18	28	10	18	28	6	22
Ukraine	182	62	120	192	55	137	172	61	111	208	81	127
United Arab Emirates .	5	-	5	D	-	D	4	D	D	4	-	4
United Kingdom	479	179	300	719	201	518	501	207	294	327	164	163
Uruguay.	173	49	124	170	52	118	169	65	104	172	69	103
Uzbekistan.	56	9	47	89	5	84	81	17	64	62	12	50
Venezuela	412	120	292	499	130	369	391	133	258	308	118	190
Vietnam.	30	8	22	52	29	23	38	9	29	53	26	27
Yemen.	44	10	34	53	14	39	40	10	30	39	14	25
Zambia	20	7	13	16	7	9	23	5	18	11	D	D
Zimbabwe	43	3	40	27	3	24	33	6	27	34	16	18
All other countries . . .	72	23	49	85	34	51	95	38	57	67	30	37
Unknown	160	10	150	73	13	60	59	19	40	78	13	65

See footnotes at end of table.

Table 41.
ALIENS REMOVED BY CRIMINAL STATUS AND REGION AND COUNTRY OF NATIONALITY: FISCAL YEARS 2004 TO 2013 – *Continued*

Region and country of nationality	2012 Total	2012 Criminal[1]	2012 Non-Criminal	2013 Total	2013 Criminal[1]	2013 Non-Criminal
REGION						
Total...........	418,397	200,143	218,254	438,421	198,394	240,027
Africa	1,434	673	761	1,164	592	572
Asia	4,331	1,469	2,862	2,933	1,110	1,823
Europe	2,743	1,275	1,468	2,009	1,074	935
North America	402,022	193,320	208,702	426,270	192,704	233,566
Oceania...........	256	189	67	237	193	44
South America......	7,577	3,204	4,373	5,775	2,705	3,070
Unknown..........	34	13	21	33	16	17
COUNTRY						
Total...........	418,397	200,143	218,254	438,421	198,394	240,027
Afghanistan........	21	D	D	10	5	5
Albania...........	112	37	75	56	30	26
Algeria...........	19	9	10	5	D	D
Angola...........	7	D	D	18	D	D
Antigua-Barbuda.....	39	24	15	21	16	5
Argentina.........	217	110	107	146	83	63
Armenia...........	56	37	19	30	27	3
Australia	37	14	23	46	24	22
Austria	8	4	4	14	5	9
Azerbaijan	7	-	7	7	D	D
Bahamas..........	108	90	18	96	79	17
Bangladesh	73	20	53	52	11	41
Barbados..........	50	42	8	26	23	3
Belarus	29	12	17	13	10	3
Belgium...........	15	9	6	13	6	7
Belize	209	148	61	177	118	59
Benin	8	4	4	4	D	D
Bermuda	8	4	4	10	10	-
Bolivia...........	151	94	57	117	64	53
Bosnia-Herzegovina ..	53	49	4	73	67	6
Brazil............	2,397	424	1,973	1,411	366	1,045
Bulgaria...........	52	23	29	36	24	12
Burkina Faso	9	3	6	8	D	D
Burma...........	7	D	D	4	D	D
Cambodia	89	81	8	16	10	6
Cameroon	47	25	22	29	17	12
Canada	965	383	582	793	376	417
Cape Verde	10	4	6	D	D	D
Chad............	D	D	D	D	-	D
Chile............	105	62	43	96	57	39
China, People's Republic	1,039	208	831	691	167	524
Colombia..........	1,591	1,055	536	1,421	956	465
Congo, Democratic Republic	13	4	9	D	-	D
Congo, Republic.....	10	4	6	6	D	D
Costa Rica.........	400	132	268	319	125	194
Cote d'Ivoire	26	8	18	17	9	8
Croatia	18	11	7	9	6	3
Cuba............	62	54	8	37	26	11
Czech Republic	48	20	28	6	-	6
Czechoslovakia, former	19	6	13	37	18	19
Denmark..........	15	3	12	D	D	-
Dominica..........	22	17	5	17	9	8
Dominican Republic ..	2,868	2,182	686	2,278	1,805	473
Ecuador...........	1,763	706	1,057	1,491	580	911
Egypt............	100	28	72	63	23	40
El Salvador	18,993	8,674	10,319	20,862	9,440	11,422
Eritrea	10	-	10	D	-	D
Estonia	16	8	8	16	9	7
Ethiopia..........	58	30	28	39	23	16

See footnotes at end of table.

Table 41.
ALIENS REMOVED BY CRIMINAL STATUS AND REGION AND COUNTRY OF NATIONALITY: FISCAL YEARS 2004 TO 2013 – *Continued*

Region and country of nationality	2012			2013		
	Total	Criminal[1]	Non-Criminal	Total	Criminal[1]	Non-Criminal
Fiji.	30	15	15	22	16	6
Finland	8	D	D	9	3	6
France.	107	42	65	78	32	46
Gabon.	7	-	7	D	D	D
Gambia	21	4	17	12	5	7
Georgia	28	15	13	31	15	16
Germany	113	58	55	81	48	33
Ghana.	179	79	100	100	53	47
Greece	27	14	13	25	13	12
Grenada	28	15	13	11	5	6
Guatemala.	38,900	13,494	25,406	46,866	15,365	31,501
Guinea	27	4	23	10	D	D
Guyana	175	147	28	150	134	16
Haiti	703	568	135	508	448	60
Honduras.	31,740	13,815	17,925	36,526	16,609	19,917
Hong Kong.	25	15	10	16	8	8
Hungary.	72	24	48	65	29	36
India	577	160	417	403	129	274
Indonesia	224	20	204	81	21	60
Iran.	36	13	23	28	10	18
Iraq.	26	15	11	27	14	13
Ireland.	45	24	21	47	20	27
Israel	191	43	148	124	33	91
Italy.	119	49	70	113	50	63
Jamaica.	1,319	1,150	169	1,101	993	108
Japan	39	17	22	45	16	29
Jordan.	95	37	58	58	31	27
Kazakhstan	38	13	25	21	8	13
Kenya	145	94	51	93	64	29
Korea, South	343	181	162	247	131	116
Kosovo	25	15	10	21	13	8
Kuwait.	5	-	5	5	D	D
Kyrgyzstan	15	D	D	8	3	5
Laos	11	3	8	9	3	6
Latvia	21	11	10	39	10	29
Lebanon	66	29	37	38	18	20
Liberia.	26	10	16	40	36	4
Lithuania	40	23	17	40	26	14
Macedonia.	30	9	21	15	7	8
Malawi	4	D	D	3	D	D
Malaysia	30	12	18	22	10	12
Mali	14	5	9	10	3	7
Marshall Islands	21	D	D	24	24	-
Mauritania.	10	D	D	6	D	D
Mexico	303,745	151,444	152,301	314,904	146,298	168,606
Micronesia, Federated States . . .	76	D	D	79	D	D
Moldova	58	24	34	32	19	13
Mongolia	55	22	33	22	14	8
Montenegro.	12	8	4	18	9	9
Morocco	58	37	21	44	30	14
Nepal	38	9	29	39	12	27
Netherlands.	42	27	15	41	22	19
New Zealand	34	17	17	16	7	9
Nicaragua	1,400	731	669	1,337	691	646
Niger.	16	7	9	6	D	D
Nigeria	303	162	141	346	137	209
Norway	10	D	D	5	-	5
Pakistan	173	61	112	121	38	83
Palau.	15	15	-	16	16	-
Panama.	119	92	27	124	81	43
Paraguay	19	6	13	21	6	15

See footnotes at end of table.

Table 41.
ALIENS REMOVED BY CRIMINAL STATUS AND REGION AND COUNTRY OF NATIONALITY: FISCAL YEARS 2004 TO 2013 – *Continued*

Region and country of nationality	2012			2013		
	Total	Criminal[1]	Non-Criminal	Total	Criminal[1]	Non-Criminal
Peru	772	414	358	634	318	316
Philippines.	480	292	188	349	217	132
Poland.	413	162	251	217	107	110
Portugal.	136	86	50	81	56	25
Romania	197	85	112	186	87	99
Russia.	177	81	96	115	64	51
Rwanda	5	D	D	4	-	4
Saint Kitts-Nevis.	37	33	4	14	10	4
Saint Lucia	23	12	11	26	10	16
Saint Vincent and the Grenadines	28	25	3	22	17	5
Samoa	5	D	D	10	6	4
Saudi Arabia	36	17	19	47	17	30
Senegal.	34	9	25	40	16	24
Serbia	17	12	5	D	-	D
Serbia and Montenegro	23	4	19	19	7	12
Sierra Leone	35	28	7	16	10	6
Singapore	D	D	-	7	D	D
Slovakia	26	7	19	23	8	15
Slovenia	4	-	4	3	D	D
Somalia.	41	5	36	52	32	20
South Africa.	43	25	18	33	17	16
South Sudan	-	-	-	38	38	-
Soviet Union, former. .	D	D	-	4	D	D
Spain	93	37	56	92	30	62
Sri Lanka.	100	10	90	47	5	42
Sudan	29	18	11	16	11	5
Suriname.	5	5	-	13	10	3
Sweden	33	16	17	22	13	9
Switzerland	13	4	9	8	4	4
Syria	16	D	D	16	3	13
Taiwan.	47	15	32	46	14	32
Tajikistan.	16	6	10	9	4	5
Tanzania	15	9	6	25	15	10
Thailand	70	25	45	56	18	38
Togo	16	7	9	7	D	D
Tonga	33	27	6	21	D	D
Trinidad and Tobago . .	233	177	56	169	134	35
Tunisia	17	12	5	12	7	5
Turkey	121	33	88	83	29	54
Turks and Caicos Islands	10	5	5	9	3	6
Uganda	10	3	7	19	9	10
Ukraine	169	84	85	109	71	38
United Arab Emirates .	D	-	D	D	D	D
United Kingdom	323	183	140	219	144	75
Uruguay.	111	59	52	79	45	34
Uzbekistan.	26	8	18	27	9	18
Venezuela	271	122	149	196	86	110
Vietnam.	62	28	34	63	38	25
Yemen.	37	11	26	16	9	7
Zambia	20	13	7	10	D	D
Zimbabwe	12	5	7	13	9	4
All other countries . . .	60	27	33	46	23	23
Unknown	34	13	21	33	16	17

X Not applicable.

D Data withheld to limit disclosure.

- Represents zero.

[1] Refers to persons removed who have a prior criminal conviction.

Note: Beginning in 2008, excludes criminals removed by Customs and Border Protection (CBP); CBP ENFORCE does not identify if aliens removed were criminals.

Source: U.S. Department of Homeland Security, ENFORCE Alien Removal Module (EARM), January 2014, Enforcement Integrated Database (EID), November 2013.